HEAL
to
Live

A guide to bliss, love, and light on earth
using your intuition and inner guidance

"Go within & let the healing begin"

KERRY CLANCEY

BALBOA.
PRESS
A DIVISION OF HAY HOUSE

Balboa Press books may be ordered through booksellers or by contacting:

Balboa Press
A Division of Hay House
1663 Liberty Drive
Bloomington, IN 47403
www.balboapress.com.au
1 (877) 407-4847

Because of the dynamic nature of the Internet, any web addresses or links contained in this book may have changed since publication and may no longer be valid. The views expressed in this work are solely those of the author and do not necessarily reflect the views of the publisher, and the publisher hereby disclaims any responsibility for them.

You should not undertake any diet/exercise regimen recommended in this book before consulting your personal physician. Neither the author nor the publisher shall be responsible or liable for any loss or damage allegedly arising as a consequence of your use or application of any information or suggestions contained in this book.

The author of this book does not dispense medical advice or prescribe the use of any technique as a form of treatment for physical, emotional, or medical problems without the advice of a physician, either directly or indirectly. The intent of the author is only to offer information of a general nature to help you in your quest for emotional and spiritual well-being. In the event you use any of the information in this book for yourself, which is your constitutional right, the author and the publisher assume no responsibility for your actions.

Any people depicted in stock imagery provided by Getty Images are models, and such images are being used for illustrative purposes only. Certain stock imagery © Getty Images.

Print information available on the last page.

ISBN: 978-1-5043-1671-2 (sc)
ISBN: 978-1-5043-1672-9 (e)

Balboa Press rev. date: 03/22/2019

CONTENTS

FOREWORD

By Dr. C. P. Asghar
BAMS (Kottakkal), PGDYT (KMC Manipal) Founder/
Director of Greens Ayurveda, Kerala India

It gives me great pleasure to write this foreword for Kerry Clancey's book, *Heal to Live*, a book I believe will help many people live enlightened lives, through its guidance and practice.

I met Kerry in 2015 when she came to Greens Ayurveda, India, to study Ayurveda and Panchakarma. Over the years she continued to study, sharing her knowledge and passion for Ayurveda. Kerry completed Ayurvedic Lifestyle Consultancy in 2017 at Greens Ayurveda. She received training in theory, Ayurvedic principles, classical and Kerala Panchakarma, different therapeutic application as well as therapeutical yoga. These included observing clients, evaluating assessments, treatment plan preparation, rejuvenation therapies, marma massage, nadipareeksha, and Ayurvedic cooking training. During many months of living at Greens Ayurveda, while undergoing many of these intense studies, Kerry also received practical training.

Kerry came to Greens on the spiritual path after a 'Near-Death Experience', needing to search for ideal ways to learn more about Ayurveda and why she was so easily able to find 'the Light'. Not one to be content with one way of learning, she has travelled to work with quality healers around the world, some of whom she met while studying Ayurveda at Greens.

Through her studies and the NDE, she has knowledge, wisdom, and awareness of mind, body and spirituality that sometimes takes a lifetime to learn.

Kerry follows her inner guidance to navigate her own life. It was during meditation that Kerry received 'a calling' to go to Greens Ayurveda to study and learn, though at the time she had no idea how profound that would be. Bringing further credibility to this remarkable healer, Kerry also studied with Professor Padmanabhan from Kannur University, Kerala.

I have witnessed her healings and spiritual guidance to help many people. Mostly they have healed; been alleviated from deep emotional suffering and pain, to live harmonious fulfilled lives instead of just existing. I hope that she continues her work to help as many people as possible, creating peace and enlightenment wherever she travels.

Dr. Asghar is the Founder and Director of Greens Ayurveda at Mahe, Kerala India. He is a dedicated Ayurvedic Doctor, and as a Chief Physician at Greens Ayurveda, he is providing his clinical knowledge and expertise at Gandhi Ayurveda Medical College, Mahe as a Medical Officer.

Dr. Asghar considers his calling to be a spiritual one, a mere instrument of the almighty and his blessings, and it is believed by the locals that his tender touch holds sacred healing qualities. In addition, his reputation has crossed the seas to clients, patients and students from all over the world.

DEDICATION

Thanks

This book is dedicated to my parents. I would not be here if it weren't for them, especially my father, as without him, I could not be the strong, resilient, spiritual woman I am today. Also, my mother, who gave me life by giving birth to me. Like walking a path that has no end, life keeps happening no matter what transpires.

I want to especially send loving prayers and blessings to my children and grandchildren.

They are my biggest life teachers. Without them, I would not be able to write this book. They are the catalyst for the emotional pain my family suffered over the years. If I could heal others, surely my children could be healed too.

My grandchildren are my inspiration, my determination, and my heart. As any grandparent will know, my love for them is deep and full. I have grown because of you, my special little (Angelic) people. I believe all children are sent as angels with unconditional love and purity. We were all filled with unconditional love when we were born; all little yogis doing yogic asanas and yogic breath. We are deeply connected to divine, consciousness, creator (god) and are filled with unconditional love. We are filled with light and love, we are the light and we can shine our inner light at any time. Knowing how to shine is empowering and powerful. Coming into our light is nourishment for our soul (inner spirit), shine bright dear ones. We hold no FEAR, judgement, jealousy, prejudice of others, or negativity when we shine. We are all full of Unconditional Love. We disconnect from who we are at a young age and become what others expect us to be. Our love and light becomes conditioned and we are told to be something outside of us, however, this is far away for our truth. All our answers are within us, inside our inner guidance system is the truth. I am hoping this book is only part of the legacy I leave for you, my children, my family, and my dearest friends.

This is for anyone in need of releasing emotional pain or blocks. If you are suffering from anything that is stopping you from moving forward or finding life purpose, I hope you too will grow to understand the meaning of life.

There may be tough times, some darkness and shadows, some highs and lows, but remember there is always light shining through the darkness. There is always the light of day after night. The darkness does not come to the light, the darkness becomes the light. In a room full of darkness, if you light a candle, only the light within the candle will be seen. No matter how hard it gets, how dark it seems, there is always a *light*.

We cannot reach the *light* without the lows, darkness or shadow. I became light-hearted, once I stopped feeling the fear in my heart. I release the past emotional pain and was able to understand what it means to live. Past emotions come from subconscios mind or belief system and is where we store past emotions. We must push through the stale old painful emotions and gain back the true loving, light way of being. FEAR is the main cause of our suffering mind. Once I realised the FEAR was coming from my thoughts and mind I was able to heal. My Near Death Experience was clear. The reasons why were understood. My life is *light*. You will find the *light* too. I came to release fear and know that the answers are inside us, not outside us.

ACKNOWLEDGEMENTS

The people who contributed to this book

Thank you for your teachings Dr. Asghar and staff, Founder and Director of Green Ayurveda, Kerala India. Professor Padmanabhan, Kannur University, Kerala India. Meghan Pappenheim (friend and mentor), Owner and Co-Founder of The Yoga Barn, Ubud Bali. Charley Patton, Owner and Co-Founder of The Yoga Barn, to the many Spiritual Healers and Yoga Teachers at The Yoga Barn Bali. Credit to Punnu Wasu. Dr Sandeep (Ayurvedic Dr), Professor Padmanaban, Kannur University, Kerala for your teachings, Dr Deepu (Ayurvedic Dr), who gave me permission to use some of his words for chakras chapter. Madya Lila, Ashraya, Australian School of Yoga and Meditation, Gold Coast Australia. Brahma Kumaris, India, Bali, and Australia.

To my beautiful clients who inspire me every day to continue my work and are looking forward to reading this book.

To the women who have encouraged me towards writing *Heal to Live*. Michiko Hayashi, Emoto Peace Project Japan; Heidi Hennerman, New York; Abigail Holman, UK; Donna Munro (author and ghost writer), Gold Coast; Simone Hickey, Community Service Worker (friend), Gold Coast Australia; Fiona Irvine (friend) Speech Pathologist, Gold Coast Australia. I love you all so much. Thank you for being my inspiration. To all my beautiful friends who have encouraged and supported me to never give up and keep moving forward. I found the *light* once and now carry it with me everyday.

CHAPTER 1

Living in the Light
Bridging Science and Spirituality

"As we work to create light for others, we naturally light our own way."
—Mary Anne Radmacher

Touching the *light* while you're alive is a blissful experience. I know because I first died to find it. I was part of it. It was part of me. We are all love and *light*. Each of us is full of unconditional love when we come into this world. When we leave it, we return to that same absolute love.

I believe we are all here to *HEAL* from the beliefs of others. From a very early age, we are conditioned by our parents, sibling, society, teachers, and peers. Views imposed on us disconnect us from who we truly are.

Once we *HEAL* these beliefs, we return to love and peace. Doesn't *love* feel *light* even when we say it? It is the light of who we really are that is inside us. We are all full of light. Love and *light* both sit comfortably with our heart and soul. Like reclining on a comfy couch with a warm blanket or looking out at the ocean on a beautiful sunny day, watching the diamond-like sparkles on top of the water streaming down from the sun. The *light* is also known as our higher intellect, higher self, this is where we find life purpose.

Knowing this, I found my purpose. I became a spiritual *healer, teacher and guide* to show and empower others to find their inner strength. This power within can create magical moments if we align it properly. If we are intuned with this power, we can find cosmic consciousness and open up our psychic. When we are at that point nothing and no one can take us from that wellbeing and inner peace. We connect to the universal life-force energy that flows through each of us.

Some call it a rush of energy or Kundalini experience. A practice where we open up, connecting to divine love and *light*, where you go to, what I call my happy or my joyful place. Through sacred heart meditation, I visit this place where I connect to my inner self, my heart and my universal divine forces.

It sounds surreal. To phrase it; *all that we know is everything we do not know.* That means, whatever we have been told from a very young age to do, act, undertake, accomplish, accept, follow, succeed, create, perform and achieve are not who we really are or what we are here to do. It is tucked away in our subconscious (like a database) and is part of our belief system, which forms our values. These are easy to change if they don't serve you or make you feel good.

Both living and dying, we are extraordinary beings with higher potential and power. We are not taught to tap into either. However, once we learn to, we can manifest, create and have whatever our heart desires. To do this, we need to understand who we are and where we have come from.

Since my near-death experience, it makes sense when someone says, "I'm dying to see that show," or "I'm dying to see that person." For me, it was, "Dying to see the light."

Metaphorically, it means they are happy, blissful or joyful when they think of seeing the show or person. Next time you hear or say something similar, consciously feel behind the meaning. You will experience an awareness that you may never have had before.

It is my desire that this inspirational book will teach you how to use, your own inner *light*; the *light* that lies in your heart. The heart is the gateway to your soul and spirit; both one and the same. Let me be your guide. You can unlock the door to your true potential and happiness by bridging science and spirituality. Our spirit is who we truly are, we are physical and non-physical; that is why I died.

Many books guide you through meditation, teach yoga, touch on Ayurveda science, discuss manifestation, gratitude, health, and happiness, they may even embrace finding the *light*. What they don't do is give you the full explanation of how you get there. How do you align your personality's destiny with your soul, to find your true purpose in life? How to find inner peace? I want to show you how.

Perhaps other books haven't found the *light*, or they have found it, but are unsure how they did it. They may not know how to pass on this knowledge. I have been asked many times to write such a book to share my secrets. Though they are not secrets at all. We are divine light.

Our hearts are everything; who we are, how we connect and how we feel. We are 'feeling beings', not 'thinking beings'. Our thoughts, if we allow them may take us to places that are unsatisfactory. When we allow ourselves to release our thoughts and come into our hearts, we let go and become who we truly are. Loving, beautiful beings filled with love and lightness.

Letting go is not easy at first because we are taught, we must be, do or have material things, reach a status or be something outside of who we truly are. Daily practice and healing affirmations sustain who you truly are, and the process of seeing and feeling who you truly are is ignited. *Ignite your flame and release the blame.*

Blaming, shaming and naming are things that take us away from our light. They extract the living lightness and crucify the bliss.

Most of us are taught 'thoughts' not 'feelings'. If you ask someone, "How do you feel when you eat that sandwich?" they may look at you strangely. Feelings don't come into eating, you might think, but they do. I feel less hungry. I feel satisfied. The flavour is delicious which makes me feel good.

You ask someone, "How are you?" They'll probably just answer, "Fine."

You ask someone, "How are you feeling?" It is more intimate, and you'll probably receive a heartfelt answer.

The way someone feels is what makes them either be at peace within or at peace without. If you have peace within yourself, then you won't let the outer harmony not be at peace. I guess we all need to ask ourselves, "Am I at peace?"

What I learnt through the practice of Ayurveda, yoga and deep meditation, about my inner-being or inner peace, was the ability to find the bliss at any time. Ayurveda (and its principles) is one of the oldest holistic medicines. The ancient Veda's Shiva, Vishnu, Brahma all understood this knowledge. Ayurveda has been helping people for over 5,000 years, perhaps longer. I hold many beautiful teachers in great regard after having learnt from them. They helped me generate my own way of finding the *light* while living. Simply put, there isn't a book that brings you towards the *light* in a way most people can understand, but this will.

When I first travelled to Greens Ayurveda, in Kerala India, it was a new, yet exciting experience, where I was irrevocably drawn to the ancient knowledge. There I understood the part of my near-death experience that wasn't making sense; the unknown spirits.

When I meditated, I would have visions and channel Indian deities and loved ones which had passed on. Afterwards, I would feel light, wanting to stay this way forever. Overtime, I learnt how to ground the experiences to only take on what I needed. That included spirit guides. By sharing this healing energy with others, I feel better, and my energy is balanced. As I share this knowledge and wisdom I become lighter and joyful. I believe we fill our light heart cups first then we are able to expand and give to others. We have had it wrong for many years. If our light and heart are full then those around us shine "shine your light on others". Always you first, then share it!

It's a misconception to think that only when you die, can you discover the absolute bliss of the *light*, the pure *light* within us. I used to think the same. That experience of my near-death experience ensures that you don't have to.

I remember the day I died very clearly. What a euphoric blissful moment for me to be given an opportunity to see what would happen if I went into nonphysical realm. I didn't always feel full of purpose like I do now, since that experience. This is why I want to share it with humanity. I want to do good for mankind and the planet. That's my life purpose.

Previously, I was confused about not knowing my destiny. *What should I do? What do I seek? What is my destiny in life? What is my life purpose? Why am I here? At times seeking answers from others, however, I learnt everything is within me. All the answers are there inside.* I seem to always look outside myself for answers. What I didn't realise was all my answers are within, within all of us. All I knew, from the moment of my near death, was that I was connected to divine source energy or divine god.

Divinity is real. Divine, Universe, God (they are one of the same) has me here for a purpose. You may choose to call it 'the divine' or 'universe'. It doesn't matter what we call it. We are deeply connected to something outside of us, which is also inside every one of us. We are full of love and *light* and were born with it. Each of us leaves with it. We are all born filled with unconditional love and peace. When we cross over we return to that of light. We are here on earth to learn, heal and live in harmony, peace and love. We can learn from each other by becoming aware of our potential to thrive and rise. We can uplift to higher dimensions just by using our thoughts and connecting to our hearts (inner being). We can become an uplifter and uplift others. We then become the Universal Masters of "Self Love". It is then we become the Spiritual Teacher of our Soul. This is how we can not only change our environment but how we perceive ourselves and others, how we can heal old paradigms, ancestoral pain and even change our DNA. On a cellular level we are consciousness. We are truly remarkable as humans. Our inner power/guidance system was not enhanced as children, it was the opposite and was dumbed down. No one is to blame for this, its just they didn't know any better – Our parents, Social groups, government's, it doesn't matter. What matters is we are both, physical and nonphysical and we can access our nonphysical (Spiritual) at anytime and connect with the higher self (Spirit within) and connect with others who have been hear before us. What I mean is once we are in a place of love, we can heal and connect with our true being which is connected to the Universe and where the energies of the past (spirit) reside. We are all connected in this way, we are connected to everything and everyone, we are connected to the Universe (Divine or God). This is who we are. Some might say not. Some might say maybe. Some might say YES because they have had experiences similar to mine or are in the work of healing or psychic medium work.

Our purpose is to *HEAL* those things inside us that don't align with *LOVE*. We must shift into a more loving heartfelt way of being. This is not just good for us but those around us. Once we shift into this conscious state, we become lighter, fuller, more at ease with self. We become happier. Those around us notice the happiness. It then impacts them and the planet.

As we become more loving, we attract additional love. This puts us into the *light* state where we feel connected to everything, including Mother Nature and the planet. Without Mother Nature, we would not be here. Mother Nature provides us with life force energy, air, oxygen, prana; they are one of the same.

We let go of our true being and who we really are. This is when we start to put conditions on ourselves. It affects the way we feel about things and the world in which we live. We judge others and ourselves, we self-loath, finding faults in much, including ourselves. I call this the dark or shadow, a bit like the Hitler inside us, but what we really want is the Mother Theresa. Well, guess what, we are all Mother Teresas and Mother Marys. We are pure bliss, pure love, and pure *light*.

For example, all babies are born with untainted love and joy in their hearts. It's other people's opinions, perspective, beliefs and guidance that can alter that pure love and joy; plus the expectations of parents, grandparents, siblings, adults, and friends; placing conditional thinking on them.

I believe my granddaughter will turn out to be my greatest teacher. At three years old she was an angelic cherub of child. I said to her, "You are too cute and beautiful."

She seriously replied, "You are too, Nan. You are cute and beautiful."

Isn't that adorable? What an amazing soul she is. It did something special to my heart, opening it wide.

As she grew older, her ego and opinions of others could dampen that pure little soul? It may be ego and other factors, but the pure love and joy often gradually dissipate. My granddaughter became sad while we were watching a children's movie together. One day she said to me, "I feel so sad, and I don't know why?"

I know why; she was already losing touch with her inner child. I wanted to help her keep it. Sharing my love and guidance through meditation brings back the pure love and joy.

Meditation is the way of connecting with your inner-guidance system or inner being. It helps you to understand why you are feeling sad. We're not taught that thoughts are connected to feelings. It's outside ourselves, but it's inside ourselves. We do not have to live by our conditional influences we can teach ourselves to be our true selves.

It's not just my granddaughter, but all children who gradually lose their inner child. Our inner child is sacred and soulful, it is the part of us that likes to have fun and joy. To laugh and play happily without judgement or care. We move away form this side of us and forget who we were and where we come from.

They may feel gloomy and don't know why. Perhaps they were asked to stop doing something they were enjoying. An action that was allowing them to be themselves, like skipping with joy. Perhaps they can see what an adult cannot see, something far greater than what we know as an adult. The higher-self knows the higher intelligence which we all are born with.

One day my granddaughter was jumping on my lounge. I said, "Please stop doing that." She kept doing it, about three or four times.

I then asked, "Why do you keep doing that?"

"I don't know why I do it." Obviously, she wanted to keep jumping but did not understand why.

"Maybe just stop because it's not a good idea," I said, then thought about it for a bit.

Was she just being her true joyful self? Was bouncing on the lounge fun? Was she spontaneously doing a fun-filled thing? Did I just try to condition her to do what I asked of her?

With my professional skills of knowing personalities, I pondered if this was only childlike. My granddaughter was playing, being a little child. We all do it at times, we revert to our inner child when we are playful, dancing, joking, playing games and laughing.

Young children are here to take us back to our inner child. Sometimes we should let them. Many of my clients have amazing releases when I take them into their inner child during meditation.

Live in peace and harmony

That is why I wanted to share what I have learnt with you. Through my experiences, my travels and the people I have met on the way, you can study to take your own path to the *light*. Through my journey, I was able to gain clarity. I now feel a sense of 'self' and realise I am the only one who creates who and what I think. The power is mine.

Hence; when the mind, body, and spirit are connected, something magical happens. We can access our inner guidance system, higher intelligence and life purpose. We can access the *light*. We can awaken our souls by going inside ourselves, (I'll give you the full story in chapter five). We have the power to understand consciousness, forgiveness, healing, past life healing and how we are vibrationally energic beings.

The highs and lows of our energy and thoughts determine our feelings; our vibration. If our vibration is low, we cannot connect with who we are. Forgiveness is powerful. Once we forgive ourselves and others, our hearts *light* up. Our soul sings to the sound of vibrational divine energy; *bliss*.

Let me explain my near death briefly (I'll give you the full story in chapter five). I had suffered an anaphylaxis episode, which is a serious allergic reaction. I first realised I was dying when I saw myself on a hospital bed from above. Doctors and nurses were talking to me. One nurse held my hand and was gently slapping my face saying, "Open your eyes, Kerry. Stay with us."

Mmmmm, I thought, *but I'm dying, and it's a beautiful feeling*. It was so gorgeous and blissful that I can only describe it as pure-unconditional love.

Once, I left my body (the near-death experience was over), I transitioned into a place with my three children present. They looked very upset and sad and confused. I said, "I'm dying, and it's going to be okay."

I remember feeling pure happiness and joy inside my heart. I felt free and at peace. I was perfect and everything around me was perfect. I was full of unconditional love. My children's emotions of pain and sadness did not touch me. It felt like negative emotions were non-existed, and nothing could interfere, or shift what I was experiencing. It was a magical moment of *joy and bliss* for me. I am forever grateful, as I don't fear death or transition because of the experience.

Once I saw my three children, it was like moving to another level or dimension, where I transitioned into something of a higher power. I explained to my children that they did not need to fear death, they needed to embrace it when it was time. "You need to live. Do not worry about me as I am fine," I said to them. I was happy, in a good place; a place of perfection. In this state, I became me, who I truly am. I then moved to another dimension of *light*. Bright, white *light* that was part of me. I have never forgotten the *light*. When I meditate, I can bring the *light* through my entire being. I feel the essence of freedom and unconditional love. Angelic energy courses through me.

I have developed my own meditation that allows me to be able to bring myself into this blissful state again and again. In meditation I connect back into the experience, surrounding myself with the *light* to connect to universal energy, the 'Oneness' and higher perception of love. It brings me into a state where I virtually feel total bliss, similar to my near-death experience.

Being able to do this I choose to share it with others. Sharing it with others is the one thing I am sure of. I am here to share my meditation. You too can experience *light* and pure lightness in your heart. I want you to feel the blissful energy, source energy. Allow it to flow through every cell, every tissue, every muscle, every organ, every part of your being.

During my near-death experience, I remember feeling weightless, blissful, *light*, freedom. I embraced abundant love and wanted to stay in the blissful state. It was moments before I found myself back in my body. The nurse said, "Thank God you're awake."

I thought to myself, *you wouldn't say that if you knew where I have been.*

With no idea how long I was in the euphoric state, I realised that there was no time outside the physical, material world. As beings, we are both physical and nonphysical. We are spiritual beings in a physical body. *Yay!* It felt so good to write those words. I hope this book gives the understanding of this gift.

Once I had recovered enough, they discharged me. I was at my home lying on my bed feeling exhausted. I asked God, "Why did you do that?" Meaning, I asked why I had that life-changing experience. I cried and felt helpless because I didn't understand, feeling stuck and confused. I felt connected but disconnected at the same time. At the time I didn't feel there was anyone I could share it with or question it.

"What did it mean?" I asked myself, for months. There was no clarity or confirmation.

I'm not a religious person. I'd call myself spiritual, believing religion has its purpose. Religion must radiate love, whatever that devout belief may be. I trust I made my deep connection with the spirit world by calling to Universe/God, or the divine. Everywhere in my room, I felt and saw angels. They were part of me and I part of them. The experiences lasted for a few months. I didn't want to leave my room, wanting to stay in the divine heavenly state.

At times, I could feel someone or something. It was as if someone wrapped their arms around me, hugging me tightly. At that point, I knew I was going to be okay. It was reassuring. That is what it means to feel angels or be touched by angles.

You see, I had to have a NDE to find the *light*, which is why I call this book, *Heal to Live*. You don't have to die to find it, because I can teach you how; right now, in this world. We can all live in love and *light*. We are born to live a happy joyful life, loving our inner being (love for self). Darkness or shadow cannot overtake a body full of love and *light*, it's impossible.

Once we connect, we have a deep understanding of where we come from and why we are here. I soon realised that we are vibrational beings and we run on a frequency of love. The love was angels and spirits.

My spiritual journey began in full, after the NDE. Later, I learned to remove myself from my physical body and take myself into the blissful place of unconditional love. I researched, travelled and learned. I was a sponge tapping into all sorts of knowledge to understand more about the science behind mystical experiences, NDE, meditation, yoga, and Ayurveda and anything else that could enhance and enlighten my spiritual journey.

I am a modern-day spiritualist who incorporates holistic and spiritual practices to balance and heal the body, mind and spiritual self. I am a Spiritual Teacher, Ayurvedic Lifestyle Consultant, Energy Healer, Grand

Master of Reiki, Master of Sound Healing and Tibetan Bowl Healing, Gong Healer, Yoga Teacher and Therapist, Meditation Teacher, and Ayurvedic Masseuse, which includes (Marma & Chakra clearing massage) and author.

My soul's purpose is to heal and create awareness for as many individuals as possible while I am on this planet. I teach inner guidance to bring people to their true potential and divine purpose. I help them find the *light* within.

Blessedly, I have been taught by brilliant Ayurveda Doctors, Ayurvedic Therapist, Spiritual Healers, Swami's and Yogis, throughout the world, particularly India, Bali, and Australia. With their teachings, I have tapped into a unique potential within me that allows me to connect with deities and ascended masters. They are like angels and spirits, guiding my way to help heal and nurture as many people as I can. Perhaps, therefore, I lived after touching the *light*, rather than moving on with my soul. I like to think I am here for a purpose. My destiny; to pass on what I have learned to create a more peaceful world.

The NDE showed me that we are all connected, and we need love not fear. Fear often creeps into our lives and takes over the love. I want to teach you how to overcome your fears. *FEAR* is a False Emotional Area Resonance. I go into more detail in chapter seven, but let's start with this simple exercise.

You can't feel with your eyes open, so gently close them. Allow yourself to feel your breath. Let your breath gently move into your nostrils as you inhale. Notice it slipping down into the back of your throat. As you inhale again allow your breath to move into your magnificent lungs, feeling them fill. Aren't you amazing? You can be lying down or sitting up, be relaxed without noisy distractions.

Every thought you make has something attached to it, often it's fear. *What if I fail? I can't possibly overcome that hurdle. No one will love me. I don't like the dark. Work makes me nervous. What if I can't do it properly or What if I can't slow my mind? What if I don't meet someone else? What if I'm not good enough?* These are all fearful thoughts. You must face that *FEAR*.

With your eyes still shut, say to yourself, "Fear, you are with me, but I do not choose you. I choose instead, happiness." Recall a happy, joyful thought. For example; for me, it would be thinking of a funny time with my granddaughter. Release the fear by saying this mantra, no matter what your fear is.

Fear blocks us from true happiness and finding our potential. You'll learn about facing your fears through these pages. Connect with fear and communicate good thoughts to it. Feel into it as it brings you into your state. Remind yourself of where you should be - not in a state of fear. It's like embracing the fear to make it subside. Acknowledge that the fear is darkness or shadow. *Light* is the loving thought, kindness or mantra. Say to yourself, I acknowledge this is a thought, a thought of matter (scientific) so I want let it matter. "Change the *FEAR* thought to *LOVE* and *LIGHT*." Choose a loving thought, your heart will love you for it and you will feel so much better within yourself.

You must think thoughts like, "Oh, you're here to remind me of where I'm going." A bit like having dark before *light*. How would you appreciate *light* or understand what it is, if you didn't see dark first? We need something to gauge it with before we can experience it.

The mind is extremely powerful; however, it doesn't identify with a good thought or bad thought. Allow your thoughts to just be there. Move into the next one will allow you to become free with your thoughts. *FREEDOM* of your thoughts is powerful and liberating.

Find yourself rather than your thoughts. By becoming free with your thoughts, you will become lighter, helping you feel and see the *light*. The *light* becomes real when we can open our blocked energy centres of the body.

The energy centres are called chakras. They feed our channels, meridians, nadis, etc. Like a blocked straw, the liquid is unable to get through. It's the same with life-force energy when it cannot be released into the body. Energy comes from the earth, heaven; the universe. It is part of us and who we are. We are all one or oneness, connected to everyone and everything.

Believe me, as you'll soon discover, I have faced some horrendous fears of my own. If I can get past childhood sexual abuse, sexual assault, emotional abuse, domestic violence, verbal abuse, physical abuse, dysfunctional family issues, bankruptcy, divorce, acute anxiety, depression and other events, so can you. I don't say that to make you feel sorry for me, only to explain that it is part of my life story and a huge component of what makes me who I am.

If I chose to let those things in my past destroy me, they easily could have. Instead, I use spiritual healing, meditation, yoga therapy and practice, Ayurvedic healing; channelling, crystals, reiki, Tibetan sound bowls and follow many principles to say goodbye to my fears and enjoy an enlightened, happy, fulfilling life. You can too. Using daily healing affirmations also helps with healing. I find them very effective and have excellent results with my clients. I was inspired by one of my friends / clients Lucy to create a small handbook to give to clients. Each of my clients enjoys the exercises, I used chakra colours so that I can explain the energy and wisdom of the chakras. I also advise to look at the past (no matter what happened) as a learning to get you to where you need to be- this is life purpose of the soul. Finding yourself!! Just like your inner child, once connected Your soul says "thank you - you found me". Now let's heal together

I want to share my spiritual and scientific knowledge and classical Indian Vedic knowledge, along with various other ancient spiritual healing techniques, with you; with everybody. I believe my destiny and purpose are to hand you the healing *light*. Will you take it and *light* your way to the bliss? If we all become responsible for our own experiences by not blaming or shaming others, only then can we come into our true empowerment.

While studying, I realised many cultures carry ancient spiritual knowledge. However, most of it has been exploited or manipulated over time. It doesn't matter whether you are in India, South America, America, Australia, the Amazon or Brazil, these healing techniques are written in ancient times and all mean the same thing.

We can heal from meditation, breath, Mother Earth and connection to each other. When we need connection or support if it is given to us, we thrive. If it's taken away or not given, we fall. Some people enjoy putting out someone else's light due to their own insecurities or maybe narcissism.

I have come across people I work with, healers and clients who feel they carry healing power. Unfortunately, some believe they are above others. This is not spiritual or connection, it is a false perception and not aligned with who we truly are. Arrogance is low vibration. We all need to find our true way.

At the end of some chapters, I will give you a few golden gems for your spiritual treasure chest. There are exercises, which will gradually help you find the healing *light*. Keep a notebook or journal and write a few sentences to answer each question. The magical golden gems are a gift to keep you on a path to bliss, joy, and peace. I use golden gems and a spiritual treasure chest with my clients, and they love the concept. Golden gems are the things you do that give you joy, and the spiritual treasure chest is where you place them.

An example of a golden gem may be:

1. Daily meditation – 10 minutes
2. Walk on the beach – 30 minutes
3. Socialising with like-minded or uplifting people- anytime
4. Art/Creative Therapy - Cooking, drawing, writing etc
5. Ayurvedic Massage – weekly/fortnightly

Your spiritual treasure chest is where you keep them. Create something that you use to place in a list of things that make you feel joy or happy. Keep them somewhere you can access whenever yu feel low or disconnected. These are golden gems you use when you feel disconnected or stressed. Making your own spiritual treasure chest is empowering. Discovering your own golden gems is connection and self-empowerment. I hope by the end of this book your spiritual treasure chest will be brimming with golden gems.

I use the name Spiritual Treasure Chest because "Tools" is a word that is very masculine and once I learnt that we are embracing feminine energy then I came up with the name. "Spiritual Treasure Chest" is where we place our golden gems. They are the things that give us light or make us feel light. This is healing.

Exercise

- What do you hope to accomplish by reading this book? Spirituality, improve relationships, healing, self-worth, abundance, happiness, lack of fear, manifesting abundance, what?
- Are you ready to greet the light and HEAL ?
- Do you see yourself as a spiritual person? Why?

Golden Gem for your Spiritual Treasure Chest

This quick video at:

http://www.kerrythehealer.com/thespiritwithin shows a very relaxed me discussing briefly what I do. The video will help you gradually build your spiritual tower of strength. Let life come to you and not for you. Let go of expectations and fear.

CHAPTER 2

The Light's Way
*Spirituality – more than religion – It's a
way of life, the gateway to self*

"Spirituality does not come from religion, it comes from the soul."
—Anthony Douglas Williams – Inside the Divine Pattern

Our souls are divine love or godness (goodness). Through our hearts we connect with our soul or spirit; the gateway to who we truly are. When you remember to love yourself and others, you reconnect and become more balanced. By letting go of the voice of *EGO* (beliefs) we release *FEAR*. Fear is negative energy that stops us from loving and being loved. Please don't take this the wrong way as we do need a little ego to give us confidence. Without confidence we cannot shift or move from where we are. We are always moving and shifting our energy, this includes our thoughts. Moving forward in life with confidence is another golden gem for your spiritual treasure chest.

The best way to stay in your place of inner peace and love is to keep reminding yourself who you truly are. What I mean is; don't allow the people who put you down, make negative comments or try to manipulate you undermine your inner peace. Instead let them be a reminder of who you really are, not what they assume or want you to be. I do this daily, and it works. It is the same as when I mentioned fear. Fear can only stay in us if we allow it. People can only remain in our life if we allow them. Feelings can only stay if we allow the negativity and ill feelings. Being present with what is and allowing others to be who they are is freedom. There are many inspirational people who know this already. Louise Hay, Wayne Dyer, Eckhart Tolle, just to name a few.

Be yourself without FEAR. This will lead to an overall balance of emotional, psychological and physical wellbeing; bliss. Ask yourself, "How well am I being?" Ask yourself, is this a good way of being? If the answer is no find a golden gem and move into the now of happiness. Just one small thing can shift you into a place of joy. It's just a thought away. Such a thing is empowering.

I recommend studying the principles of Ayurveda, Yoga and Meditation and particularly Ayurveda's three Doshas; Pitta, Vata, and Kapha, to find your way to the *light*. These doshas are our constitution. We are born with them, as known by ancient Indian Monks, Vedas and Yogi's who received guidance from the spirit world. Ayurveda is the emotional, physical and spiritual connection to all things.

I would also recommend researching other healing and spiritual modalities. Study whatever feels right for you now. Each has common modalities and the same meanings, only defined in different ways. This knowledge is universal in every culture. Imagine if each culture shared and embraced each other's knowledge and spirituality. Peace on Earth would be found.

Ayurveda opened me to experiences that connected me to my NDE. Firstly, learning about the five elements Air, Fire, Water, Earth, Space (universe) and how they connect with our five senses (channels) hear, touch, taste, smell, see. We are also connected to the sun and the moon. This is ying and the yang, the masculine and feminine, the nurturing self love and go get them action type. Without the balance of both we become disconnected and out of balance. This feels like stress or anxiety, even low energy. We must balance the two energies to return to source or self. When we are balanced we feel joy and harmonious within. It's a simple process, however, our thoughts will deny us at times, to feel the inner true self or true way of being. This is what we need to heal to bring us back to source self. They represent masculine and feminine. Learning about when we are in 'masculine' and when we are 'feminine' is one way to stay balanced in life.

Yes, male or female, we each have both. Pancha Buddhas are known in Buddhism and not just the Vedas. They represent our connection with our five fingers and connect to each other. The five wisdoms. Vata is the little finger, and without vata, pitta and kapha would not move. Vata governs all movement and the mind and body. It controls blood flow, elimination of waste from the body, breathing and the movement of thoughts across the mind. Balanced vata means balanced thoughts.

Nervousness and anxiety are all traits of vata. Also, dislinking loud noises. This comes to mind when meditating, and a loud noise is heard, and the meditating person can only hear the noise and nothing else. They become irritated by the noise and cannot continue with their practice. They have allowed the noise to become their focus. Pitta kapha cannot move without it, and vata is considered the leader of the three Ayurvedic principles.

Knowing when we are in one or the other will balance us and keep us in a joyful state. Awareness and knowledge are the key. It's a good way to understand how we feel stressed, anxious, even depressed when out of balance.

Lord Shiva (Deity) who is the 'God of Yoga and Classical Dance' would receive divine messages in meditation. The messages told him which asana to do in yoga practice for mind and body healing. He would also receive divine messages of dance for healing. Monks and sages received similar divine messages. This is all part of meditation, yoga, and Ayurveda.

Once I discovered this, everything became clear. My NDE was a way of showing me; in meditation we can all access the spirit and divine world by closing our eyes, breathing and allowing our spirit to connect with the outer divine world. This is bliss, love and inner peace.

Dhanvantari is the 'God of Ayurveda'. It is common practice in Hinduism to pray to Dhanvantari, offering a blessing for health for self and others. Lord Vishnu incarnates as Lord Dhanvantari and reintroduces Ayurveda to the world to help relieve the suffering of humanity.

The wisdom was to be shared with all humanity by Dhanvantari. It is written in ancient text and scriptures from the Vedas. Learn this knowledge to be able to place yourself in a meditative state and understand your inner-self. There are many different meditations. However, there is only one that can take you into self. It must be mastered by you, for you.

Before going to India, I felt like there was one more thing I needed to learn to really seal the deal of my purpose. Finding Ayurveda and learning about classical Indian Hinduism did that.

In this book, I give you the steps and teachings of how to get to your inner being 'self' in meditation and find the answers to whatever it is you need to know about your life purpose. When we meditate, our mind calms allowing space in our observances. This space can then be filled with creative ideas or divine messages, as we are no longer in our busy minds. The average, sixty to eighty thousand thoughts we have, can settle and calm. I call this, "When the magic happens." I say this a lot to my clients because I want them to understand they have all the power and knowledge within them.

Within your heart and soul lie the answers to everything in our lives. We come into this life full of unconditional love and when we leave that returns. In between is learning, healing from our experiences to bring ourselves back into love and joy.

Understanding that we are created and connected through universal divine energy allows us the freedom to choose which one we want. Following someone else's beliefs or perceptions will take you away from the inner you, placing you instead into their energy. No one can steal your universal energy; however, we can hand it over to others through our thoughts.

Have your own conviction. Be your own power. Use your inner guidance system (intuition) to connect with universal source, life force. Be the creator and create.

Don't be a follower, become the Wellness Worrier of your intuition. Allow yourself to feel the truth from the divine running through you. Believe the truth of who you are. The power within is your guidance and connection. Swallow it. Bath in the magic of infinite divine energy, love, and bliss.

The key to love is to adore oneself first, not just the exterior but interior also. From every cell to every organ to every bone; love, love, love! Push the divine infinite into every part of you.

Trust your intuition (gut) guiding you to a better place, circumstance or person. Going into you (intuition) is like trusting whatever you feel is right. When it's not, trust the feeling. *I don't feel good about that*, is your intuition guiding you to life purpose, people and the environment. Don't allow your energy to split. If it feels good, it is good. This means you are in tune (intuition) with what you are here to do.

Without loving within, your intuition cannot flow. It will become blocked. Have faith that all the answers you ever need are within you. There is a Kundalini yoga mantra, "Sat Nam," which is Sanskrit; the yogic of the mind, It elevates consciousness through song, rhythm, tone, and reflexology, because of the way our tongue is placed on the roof of the mouth with the sound.

Sat Nam in English basically means I honour the god or goodness in me. I honour the god and goodness of the universe. I honour the good and goodness in you. I know that I am part of this universal energy.

There are many kriyas, mantra, yogic postures and breathing techniques that can activate energy centres (chakras), meridians and marmas; by breathing, moving the body and saying mantra (sounds).

Another way to tap into (intuition) is to play music. There are many types of music to expand and open your intuitive side. African music, Christian hymns, and many Indian Mantras are played or sung, they can stimulate emotional, physical and psychological. The resonation of the song, vibration (hertz) and conscious words is what makes us feel good. While chanting or singing mantras, it is no different to how we feel if we do good or receive good.

If you are in tune (intuitively switched on) you will activate your internal psychic energy force, connected to universal life force. Using your intuition, you will then be able to tune into your inner guidance and energy. It will allow you to create and manifest whatever your heart desires. You will also connect and understand your life purpose and why you are here. You'll come to the realisation of what it is you are here to do.

It took me sometime to fine tune my intuition by working at it. Soon I realised it was guiding me to where and what I needed to do. This had led me to help change lives by teaching people how to use their intuition.

Simple techniques can be practised daily. Sitting and breathing with your eyes shut can activate your intuition. If you create a state of calmness it is the start of *bliss*; the beginning of internal intuitive integration.

Using Kundalini techniques has given me the inner body methods that bring me back to my inner-self-awareness. When kundalini energy is roused, we become awakened. When we are awakened, we are intuitive, psychic, loving and blissful. We become all of who we are (oneness) not what others expect us to be.

It is said, that when we activate our kundalini energies a deep meditation occurs which results in a feeling of enlightenment and bliss. This type of yoga is one of the methods I use to keep me balanced in my life of healing. I could not do what I do unless I used these techniques to keep my intuition, psychic abilities and spiritual strength balanced.

When I feel like I'm out of balance kundalini yoga is what I choose. I find my chakras return to balance and psychic energy flows. My intuition is in tune, and my insight becomes aligned with the loving, peaceful energy of divine, god-like, goodness. I become infinite with who I am.

Inner Guidance

'Inner'; meaning *inside* or *inside you*. It is known as the inner work, meaning to love one's self within. You cannot love others if you do not love each part of within you. It is never ending unconditional love for self. Don't put yourself down or think you are unworthy. We carry some of these traits because we are taught to honour others before we honour who we are. This is not a true or useful teaching.

One of my clients said to me, "I don't know why I feel so lost and not worthy," thinking her recent break up that was causing the way she felt. After a short discussion, I began sacred heart and inner-child meditation. I placed my hands on her heart and was able to help release her emotional pain suffered as a child. As a child, she felt lost and confused, not understanding why. It was carried with her, and it affected a future of positive relationships.

Even while practising yoga, she felt like she couldn't relax and enjoy it. She did not feel worthy of allowing herself to relax and enjoy something for her. By building walls around her heart, she couldn't access her beautiful, loving heart or feel peaceful or filled with inner peace.

By reconnecting with her inner-child to re-feel the emotions of being lost, unsafe and confused, it allowed her to reconnect. As she held her inner-child close to her heart, it healed the painful emotions.

We cannot change unless we shift. By shifting emotional pain, we remove it from our body, handing it over to the universe to heal. If we tune into the emotion, understand where it is and what it comes from by using our imagination (inner-power), we can hold our inner-child close to our hearts. Hold your arms around the child to heal.

It's very powerful, bringing out the old emotions to renew the new ones. This is an inner strength, full of power, filling your heart cup up with delicious soup for the soul. I have healed, and I have healed others through this process.

We need to honour who we are, teach others how to love themselves and honour who they truly are. This is the way, your intuition, your inner guidance, become your GPS (global positioning system).

Learn to vibrate so high that your *light* can be seen around the World. Once you have achieved that, teach others. It's simple once you get the hang of it. *Light* or *dark*, Hitler or Mother Teresa, Jim Jones (Cult leader) or Buddha, peace or fear; pick one.

In this book, you'll learn some of the principles of yoga, Ayurveda, Reiki, channelling, Tibetan bowl sound healing and crystal healing. They will help you release emotions that do not serve your life and purpose. Learn how to implement these practices into your daily life to revitalise, rejuvenate and replenish your body. You will be taught how to feel your inner being, your true inner self, the inner you.

Mostly you will come to the exact understanding of, 'What we think is our thoughts, are just words grouped together'. Like a train with carriages, each one connected to another and moving along. Why wouldn't we choose a good thought over a negative or not so good thought? The mind does not know reality from fantasy. So why wouldn't you want to get playful with your thoughts and have fun with them to create happy, joyful thoughts? Use your inner child to create joyful thoughts.

I tell my clients:

- "Feed your mind delicious thoughts, so it thrives on goodness, not darkness. It is only you that give them meaning." Your heart will fill with feelings of bliss and harmony. Strive for inner peace; inner wellness.
- "Your mind is just matter (scientific). So, don't let thought matter, just be aware that they are there." Allow them to come. Let them go if they do not fit with your spiritual alignment. They are energy, either low or high. "Let them be and you will see."
- "If you're going to have one thought, make it a good one."
- "You cannot hold thoughts in your hand and see them because they are matter, so why let them matter."

Exercise

- Have you ever thought something was going to happen and then it did? Like the phone ringing or a friend suddenly calls and you have just thought of them.
- Do you wake to a new day feel happy that you are alive? Explain why?

Golden Gem for your Spiritual Treasure Chest

Your Spiritual Treasure Chest maybe a small box which you have created or a jewellery box which love to look at. Find something that inspired you heart and create it. This is you Spiritual Treasure Chest. Fill it with your Golden Gems.

Think up a thought that makes you extremely happy. Write it down. Place it in your spiritual treasure chest for times you want happy thoughts to replace fear or unhappy feeling.

You'll also find this one to add to your spiritual treasure chest:

http://www.kerrythehealer.com/chakrahealingyoga

CHAPTER 3

Inner Child
Universal Connection

"You will find more happiness growing down not up."
—Author unknown

"In every real man a child is hidden that wants to play."
—Friedrich Nietzche

Our souls are divine. Through our hearts we connect with our soul or spirit; the gateway to the inner-child; universal connection. It's important to have fun with your thoughts by harnessing your *inner-child*. Everyone has an inner-child within them. You'll find it by laughing, being playful, joyful and having fun.

Be lively and joyous in every moment; just like a child. Deep inside each one of us is that child. The kid who used to play and have fun enjoying simple things; like the shower of a summer sprinkler on a freshly mown lawn, catching tadpoles in a creek, dancing when there is no music, collecting shells along a beach, blowing bubbles or jumping on a trampoline. The child who giggled, frolicked and lived in the moment, did not have a worry or care about anything or anyone's judgment. As children we just were.

If you observe little children, notice they don't worry about the size of their body, how their hair looks, if they are dirty with mud, the colour of their skin or that of their friends. They are happy with life.

Disconnecting from your inner-child is what causes us to become someone outside of our true self. We should not be others' perceptions, judgements or conditions. We are authentic and unique. We each came into this world knowing our purpose. However, we become disconnected by someone else's beliefs, and perceptions often felt with fear and anxiety.

Thoughts are energy. Each is connected to everything, including cells within us. We have over 100 trillion cells we are uniquely connected to in our body. Even Science has suggested we can change our DNA by thought. Yes! We hold the power. If change our feelings by thought, we change our direction in life. Directing our thoughts to something and somewhere else by focusing, meditation and allowing make it possible. How amazing is that!

Yes, we all have a magical gift. As babies and small children, we knew it. Once we reached a certain age, we are told we must become something and some else. This is a mistruth. We are not a status, thing or object; we are pure divine love.

When we were children, we were at peace with ourselves, playful and very much in tune with universal laws. We knew how to communicate with these laws. As I mentioned in the first few pages of this book, my granddaughter, Scarlet, is my biggest guru - she knows things adults have lost the ability to understand.

Scarlet told me, "Fairies live in gardens." And unicorns live in the mountains and angels live in the clouds. Through my research, I found fairies and unicorns do exist. I have my own personal experiences with angels.

Again, it's universal. The universe responds to every thought, hence the 'law of attraction'. Thinking about fear creates *FEAR*. *FEAR* is an emotion that is false because it hasn't happened yet. Fear stops us moving forward and provides negative thoughts in our minds. Our mind tells us to *FEAR* this and that even though it is yet to occur.

Our minds are so powerful that they don't know a good thought from a bad thought. Fantasy or reality. For example, using the law of attraction and thinking about lack or lack of something creates more of that. Thinking and feeling love will create just love.

Working on your thoughts is just as important as working out at the gym, doing yoga, meditation, or toiling on something to achieve results. For instance; doing a body detox does not include thoughts. If you fail to detox your psychic, then you will move no further than reducing a few kilos. Emotional detoxing is an important part of healing to live.

As a child, thoughts were placed in our belief system. Like a filing cabinet, each thought, incident, and experience are kept in order. The belief system determines our personality. It is greatly connected to our guidance, nervous and immune system. You must love and nurture your inner-child because it is who you are deep inside you.

Look at your inner-child by gently closing your eyes. Through the power of your imagination, visualise yourself as a seven-year-old. Walk towards the child. Reach out and hold their hand. Pick them up. Embrace them by holding them close to your heart. Gently, through your thoughts (mentally) tell them, "I love you and you are safe".

Your inner-child will let you know what it needs. Sadness, regret or anger may arise. Many emotions can be brought to the surface with the inner-child connection.

When I first used this technique on myself, it was like my inner-child spoke from inside me. My inner-child said, "You found me." It was emotional. Once I began using the technique it soon became part of my spiritual practice with my clients.

Once I worked with a client for many hours taking her back to as far as a one-year-old. She remembered her mother saying she didn't want her anymore. This left a broken heart string on the inner child's heart. It needed to be repaired. Through my guidance, she re-connected with herself and realised who she was and what she was here to do. The guilt, shame, and blame were removed; eliminated. Hope and love were restored leaving the inner-child free and feeling safe again.

Inner-child work can be an easy process in most cases; however, it must be maintained. Making it a daily practice or routine is the difficult part. Daily telling yourself that you are a fun, loving, divine *light* is not easy if you don't practice.

At a ten-day retreat, I was counselling clients in working with their inner-child. By the end of it, I was showing signs of exhaustion. One of my clients passed me a note. Cutting it short, it basically said, I hadn't been practising my inner-child.

I realised I had neglected my self-care by taking on other's low vibration energy. If we don't allow time to connect daily and 'just be', it is easy to fall into a negative way of being. A few days away from the retreat and I was back in my usual self. I have included this example because I want you to know that it's okay to feel this way. Be fine with it and you will easily return to the person you really are.

Other's energy is just that 'other'. Don't allow yourself to get caught up with other people's negative patterns. Move quickly, gently and quietly into your own space and allow yourself to process the situation and return to self. It's empowering, freeing and over time becomes your practice. The more you do it the easier it is; with ease and with grace. With *light* and with *shadow*. Become amazing grace.

In this case, it's about working on your thoughts to achieve the *light* within; the connection the spirit within us all. Once we are aware of this and how our thoughts influence our feelings, we can work toward feeling good most of the time.

Feelings are who we are. When we breathe, we don't ask ourselves, why we do it. We just breathe and allow our breath to do so without being conscious of it. I call this higher consciousness, knowing that there is a higher intelligence that just breathes in and out. We don't do anything it just happens. Our breath comes from Mother Nature, plants and trees. Our breath is another key to our soul; our life force, a gift from Mother Earth. It is where answers to finding the *light* lie.

Golden Gem for your Spiritual Treasure Chest

This Golden Gem is a video explaining the wonder of your inner child: http://www.kerrythehealer.com/innerchild

CHAPTER 4

Universal Laws
How to attract what you want.

"All that we are is a result of what we have thought."
—Buddha

Thinking about prosperity and abundance creates prosperity and abundance. Like attracts like, love attracts love and so on. Fill your heart with love; you will attract love. Fill your house with loving vibrational energy and you will attract loving people into your home. If your mind tells you this is silly, or it doesn't work, then it won't. Simple!

Never think of lack. It is detrimental to us, to who we are and how we want to be. Lack attracts lack. This is law; universal law. What we think we will attract, good and bad. For example; don't gossip about others, don't negatively speak about people, and don't get caught up in greed or unconstructiveness. Otherwise, those things are what you will attract.

Love everything and everyone. Live in the now; the moment. Enjoy every experience in life as if it were your last. The need for greed is exactly what it is. If we need more and it causes stress, then that's what you will become; stressed. If you always need, always want and will continue to put yourself under stress. This is not God's way. It is not goodness (Godness).

I have tested the law of attraction many times and have manifested countless things. My home, where I work and best of all many beautiful friends around the World. They are from diverse countries and backgrounds, several walks of life, from highly successful business people to extremely respected priest and priestess.

Trust! Have faith and life will take you where you need to be. Trusting your inner guidance system (GPS), have faith (universe), and all will be delivered. Once I manifested $10,000 in twenty-four hours with meditation, alignment, and manifestation. I said to the universe, "If you want me to continue the work I am doing, then you better make it happen." I trusted, believed and I received. It never fails. There is an abundance of whatever we need. When we understand the universal laws, we can have whatever we want. Without the need for greed, there is enough for all.

One other thing I would like to share about the *Laws of the Universe* is when using the 'Law of Attraction' you will not manifest while you are in low vibration. Low vibes create negativity. So, it's best to ask when your vibe is high. Clearing and cleansing stale energy from your body is the best way. Using *Sacred Heart Meditation* is easy and doesn't take much time. Having a shower or swim in the ocean is another way to clear unwanted energy.

I do these daily. It makes me feel good and lifts my vibration to clear out negativity. I love how I feel when I do high-vibe things. Afterwards, I sit quietly with a relaxed breath, using my imagination to create and manifest. Try using inspired action to manifest what you want. Don't act until you feel joy in your heart. I wait for the feeling of inner love and inner peace to come. Once it comes, you can manifest anything.

As I said, I am not religious, but I am deeply spiritual. Some people call the creator God, Allah, Jehovah, Krishna, and other variations. For the sake of this book, I'll call it the Universe or Divine. Whatever you want to call it doesn't matter (call it what you wish), what matters is that science has proven, what Ayurveda, Aboriginal (indigenous Australians), Healers, Psychics, Mediums, Channellers, Sharmans and Yogis and others have acknowledged for thousands of years. That is, we are all connected to each other, flower and fauna, our Mother Earth; the Universe; the Galaxies. The whole planet and other planets play a symphony of vibrational sound music. All are connected to us on a cellular, vibrational level which also connects to deities. On a cellular level, our cells record sound and hold memory connected to our muscles and tissue. Each cell is connected to a vibrational sound – which is connected to keynotes. For example, the note C# is connected to the heart chakra and played in the frequency can that resonate with the planets and universe. Sounds are part of who we are.

The sound OM, when used as a mantra, will resonate with the universal planets. Hitting a sound of frequency using any instrument will also resonate on a cellular level. It's like giving our cells a sound bath or a massage of the soul. We are universal energy connected to sound frequencies vibrating through us and to us.

The Sun and Moon are also part of this vibration. The Sun is like a charger for our cells. Just like recharging our cellular phone, the Sun is part of source energy or the universe. Align with all of these, and you will manifest and create whatever your heart desires. Once you set your desire, align it with the feeling of what it would be like to have it. Use the power of your imagination. As Einstein said, "Imagination is everything. It is the preview of life's coming attractions."

You will create it. You are universal energy. Your powerful inner guidance system can be aligned to the universal law is in charge. Every major organ is also connected to the universe. We have many marma points, pressure points and energy centres throughout our bodies. Our chakras are also a part. If one is blocked, others block. We need to understand how our systems work and in what way they are connected to the universe, Mother Nature and each other.

Bringing spirituality and science together will make more sense to you as you read this book. In an ideal world, if science, spirituality and western medicine all came together, imagine the impact. Healing would happen around the world. There would be more spiritual healers, and people would learn how to heal themselves. We all have this ability. Our planet would heal. We would live in harmony with who we truly are. Just imagine that!

I love sitting by myself listening to John Lennon singing 'Imagine'. The lyrics of the song are so calming and blissful, especially if you do really take a moment to feel into them. What I mean is; imagine the planet living in peace.

If we looked at our inner-child as a part of God (universe), then we would realise that God is our inner-child connection. We are born with it, the pure innocence and unconditional love. A non-religious background was part of my life, though I always had a deep knowing that I was connected to something. The name God, but I believe it is the universe, and we are all connected to it.

Living in the *light* of love, bliss, joy, and inner peace. It's hard to describe how beautiful it is. It's a place we don't want to leave. I am not afraid of dying or transitioning. I know and understand this is how it was meant to be. How we come into the world is how we go out. How we live is a choice. If we choose to live in the *light*, we will live a life of love. We will always be loving within and continuously giving love to others. This is the key. How we live is how who we become.

Someone said, "What if people want to die, or transition earlier, because of you writing about your near-death experience?"

I reassured them, "The state of bliss can be reached in our physical world. We don't need to die to go there, once we understand why we are here." Writing about the NDE is teaching people to live.

I feel like I'm in heaven, is a statement uttered when someone is happy. There needs to be feeling behind each word we think. Heaven is beauty and joy. When I am travelling to other countries or flying interstate, I love looking at the clouds, feeling closer to heaven. I use my travel time in the air to meditate and connect with who I truly am.

Look at the blue sky and the pictures in the clouds; feel the connection. Place your feet on Mother Earth and see how good you feel. Sit quietly in a garden or anywhere where there are plants and trees. Observe by using your senses, see the beauty, touch the leaves, smell the fragrance, hear the melodic bird calls, feel the sun on your shoulders, the wind through your hair. You will find a connection.

As a child, I was beaten and sexually abused. It was tough. I was terrified and still have flashbacks. Back then I talked to God asking him why it was happening, though I had no understanding of why I did so. "These abusers hurt me all the time. What are my lessons?" I would ask.

I often communicated with God. There were days I wondered how I got through. I was attracting that because I had to heal and come out the other side, a different person. The universe finally showed me that it was here for me (as it is for everyone) but I still had work to do. I remember saying to my mother once, "I must be adopted because I don't fit in this family." For some reason, they didn't know how to be around me, or I near them, because we were dysfunctional.

I had no one to talk to about my abuse. No one to explain why it was happening. That's why I conversed with God.

During my NDE 15th February 2011, I looked down at the medical staff as I suffered anaphylactic shock. I was the light. I was the universe. I was *IT.* Later I shared how I had left my body with one of the nurses. I told her I could see the medical staff working to keep me alive.

I said, "You were touching my face and my hands and telling me to wake up. I had no control over my body, but I blissfully watched on." This nurse now uses what happened to me on that day when she is lecturing students.

The same experience can happen in meditation with your inner being, your true self. We can all go into a state of higher consciousness or higher self to connect with ourselves and connect with the spirit world.

I read that a human being is a part of the Universe. Albert Einstein said, "A human being is part of a whole, called by us the 'Universe' – a part limited in time and space." He experienced his thoughts and feelings as something separate from the rest, a kind of 'optical delusion' of his consciousness.

This delusion is a jail cell, as Einstein said, "Restricting us to our personal desires and to affection for a few persons nearest to us. Our task must be to free ourselves from the prison by widening our circle of compassion to embrace all living creatures and the whole of nature in its beauty." Nobody can completely achieve this. Striving for such attainments, it is a part of the liberation and a foundation for inner security.

We let go of all negative human experiences to become *light*. Letting go of the heaviness is imperative. Why would anyone want to feel heaviness when they could feel lightness? We are all here to live in the *light*. I have come across numerous people in my work who were suffering daily in their thoughts. It made me want to continue my work further, spreading this message to as many people as possible.

We are supposed to live here in the present moment; love, *light*, bliss, kindness, and compassion. The more we do it, the more people around us will also. Saying it and speaking it will make you feel happy that you've shared the experience.

Singing it is another way to achieve joy and bliss. Notice how you feel when you croon your favourite love song, or you sing a mantra of the love of all these things. It brings you closer to who you really are.

As far as I can tell there is only one main thing that needs to change and that's our beliefs. Beliefs in separation, from each other, from other living things, from our highest self and from our source energy or divine.

I sang at a world peace event in Bali with Baba Ji from India. We had so much fun. Though I had never sung in public before, I sang about world peace. Taking a moment before I stepped on the stage I talked to my fear. "I am going to do this," I said, realising it was not about my voice, but about my message of world peace. As I kept telling myself that, the fear of singing in front of people left me. It was replaced by an overwhelming feeling of connection with the 500 people there.

I used to tell my children, "If you say you're going to fail something then you will. If you say to yourself you are going to succeed and just do it, you will succeed."

Near-death or death, it doesn't matter the *light* is available. I know that I am the *light*, we are all the *light*, connected to the universe. I know there is something I'm connected to, it's the placement of love, non-judgement, and happiness. I'm linked to my source (me) and the universe. When I feel resentment shame and guilt, I am then separated from who I truly am.

What does it mean to find happiness? It's tapping into your heart space and soul. Separate the two; thought and breath. Take your breath into your thoughts and then connect with your heart. Let your breath control your thoughts not the other way around. Tap into your inner being. Find your life purpose and what you are here to experience.

Contemplating how I feel now about my spiritual journey

My journey felt like a homecoming into who I really am. I am an internal being filled with *love* and joy. This is what resonates with me when I write about my NDE. I used to be a person who had lots of energy, fitting as much as possible into my day. Like a mouse on a wheel, I rushed around. Most days I would exercise, go on long brisk walks, work out at the gym, do boot camps, run marathons and really beat myself up if I didn't do these things. It dawned on me I was doing these things because I thought I had to because I was told to; TV, media, peers, others etc.

Some of the writing of this book was done when I was in Bali, at one of my happy places, The Yoga Barn in Ubud. I love teaching meditation and intuitive classes at The Yoga Barn. I also receive from my clients. When I receive insight comes through which guides me to my next step. The Yoga Barn is a regular pilgrimage where I learn and teach. A stunning place where I've enjoyed some of my most beautiful spiritual moments, which I'll go into in later chapters. As I paused from a half-written page, I sat quietly, looking at the pool outside my room in Bali, listening to the birds and inhaling the sweet smell of frangipanis. I went into a state of deep thought as I remember the person I had left behind.

There was personal grief as I looked back at the person I used to be. I experienced loss of self, loss of self-worth and loss of materialistic things. Typing and contemplating, I wondered where I would be if I didn't have an NDE. Where would I be living? Would I still be a social worker? Would I carry fear around me like a shadow? Would I think I wasn't worthy or anything good? I can tell you we are all worthy. We are all love with a beautiful heart.

Wow! Coming to a realisation, I said, "Look where I am now. I am grateful for everything since. I do not hold fear anymore." I'm certainly not afraid to die or crossover. My first-hand experience in NDE was of wellbeing, happiness, joy, and bliss. It was inside me, part of me and I was the *light*. Who wouldn't want that lovely understanding? And who chose not to live that every day on earth?

We all have different experiences and hold diverse thought; however, we have the power within us to change and find our higher being (higher self). Sometimes you may feel negative emotions. They are not good for you or for anyone around you. You may find yourself bristling with anger at someone, being afraid or feeling guilty about something, past or present. It is normal to feel that way. However, if you hang on to such emotions, you are not honouring your true self. Be worthy to yourselves.

You sabotage the goodness inside you by giving power to thoughts attached to negative feelings. By asking yourself, "How much awareness do I have?" You are I letting your thoughts control you, giving them the power to exist.

If you find yourself, feeling negative about someone else, find something good about that person. It may be their smile or their clothes or even the colour of their eyes. This will immediately change your thought and alter the feeling of anger to a feeling of goodness. Wouldn't you like to give that feeling to yourself; a feeling of goodness instead of a feeling of anger? You will feel better inside, and your inner being will love you for it.

Being kind to yourself it sometimes not easy, however, it's much like anything else we do. Once we do it many times, it becomes a normal way of living. Make it a habit. Try and do this exercise next time you feel angry or upset with someone. You are giving to yourself when you do so. It's a gift to self.

When I meditate, I ask myself if a thought is good or bad for me. The awareness brings me into a better place. I celebrate in my mind and say, "Yay! I've banished another negative thought. How awesome am I!"

Sometimes I do a little dance or throw my hands in the air like I just won something. I did win something, my sense of self.

My subconscious knows the feeling is good for me. I do this until negativity has disappeared. Once it has, I am ready for my day. Importantly, I have learnt that uncomfortable thoughts don't come from others; they come from my subconscious mind. If I let them dominate my thinking, inappropriate thoughts will continue to take over. It will impair my ability to be at my best and will harm my skill to make good decisions for me and my life purpose.

Negative thinking will pull you away from your life purpose. This is its job. Our job is to change it. Change the way we think.

Fear can bring on so many uncomfortable emotions. However, once we understand it, we can allow the thought to pass over. When it passes over, it doesn't return until we have the next one. It's something that needs practice, though it is attainable through daily meditation. My daily meditation practice is what has got me to where I am today.

I believe my NDE showed me; letting go makes room for the good to come in, letting go of money issues, relationship problems and any other thoughts that do not serve you. Once the good comes in, you create magical things that will make your heart sing. Have fun with your thinking. The Universe loves it. Go into your inner-child and feel the love inside you as you go on your way to creating and manifesting what your heart desires. The mind does not know or understand fantasy from reality, so go for it. What do you want?

I believe I was shown the *light* (through my NDE) to pass the knowledge on to as many people as I can. Absolutely I want everyone to experience happiness and joy here on Earth. I live with feelings of bliss, joy, and happiness, anyone can. You just need to understand your thoughts (ego) and feelings (emotions) create your happiness and joy. Knowing when to play and party with your mind and when to work on it will take you to the playful, joyous, place of merriment.

A typical day for me is filled with, meditation or yoga, looking at the sun, moon, stars, clouds and sky. I enjoy the beach, bush, Mother Nature and what she provides. They are my favourite things. Life was not always like that, and my journey was one of victim, forgiveness, survival, and resilience. My inner strength is one that (sometimes) I feel like a warrior princess or a goddess. Other times not so much. It's then when I sit quietly and say to myself, you are ok, the universe has your back.

I find solace and interconnection during my quiet time. It gives me a chance to connect with my inner wisdom, who I am. It gives me a chance to seek inside myself and tap into my in-tuit-ion (into one). These days, you will see me practising meditation, yoga, writing, reading or just relaxing. I'll be planning my next manifesting-magical moment. I try to be playful with my communication to myself (keeping my inner-child). This retains well-balanced self-esteem.

Motivational speaker, Louise Hay, was an inspiration when it came to increasing my self-worth. She told people they were beautiful and to look in the mirror and say so. I look in the mirror most days and say, "Kerry you are beautiful, and I love you." It works. I also ask my inner being, "What is it you need? Or what is it you need me to do?" I always get a response from within. It's like speaking to an extra person, the one, the inner-being of creation.

Quiet time connecting with my inner wisdom is enjoyable. It grounds me as I ask my inner-self how to deal with whatever is bothering me. I prefer this to waiting for things to manifest into something bad, by asking myself to be receptive to receive, inner, universal and spiritual guidance. It isn't surprising that the answers always lie within. Wouldn't it be wonderful if it were taught in schools? Young children already have an inner knowing, let's help them keep it. We only lose it as we age.

Keeping myself joyfully in a place of unconditional love does take effort and consistency, just as much work as being a spiritual teacher and healer. Energy shifts and moves all the time and thoughts do the same as they are energy. Re-grouping holistically can be challenging somedays. It's not easy knowing I am a spiritual being in a human body.

Try to and find something positive in most things in life. Sometimes it's challenging dealing with people's perspectives and opinions. Ask yourself, I wonder what's going on with that person's thoughts. I often share my joy only to have it slammed to the ground as if some people enjoy jumping all over someone's happiness and trampling it – destroying it.

Not everyone believes my joy and enthusiasm is real or understands that I want to share it. I ignore the naysayers because I want to share my bliss and show people how to heal. In this world, many individuals need healing. There are plenty, like me, who have the power to heal others. It's exciting and in many ways, is my passion.

Since my NDE I have changed many of the things I used to enjoy in life. I no longer view television. I don't watch the news to get caught up in media hype that is often swayed with negativity. I would rather read, write or meditate. I spontaneously walk by the ocean or to dine by myself, enjoying my own company. Don't get me wrong, I also like the company of others. Some say I'm bright and bubbly when out socially. The thing is, now I know when it's time to leave. When I need my time, I go home to meditate. You'll learn what is helpful for you as you turn these pages.

Exercise

- What are three things you like doing that makes you feel more connected or happy?
- Do you have a deep connection with others? Do you feel people's pain or are you unaffected by it?
- Do you feel you are an empathy or apathy?
- Look in the mirror. Say to yourself, "I am beautiful. I love you." Do it for a week and on the seventh day write down how you feel.

Golden Gem for your Spiritual Treasure Chest

This Golden Gem will make you smile: I regularly post uplifting messages to Instagram, these can help you to find the light. Follow me @ kerrythehealer or kerrythehealer@gmail.com

CHAPTER 5

Dying to find the Light

How I died and came back to find that bliss was already here

"The best and most beautiful things in the world cannot be seen or even touched. They must be felt with the heart."

—Helen Keller

Normal days can lead to extraordinary events

I lived in a glorious part of the world, the southern Gold Coast, Queensland, Australia. With above average sunshine, pristine waters and beauty abounding. A national park was at my doorstep where water dragons sunbake along the sandy path and blue water twinkles between the pandanus palms. I even had a creek, brimming with fish, in my backyard which led to the ocean.

The fifteen February 2011 was a day like any other. It was summertime warm. The sun shone brightly in a cyan-blue sky. Birds sang a melody outside at the edges of the creek and in the trees in my garden. I was readying myself for work and wondering what I was going to wear. For some reason, I chose a beautiful, colourful dress that made me feel good.

I left for work. On the way, I stopped at my doctor's surgery first, for my fortnightly allergy injection. Being a chronic asthmatic also triggered allergies, sinus pain, eczema and most of the complications. An allergist tested me, taking blood for analysing and designed a vaccine. I was recommended injections to desensitise my allergic reactions. The vials were sent to France, and a vaccine manufactured there, then shipped back in two month's supplies to Australia. This inoculation, designed for me, was like a small dose of the allergy to help build up immunity.

The nurses gave me the usual check-up, then readied for the injections, as I sat propped in a chair. A medical student from a local Gold Coast university doing some practical training, sat beside me. Enthusiastic to learn, she chatted to me about my treatment.

A nurse explained to her, "This is Kerry. She's been coming here for about eighteen months for fortnightly injections. Everything is going well. I'm going to give her the injections. You can sit with her and speak to her." I felt the quick prick sting of the needle. Then, a normal day turned irregular.

Odd sensations tingled through my feet like something was pulling them to the floor. I said to the medical student, "My feet feel funny." Severe pain ebbed throughout my whole body.

She opened her mouth, then frowned watching my pallor. Touching my clammy arms, she asked, "Are you okay?" Quickly assessing the situation, she called for help as I became semi-unconscious. The pain doubled me over. I clutched everywhere that ached. Medical staff came to assist me to the nearby bed. I managed, on wobbly legs, to make it on the bed, grimacing in pain.

I scrunched my eyes trying to block the pain, but it was unbearable. The agony was horrific, rushing throughout my body from top to toe. The pain in my back was so severe it made me nauseous. I was suffering anaphylactic shock.

Anaphylaxis is when your vital organs begin shutting down. *This all makes sense now as our vital organs are connected to our energy centres (chakras, marmas) etc. and we are connected to the universal energies one of which is light.* The nurses were trying to wake me. One was gently tapping my face saying, "Kerry, open your eyes. Stay with us." The agony distracted me from this tiny task. I could hear her, but I was unconscious. I couldn't react to anything with my body. It was like my body was taken over.

I thought, what's going on? I lost all control over my bodily functions.

Weirdly, I began to feel no pain. It dissipated, and it was like I was outside myself looking down on the doctors and nurses around me. They were endeavouring to keep me alive, but I was in this ethereal place, a mystical place, where it didn't concern me that my body was on the table and I was out of it and dying. I observed them, but went into myself, feeling euphoric. There was fearlessness and peacefulness, as I floated drifting into a lightness; like a piece of paper when if falls, it floats peacefully and silently.

I said, "I'm dying," but instead of being scared, it was like a 'wow' moment. Like, "I'm dying, how beautiful." Any worry, concerns were gone.

It was odd. I felt calm and connected. I felt light filling my every cell. Though alone except the doctors and nurses in the room, somehow my children appeared while I travelled into total lightness, pleasure, and blissful angelic, superconsciousness. There were perfect happiness and great joy. It was as if I was taken to another dimension with my children, yet they were not my support, instead clearly distressed that their mother was dying.

My daughter, my oldest son and my middle son were in a row, like when teachers line the children up at school. I told them, "I'm dying, but it's beautiful. Don't worry about me. I'm okay. Everything is good. Everything is beautiful. There is no pain."

Their faces showed fear, anguish, and grief. I'm not sure they knew I was dying, but they could not connect with what I was saying as I described my blissful state. Though I told them not to worry about me because dying was a perfect place of bliss, they couldn't hear it. They remained sad. I tried again to convey to them that I was in a good place; a place of perfect harmony.

Why didn't I feel their emotional pain? Normally I feel it intensely, especially with my children. I am an emotional being and a clairsentient. A clairsentient can feel the present, past or future physical and emotional states of others. Energetically, clairsentients can feel others emotional pain.

I didn't identify with my clairsentience or clairaudiece until after my near-death experience. Now that I know how to harness it I use it in my healing work today. Because of my high state of energy, I know that we vibrate at a frequency which can be measured in love, joy, and peace. I now understand that when we die, we return to the source energy. Source energy is universal life force; our connection with each other and the universe.

Forgiveness also plays a huge part in our vibrational frequency. Once we forgive those who hurt us, we can return to inner joy and love. Without forgiveness, we stay stagnant. Release to be at peace, make this your daily mantra.

Reminding myself, "If someone knew better, they would do better," is what I say to myself when someone hurts me. I understand they don't know any better. It is their way, not mine. Once I forgave my father it was easier to forgive my mother. Pondering what her life was like as a child, made me realise her fear. It was difficult for her to express emotions. I acknowledge her fear. If she had known better to face her fear, my childhood would have been different. Anyhow, whatever it is, I am happy with who I am today.

When we leave our bodies, we leave all the negativity, fear and pain behind. All the undesirable emotions; guilt, shame, blame, pain, jealousy, frustration, fear, doubt, anger, judgement, and depression are gone. We become fearless, letting go of any negative emotions, no longer suffering the emotional pain that our thoughts can create.

Also, we don't feel the pain of loved ones or those we have hurt. Pain does not exist during the nonphysical spiritual side of us. We leave it behind. I experienced an epiphany, knowing why I could not feel my children's pain was because in the nonphysical we are love and bliss. Negativity and low vibrational feelings do not exist in the nonphysical. They can only experience this in the physical. Wow!!

What a day! I was nonphysical in a body, though somehow, I knew I was both physical and nonphysical. My inner being both soul and spirit connected with everything in the universe and all things on the planet; everyone. How cool is this knowledge?

Countless ancient cultures know this. Through time, however, the knowledge has been dumbed down, destroyed, manipulated, misinterpreted or lost.

While I was dying, I felt so pure and full of love. There was positivity, clarity, euphoria, joy, empathy, serenity, hope, awe, kindness, forgiveness, inner peace, confidence and most of all deep love for everything. Heaven is wonderful, so is living. We just need to let go of ill feelings and beliefs we have been conditioned with. The reasons we think in certain ways. Our way of thinking is developed through other's beliefs. We were not born this way. Find a reason to want to change, and everything will change around you.

Think of intense feelings of joy you've felt, like holding a newborn baby for the first time after giving birth or falling in love for the first time. Intensify that to understand the bliss of the light. When I was a child of about nine years old, I won a basket full of chocolate Easter eggs. You could imagine the joy I felt when receiving such an unexpected gift.

We are born to enjoy feelings of love as we live. Unfortunately, most of us produce pain by our thoughts (negative ones) and beliefs. All that is irrelevant and does not exist, if you allow yourself to let go of negative or shadow thoughts.

During my experience, shortly after I spoke to my children, I seemed to drift, in spirit form, to somewhere else. My children would be okay. I was experiencing such a beautiful thing and how could it be otherwise? I didn't think about never seeing them again. Instead, I wanted to share the bliss with them. They could feel it too, becoming fearless and living a life of joy and happiness. Happiness lies within each and everyone of us. It's not in someone or something else. It's in you. I explain more about this further into the book.

My children became indistinct as I drifted towards a bright *light*. It was white, bright and more incandescent than anything I'd ever seen. It drew me to it, to become part of it. I felt it enter me. I floated in it as part of it, not in physical form. The no-nonsense voices of the doctors and nurses muted. My children's images disappeared. I became the *light*. It was part of me. It was everywhere. No one and nothing existed where I was. I will never forget the feeling. Disconnected from my body and in spirit, I was ethereal. I was the *light*.

It was timeless. Time was not part of my experience. There was just lightness, love and forgiveness for everything. Pain towards my children, because of things we have been through, dissipated. Anger, guilt, and shame was gone. I let go of antagonism and resentment. It did not exist anymore. There was a deep love for myself and my children. As I saw them briefly again, I encouraged them to embrace love because it's such a beautiful thing. I have many similar euphoric experiences in meditation.

For whatever reason, I was suddenly back in the doctor's surgery. No one told me to return to life. However long it took, I found myself on the bed, in my body, trying to open my eyes.

The nurse said, "Thank God you're here." Little did I understand that it was God like experience (or whatever you call it) putting me back in the physical.

Gradually, I came back to the living. Waking slowly, I glanced at the walls, the lights on the ceiling, and the doctors and nurses astonished faces as they surrounded the bed. To see if they were real, I clutched the white sheets with my hands. *I'm back. I'm here. Why?*

I asked the doctor, "What happened to me? Why did I feel so much pain at the start and then none?"

He said, "Your internal organs were shutting down. Your kidneys and liver would have been the pain you felt."

I asked what had happened after that. They had given me two shots of adrenaline and an allergy shot, gradually bringing me back from the brink. None of which I recollected. It didn't explain everything. I was unable to verbalise my near-death experience to them.

I rested in the doctor's surgery for a couple of hours to recover. They phoned my husband (now ex) to come and get me. He entered the room and sat holding my hand. Speechless for a while, "We nearly lost you," he said, in disbelief.

I couldn't talk either. It was like I was still in my body, out of my body, back in my body. I felt like I'd been slammed backwards and forwards like a tennis ball against two rackets. It was impossible to process what had happened.

Once we arrived home. I went to bed to rest and recover, as suggested by the doctor.

When I woke up, I cried bucket loads of tears. Crying, because I wanted to go back to the *light*. Sobbing, because I couldn't understand what had happened. Crying, for reasons unknown. I looked up to the ceiling and said to God Universe, "I know now that you are real."

Clenching the sheets in my fists, I was confused about what had happened. "If you want me here for a purpose, you need to show me because you didn't tell me what it is, I'm am here for," I yelled at the Universe. From that day on things changed.

Something shifted in me. Looking up at the fan above my bed I was thinking, I wish I were a fan. All I'd have to do is spin all day. I wouldn't have to worry about anything else but spinning. Then if someone didn't want me to spin, they would turn me off and I could rest. It was weird how I suddenly looked at an inanimate object and had these thoughts. It was as if I'd become one with it.

In those reflective moments, I realised I was a part of everything. Part of a fan even. Everything is energy. We are energy; all part of it. I said to the Universe (God), "Why did you do that to me?"

I cried. I wanted someone from that dimension to come to me. I kept asking anyone in the divine realm to tell me why they had given me a blissful experience, only to send me back away from the divine *light*.

I believe divine energy (she or he) did that because I didn't know why I was here. They wanted me to complete some purpose in my bodily form before I could return to the spiritual soul being. There was this feeling that I was going to be okay. It was like I was embraced in a huge hug. My bedroom was so full of love. I thought, this is where I need to be, this is home, this is me.

From that day on I have never felt lonely again. I felt part of everything, earth, trees, the ocean. A deep, deep connection to the moon, sun, universe. For the first time in my life, I felt whole, as a human-spiritual being. I realised this is who we are. We are both physical and non physical beings, we are emotional beings. When filled with love we became WHOLE or 'at one' with who we truly are. Our responsibility to our self is to fill our hearts with love. This is not someone else's responsibility.

I saw Angles for months after my near-death experience. Because of the feelings of angelic love surrounding me I never wanted to leave my room. I didn't understand them until much later, but I loved them, and they loved me. They are with all of us at any given time. Through my journey, I learnt that angels are messengers from God or Divine. That is what the word 'Angel' means.

Waking early, I could see the sun piercing through the blinds. There was silence except for birds chirping. For some reason, I needed to connect to the sun. From my house, I strolled to the ocean to feel the salty water. Birds flew above me. I could feel their freedom. The feeling of love came from all of nature.

I observed light through the trees in a new way. Everything seemed magical and special in a clear way that I had not noticed before. Sitting by the ocean, I felt a deep sense of belonging. Gazing at a tree made me want to hug it. All the elements were connected to me. The clouds became my messengers from Divine. The moon became my wisdom and the sun became my spirit within me; the *light*.

The ocean was my breath. As I sat gazing at the sun glistening over the oceans gentle waves I relived the feeling of bliss and love. It was then I had clarity that I was connected to something bigger than who I was physically. I was deeply internally connected to the elements of life; the universe, air, earth, water. Later, I would add fire when I studied Ayurveda. All of these were connected to me. Science now is proving and studying these connections within us.

It's been over seven years since my near-death experience. I still feel that deep love and inner connection with everything on our planet. I appreciate all of it and embrace it. There is deep gratitude for it and the abundance it brings to me. I have a deep love with Mother Nature and look at her as the Mother who provides our goodness being air. She purifies toxins and gives us oxygen. She asks for nothing in return, giving unconditional love.

Only a mother could love unconditionally like Mother Earth does. We throw toxins into her soil. We destroy what she provides to give us life. Rarely is she thanked. How many people have come to realise that without Mother Earth we would not be here? Our food, the air, keeps us alive.

Consciousness about Mother Earth is the only way we can slow down and stop global warming or what I call the *cause and effect universal laws*. Promoting fear by saying plastic is destroying the planet causes it to happen. Saying negative things about anything will create more of that. It's another reason why I don't spend much time on social media or TV.

Saying something like, "What can we do with the plastic? Let's come up with a solution," is more positive. It is a higher vibration. Sending out low vibrational frequency affects not only our planet but the lives of countless people. Mother Teresa once said, "Invite me to an anti-war rally, and I won't come. Invite me to a peace rally, and I will come." They both mean the same thing, however, carry a different vibrational frequency.

Tears of sadness fall down my face when I feel Mother Earth's pain. It is our pain. If we want to help her, we need to understand what consciousness really is. The words we speak either to others, through social media etc., affect us and our beautiful planet. Praying for peace with others is better than asking God to fix it. God did not do this or the universe. Man did it. The planet was created with abundance for all and look what happened. Mother Earth is inside us. Treat her with the kindness you should show yourself. Loving the planet is like loving yourself within.

Her agony as she struggles as a mother to teach us that we don't need to worry or feel scared. She will continually provide unconditionally without judgement. That's what mothers do.

Something beautiful was felt in my heart when I connected to the universe. It was, and is, part of who I am. I have developed my feelings of intuitiveness further since then.

When I walk into a room I know if someone has something going on. I can feel the energy, good and not so good. Before starting this book, I developed my spirit connections to help others connect with the loved ones who have crossed over.

When I had my NDE my grandparent's spirit was with me for many months. Looking back probably about a year I found it very easy to communicate with them and angels. Finding white feathers, looking up at the clouds and being surrounded by butterflies, birds showed me spirits connecting. This was a freeing feeling. It regularly happens to me. I never know from one day to the next what is going to happen with the spirit world. I just learn to live with it.

Sometimes it's not easy. However, once I learnt that we have a frequency of energy that is vibrational energy, it allowed me to understand further, why I was feeling the way I did around other people's energy. I learnt that we vibrate at different levels depending on where we are in life.

Often, in a place like a shopping centre, I will feel like I'm being bounced around by people's energy. I've never enjoyed shopping centres, I now understand why. At first, it was difficult to deal with. I have realised it was not good for me. I needed to ensure self-care and avoid being around multiple stimulating human emotions and energy.

Instead, I'm drawn to much of nature; fish in the pond, waterfalls in the background, soft-melodic relaxation music and things and places that stimulate my inner being. Travelling in aeroplanes, I watch the clouds. They take me to somewhere else in a meditative state. These little things are nurturing.

If for some reason, I don't feel love and happiness on a day-to-day level, something in my mind and my thoughts need to be cleared and, to bring me back to feeling the bliss. It's a beautiful awareness to be able to control that within myself. Only through the experience of near-death, could I teach others to do the same.

I don't fear death. I embrace it and look forward to it. It's like I'm on Earth living an illusion. It's such a sublime thing. I realised I came back to fulfil my destiny before I return or go back. My destiny and purpose are to show as many people as I possibly can, the way to find the *light* and return their true being of unconditional love and love for self, while they are on Earth.

Leaving our bodies doesn't mean the end – it means a new beginning. Just like butterflies mean new beginnings on Earth. There is a story about the caterpillar who feared sheading his cacoon, once the fear left, the butterfly became a beautiful creator of the planet. Who doesn't enjoy watching butterflies.

I remember when I was a child I would wake up through the night seeing snakes above my bed, as I got older I could see spirits at the end of my bed. I was told by a relative that these were ghost who had come to get me. The fear was embedded in me and I lost my connection for many years as I thought I had done something wrong and they were hear to take me away. This was not true and was someone else's perspective. Who would put fear like that into someone, especially a child. I can only say that it would be someone who is of low energy/vibration and is disconnected from higher source. When I tell people this nowadays they love it and enjoy me sharing my spiritual stories.

Exercises

- Have you ever meditated to a level of bliss or inner peace? How did it make you feel?
- Have you ever felt that angels are around you? Can you see them?
- Do you ever share you spiritual experiences with others?

Golden Gem for your SpiritualTreasure Chest

I want to give you something special from my NDE and say to you, "Do not fear death but do not fear life either. You can find the light alive or dead. Light your own light here on Earth to make your light even brighter when you are in ethereal form."

Actor Sharon Stone said her NDE was peaceful. Watch what she says while talking to Oprah at https://youtu.be/xnHK6TbZTX0. Anita Moorjami who is amazing to listen to on YouTube about her NDE and how she overcome cancer. Her father came through in her NDE and told her it's not her time. So many people have had experiences of seeing the light or feeling the bliss and love. We are all eternal beings who are living in physical form.

CHAPTER 6

World Peace
Our universal connection –'Imagine'

"We can never make peace in our outer world until we make peace with ourselves."

—Dalai Lama

Over time, we have developed an 'action and non-connection' way of life. Instead of just *being* and *allowing* we want to change things. My experiences and NDE has led me to overcome several obstacles. However, it doesn't matter what happens in life or what life throws at you, you can overcome it.

As emotional beings with vibrational energy and frequency, we can seek peace if we want it. You can then create it. Remember what Mother Teresa said about the peace rally and anti-war rally? Both mean the same thing, however, when spoken there is a different feeling to the words.

Thoughts and words are powerful energy that creates goodness and badness in life. If water and plants have consciousness and we eat plants and drink water, we need to be aware of what we are putting out. We are 80% water, what we put comes back. Everything is energy conscious, connected to us and the universe.

An organised trip I took from Bali to India went horribly wrong. I was left without a passport and was staying in very poor conditions with minimal contact with the outside world. Suddenly, what I call divine intervention, angels (Brahma Kumaris) brothers and sisters appeared one morning.

Brahma Kumaris is a worldwide spiritual group dedicated to freeing everyone on the planet from suffering in their mind and health. Founded in India in 1937, Brahma Kumaris has spread to over 110 countries on all continents. However, their real commitment is to help individuals transform their way of thinking from materialism to spiritualism. It supports the cultivation of a deep collective consciousness of peace, love and of the individual dignity of each soul.

I felt lost, fearful and alone, my first solo trip travelling to an unknown India. The brothers and sisters had somehow managed to slip into the room next to me without sound. At first, we chatted and laughed. After a few days, they were inviting me to share a meal. I jumped at the opportunity as I really wanted to learn more about what they did. They all wore white. I think of healing and purity when I see someone in white. There was a buzz of angelic energy radiating from them. I could feel how special they were. It felt easy to enjoy their way of living.

On one of my visits, Sister Sumangala Sama asked me to do a healing. Her sister sat beside her. An Ayurvedic Doctor was also there as I began. The healing was remarkable. As I held my hands over here body, I could feel a rush of energy radiating through my hands onto her. My heart filled with love as I began to do reiki channelling and bringing in divine angelic energy, using crystals to enhance the energy connection. I channelled angelic energy and ascendant masters, by placing crystals on her body. The energy that filled the room was also felt by Sister Sama's Sister and the Doctor.

As I felt the angelic energy streaming through me to her, I cried tears of joy. This allowed the angels to penetrate her body in a healing way, through me. Sister Sama lay peacefully as I continued tears streaming down my face. The healing session went for about an hour. When Sister Sama opened her eyes, she said, "Angels were everywhere. They surrounded me as I was receiving the healing."

The words she used to describe her experience filled my heart with love, and my eyes brimmed again. This was my moment of truth; the truth of healing. I was healing others, through belief and love. When you need the love of angels, they will come. Angels are here for us whenever we need them. 'Angel' meaning is messengers from God; messages of Goodness or Godness.

There are many good memories I hold in my heart from my times in India. Kindness and giving came easily to the wonderful brothers and sisters of Brahma Kumaris. I love and appreciate every minute in their presence.

It wasn't long before I visited their Ashram in Hyderabad. While there I did community work for the village people and offered meditation to whoever wanted to participate. Brahma Kumaris do 'Raja Yoga' Meditation which is linked to Hatha Yoga and its principles. These are ancient modalities to bring us deeper into consciousness and connect with higher self.

It was so much fun and very mystical. One of the practices is being happy. Being happy with self, with others and being grateful for others in your life. Every day I would wear a white sari and have my hair done in preparation for the day.

I noticed auras around the children and some adults. It is such a powerful meditation. Raja Yoga is looking into the eyes to connect with the soul. There is such a deep connection when you gaze into someone's eyes and just be. Connect with the other person by gazing intently, seeing their soul. This is an ancient practice and a beautiful one. You don't think them, the person in front of you, you feel them. Thinking causes judgement. If you just feel them, you will find their heart and soul connect with yours.

In February 2018 I was invited to attend and speak at the Brahma Kumaris Global Peace and happiness event in Mount Abu, India at the Brahma Kumaris Headquarters. This is a huge event which attracts around 25 thousand people globally.

When I arrived, I was met at the airport with a beautiful smile of the very obliging brother. I love Brahma Kumaris honesty and loving demeanour. After a 3-hour drive, we arrived. I was feeling very weary from my long trip so opted to go to bed and get up early to have a look around.

Walking out of the front door of my accommodation I was blown away by the energy coming from thousands of people who were walking the streets and smiling and saying hello. Every turn I made was like an exciting new discovery. I felt like a child in Disneyland for the first time.

Brahma Kumaris Headquarters at Mt Abu, India; a Spiritual Disneyland. Wow! I felt so blessed and honoured to be invited to speak at their global event. 'What an opportunity', I thought, to be spreading a message of love to the World.

On the third day, I met Dr. Partap Midha. He was speaking before me, so we were placed together on the stage. Kindly, he invited me to tour Brahma Kumaris hospital. This was an exciting prospect because they have

Ayurveda. Curiosity and joy filled me as we headed up the mountain to the Hospital. It's like that at Brahma Kumaris; everyone is kind, respectful and always willing to share their knowledge and love. Nothing is a chore. It comes naturally.

Dr. Midha was busy, so he introduced me to his assistant who kindly showed me around the hospital and surroundings. I felt euphoric as David Kilowasky gave his time to me for the next couple of hours. I noticed some statues of kangaroos, our national emblem, as I was staring at the sign 'Peace Park'. How wonderful it was to see a part of my home (Australia) in India.

David asked if I wanted to meet Didi (Dr. Nirmala) who I was curious about. She lived in Gyan Sarovar premises. For some reason, she wanted to know all about me. We were curious about each other. We laughed, enjoyed tea and exchanged our spiritual journeys. Both of us wanted World Peace and additional love for the planet and every living being. I was given a book she wrote, which I cherish.

I spent time nourishing myself in the mystical realm of peace and wonder as I strolled the buildings. Many were filled with past ornamental deities, like Shiva, Shakti, and Krishna. It felt like entering the water with dolphins swimming around you. Surrounded by deities and lords of ascendant masters made me feel at home. Some of the deities I had channelled, so I deeply resonated with them. The colours, the costumes, everything was sheer beauty.

After four days of the event, it was time to leave. My heart was low as I packed my suitcase. The happiness and love that was shared amongst every person who attended were magical, making it difficult to leave. I will never forget the respect, love, and generosity I had been shown.

I meditated with the Sisters of Brahma Kumaris and my heart filled with love every time I was around them. The Brothers of Brahma Kumaris were the same. Proving once again we are all one. I embraced Brahma Kumaris with an open heart.

How is it that people judge and put down such organisations that are only here to do good? They wear white for purity. I loved how I felt when I wore a white sari given to me at one of their events. It made me feel special, at peace and full of love. High vibrational energy of love and peace that Brahma Kumaris puts out created it. If you want to lift your vibe, then Brahma Kumaris is a great way to start.

I am in awe of my divine connection with Brahma Kumaris. They are on this planet to help and assist, to bring peace and harmony to our world. Wherever possible, I attend their meditation and celebrations. Their meditation and courses are free, and they offer their service. It's also one of my self-care things to do, enjoying their uplifting energy and loving environment. I know that I will be connected to them for the rest of my life.

We have moved into a time Age of Aquarius, which is a Vedic astrological term for how the planets align and how it affects us energetically. Many people have felt this energy especially this year, where consciousness has moved quickly. There will be a more dominant shift in the years to come. Many of us are awakening, awakened or becoming awakened.

We are no longer focussing on materialism as we once did before. We are choosing to trust more of our own abilities and uniqueness, rather than thinking we must conform to something that does not resonate with us.

The spiritual headquarters of Brahma Kumaris is in Mount Abu, India. Their international interest is coordinated regionally from offices in London, Moscow, Nairobi, New York, and Sydney. Though all congregate in Mount Abu for world peace.

Brahma Kumaris is the largest spiritual organisation in the world led by women. It's interesting how we are in the feminine movement. It was the founder, Prajapita Brahma Baba, who chose to put women in front from the very beginning. This has set Brahma Kumaris ideals.

Weirdly, I began to feel no pain. It dissipated, and it was like I was outside myself looking down on the doctors and nurses around me. They were endeavouring to keep me alive, but I was in this ethereal place, a mystical place, where it didn't concern me that my body was on the table and I was out of it and dying. I observed them, but went into myself, feeling euphoric. There was fearlessness and peacefulness, as I floated drifting into a lightness; like a piece of paper when if falls, it floats peacefully and silently.

I said, "I'm dying," but instead of being scared, it was like a 'wow' moment. Like, "I'm out of my body, how beautiful." Any worry, fears, concerns were gone.

It was odd. I felt calm and connected. I felt light. Though alone except the doctors and nurses in the room, somehow the connection with my children appeared while I travelled into total light, pleasure, and blissful angelic state of being. There were perfect happiness and great joyfulness. It was as if I was taken to another dimension with my children, yet they were not connected to these feelings, clearly distressed as looks of confusion lined their confused faces.

For over 80 years of leadership, Brahma Kumaris has been characterised by steady courage, a capacity for forgiveness and a deep commitment to unity.

Although women hold the top administrative positions, the women who hold these positions have always made decisions in partnership with the men. It is a partnership and consensus model of leadership, based on respect, equality, and humility. Living in peace, harmony, and happiness.

Happiness and bliss envelop me when I am with my Sisters of Brahma Kumaris. They are surrounded by *light* and *love*, sharing it with those who come into their life. As I stood beside them, I felt the *light*. I honoured the *light,* and I became *light*.

I truly believe I was guided divinely to meet the brothers and sisters of Brahma Kumaris. Without meeting them, I would never have found out about the deities that were channelling me. Travelling to India has been one of confirmation and clarification. Many of the images I received were to do with ancient traditional Indian Culture, buddism and hinduism. I didn't understand why or what was happening to me. I now know it was happening *for* me. Life happens *for* us, not to us.

We are in times of positive change, the forces of energy that align with our inner peace and love is now stronger than ever as we learn who we truly are. Angels are from the seventh dimension. We cannot live in this dimension in our human body. However, we can have moments of angelic energy flowing to us. It is the light or the brightness of lightness. Angelic energy can be felt through animal totems, life watching dolphins in the ocean or whales swimming while the sun is beaming sparkles of diamond on top of the ocean; a place of oneness or stillness, where nothing can interrupt you in that moment. You feel that you have something else that you are connected to; the water, the trees, the sky, animals, every living being is all part of us.

Say to your inner self, "Everything inside me is part of you. Everything inside you is part of me."

Feminine energy is part of the shift into the fifth-dimension; feminine energy. It doesn't mean that it is a female. We are both masculine and feminine. Feminine energy is of much higher energy, enlightened and aligned to heal us and the planet. Both male and female have this as a union.

In the fourth-dimension people awaken and are open to receive love and compassion; what we feel, not what we think. Feeling the energy of love, inner peace, compassion, forgiveness is the key.

Clearing and cleansing are important parts of shifting your energy, as you evolve and align with cosmic energy. Accept it and release the low energy. Bring in the *light* to change the masculine energy and move into the feminine energy.

When you are in this state of being it is a great idea to send that energy out into the planet, to Mother Earth and to others who may be experiencing darkness and want to shift into the *light*. Those who do not move will either be removed or put somewhere else. It is a conscious shift. They will not be able to survive in the new energy of love and light. Being part of this shift and knowing what your purpose will help you remove the low energy that once lived inside you.

The old paradigm of greed, materialism, and selfishness is collapsing to make way for the new. This has been happening since 2011. When we make way for the new, we become aware that we must work together, building each other up, uplifting and bringing in the JOY!

Those who are not interested in living in peace and harmony will not stay. Those who are in low frequency and choose to stay this way will remain that. Low frequency carries stress and resistance. People who want to work on their higher frequency vibration will see a change in themselves and the world around them. The oneness of the world has been activated.

Have you noticed any significant change in you since 2011? Perhaps a change in relationships, career or moving house? You may see life differently and see others as something else.

Exercise

- Do you experience visions or dreams you don't understand?
- Are you feeling a deeper connection to the feminine shift of nurturing/love?
- Sit quietly somewhere near nature (under a tree, near the ocean, etc.). Appreciate everything around you. Be gentle with yourself and bring in the awareness of being, enjoying the stillness or everything. Allow yourself to go deep and really feel into you.

Golden Gem for your Spiritual Treasure Chest

This Golden Gem bonus will bring forth creativity and peace. Find a quiet place and draw something that makes you feel good. If you are not so good at drawing it does not matter as it is what is in your heart as you draw. Keep the finished artwork and place it in your Spiritual Treasure Chest. Use colour to express your feelings. It's good for the soul and chakras.

CHAPTER 7

How I faced my own fears

"Let it go" - Let go of fear and magic will appear – Kerry Clancey

"Fears are nothing more than a state of mind."

—Napoleon Hill

Fear, we all have it. It's how we deal with it that matters.

Letting go of fear was not easy for me at first. I used to allow others to put their fear on me. I then found out that it was better to do whatever made happy, not what others thought I should do. Once I learnt I was responsible for my own fear, it became easier. Fear is a false emotion that appears to be real. It's not actual, because it is thought. Thought does not know what is true or false. The mind does not know reality from fantasy.

Before I went to India on my first trip solo, several female friends said, "Don't go to India by yourself. It's not safe for a female." Initially, I did let fear in. It made me nervous. The fear they spoke about then became part of my fear.

I had been working in Ubud, Bali with an Ayurvedic doctor as a healer and decided to go to India from there. In India, my first three weeks were unpleasant. I was looking for exciting experiences and to find answers, but I wasn't discovering them. I went to an Ayurvedic training hospital to learn and study about the traditional ancient plant medicine that heals our bodies within. I discovered it wasn't for me (that hospital that is). Something just didn't feel right. I was feeling the energy that wasn't compatible with me.

I moved to another Ayurveda training hospital where I met Dr. Asghar, who is the founder of Greens Ayurveda, in Mahe, Kerala. The warmth, care, and love I received there opened my heart to the people of India and especially Kerala. (You can read more about Kerala on my website).

On my first day, I was met by an Ayurvedic therapist. She was happy to be giving me an Ayurvedic massage. This massage was with herbal oil, specially made at Greens Ayurveda by an 82-year-old Ayurvedic pharmacist. Her name was Soumnya. Before my massage, I was asked to sit on a chair with my eyes closed, which I didn't mind, as I was weary from the hours of travel.

As she proceeded, I could feel calming energy shifting through my body. I opened my eyes to notice she was praying over me. There were Indian mantras playing. I have since learned that this is part of traditional ancient Ayurveda. It is done so that divine energy can flow to the receiver as part of the healing process. Once my massage was complete, I was totally in another world. I relaxed in a hammock, realising that I was in a good place. The fear vanished. I had managed to experience the letting go of fear. One I did that it allowed other things to present themselves to me.

Anxiety and Fear

I have many clients who suffer from anxiety. They suffer in their own thoughts. The truth is (a little was explained in chapter one) if a thought can change a feeling, then to release fear is to change the way you think. I have tested it many times on my clients and using CBT (cognitive behaviour therapy) and other therapies, with great success. These successes make me feel alive inside, knowing I can share these experiences to help and guide others.

Fear can be debilitating for some people, to the extent that they cannot leave their homes. One of my own experiences with fear was just before my NDE. I had recently split with my (now ex) husband. There were indiscretions, which was difficult enough, also stressful business problems forcing bankruptcy. I was 1.8 million dollars in debt. It was a traumatic time.

This situation would put fear into anyone. However, after months of enervating fear, I began working through the debt. I paid who needed to be paid. I managed to keep my home. But mostly I learned that there is something inside 'each and every' one of us. I found an inner strength, an internal direction; which I know now is our inner-guidance system. I was stronger and more resilient than ever before. Taking my own power, I no longer relied on someone or something else to make me feel fulfilled or whole. Things were perfectly aligning; I was whole.

At first, it wasn't easy. It was day-by-day, step-by-step. I managed to rise from bed daily. I worked through, not only the pain of my husband leaving, but the loss of my marriage, plus the loss of him as my friend. I believed he was my soul mate. I was a loyal, trusting person and wife. Marriage to me was forever. The biggest thing I learnt from this experience was my resilience; to life, to people, to everyday things, both good and bad. I could keep going no matter what life threw at me. I let go of the attachment to these things and I was free.

Once I realised the betrayal, I moved away from some friends. Betrayal is low frequency. I needed to always keep my frequency high. It is not necessary for me to rely on someone else to fill me. Taking responsibility for the way I am feeling is me relying on me. It's up to you not someone else to keep you happy and joyous. Daily practice leads to perfection. Fill your body with love and fear cannot survive in a body full of love.

Fear and how it's affected me.

Though I've learned to let go of fear, since my NDE seven years ago, in my early twenties I was on edge frequently. My past wasn't one of 'happy families'. It was dysfunctional in many ways.

I suffered sexual abuse, from eight years old. That was horrific enough. I was also hit a lot, surrounded by violence. I suffered physical and emotional abuse, always being put down and told that I was useless or not good enough. This not only affected my self-esteem but gave me a feeling of unworthiness for anything good in my life. I felt empty inside. Much later, I worked through that, learning not to blame or shame; to forgive. Accusing anyone didn't help me. I came to accept that they didn't know any better.

Perhaps they were only repeating a pattern of what (probably) happened to them.

Forgiveness

I once read that to forgive you need to be told what forgiveness is. You must go deep inside yourself and then put yourself in the shoes of your abusers. I visualised my father (I haven't seen either parent for many years) from an old photo when he was three years old. I stared at the photo thinking of an innocent three-year-old boy. I felt compassion instead of fear and hate. I sent him love from deep within my heart. It broke a dam of tears as I celebrated the forgiveness. I never met my grandfather, but I figured he had a lot to do with how my father turned out. I released anger towards him while realising my father probably had the same rage at him. I released any attachments to the fear, including ancestral.

To release my fears, I had to go back to when I was young. I needed to relive my early life to heal. After facing the fear, acknowledging it and forgiving those who had caused it, my fear gradually dissipated.

It's empowering to understand we hold this stuff within us. Our beliefs, values and everything we've been told in our formative years fills us. Expectations, perceptions, teachers, parents, siblings, friends all have an influence on our lives. Think of it like; your tribe is your vibe. Who, and what you are surrounded by, reflects your family, job, friendships, in fact, your life; everything.

You need to come to a point where you can say, "Wow, now I know why I did that. I understand and accept it."

Through my whole life, I was fearful. Terror of my parents, then fears of my bosses. Through my many jobs, from pumping petrol, working for Queensland Health to NSW Police, I struggled with my fears. Some bosses used power to control their workers, or just for their own satisfaction. Perhaps they were suffering inside, if they weren't, they would not put others through misery. I find it hard sometimes wondering what makes people do things to others that hurt or bring them down. When someone writes a negative comment on social media, they too are suffering. If a person puts another down, then they are probably in anguish. Plenty of people on the planet are desolate and don't realise it. They suffer from thoughts and beliefs.

Once you acknowledge it and let it be their personal problem, not yours, you release the fear. When I did so, I had an awakening. I became a confident, fearless person. You can too.

The NDE showed that we are all connected; we need love not fear. We can realise it by gently closing our eyes. You can't feel within, or our inner being with your eyes open. Remember fear is attached to a thought, such as; don't do it, you're not good enough, you'll fail, you're too old, you're too young, your too fat, your too thin, you have no knowledge. These are the stories you tell yourself. You mustn't hold on to them. Einstein was told he was a slow learner and had a learning disability. Meryl Streep was told she was too ugly to be an actress. Imagine if they had listened to what they had been told by others. It's other's opinions and perceptions that put fear in us.

Look at your fear. Say to that fear, "I know who you are. I know that you are there."

Say to the fear, "You are with me, but I do not choose you. I chose happiness instead." The word happiness could be anything if it's the opposite of your fear. Happiness sits in the heart. Hold your heart and you will release fear.

- Poverty – Abundance.
- Failure – Success.
- Loneliness – Love
- Anger – Forgiveness
- Guilt - Worthy

I said to my client Brandon, from the USA, "What if a tiger were stalking you? You would be scared." Let the Tiger eat you, and release the FEAR, it will no longer be there. Making friends with fear and allowing it to be there is empowering the path to heal. Brendon has a tiger tattoo on his leg, so I was using it as a metaphor to help him heal.

Instead of being fearful I told him to say, "Tiger eat me. I want you to be full of love and peace." Of course, it's only an example. A tiger is a wild animal, but as a metaphor, it works. We do need fight or flight in a situation that hasn't been created by a fear though. If it's only a thought it can be gone. If there were a real tiger, perhaps I wouldn't suggest the next statement.

Brandon was taken into a meditative state. He could feel me inside him cutting cords in his heart. I channelled energy to get him to release his fear. I said, "Let the tiger eat you, if it is the fear, then release it." As a metaphor that worked for him. He released the fear that he could see was a tiger, but of course was a fear of something else; his personal fear. *Read Brandon's testimonial on my webpage and at the end of this book.*

Identify the fear that is holding you back

If the fear isn't on top of the umbrella is it the shadow under it. It may be guilt or any negative emotion. What is your emotion? Anger, resentment, greed, sadness, shame? Find the emotion, close your eyes, breath slowly (I explain breath in later chapters). See it. Release it by changing the thought? We have the power within us to do it.

When you take yourself into your heart and breath, slowly gently, calmly, you'll leave your mind. You'll feel your intuition and guidance system will kick in. The mind and the breath are connected. They can slow your mind. We are not taught that the breath can do that. I will teach you how. When we slow down our breath, our mind slows and allows a space for goodness to come, goodness of thoughts and positive thinking. It then you will connect to who you really are; a spiritual being.

Negative words, like my mother said when I did something wrong, "Didn't you think about that?" A better way would have been her guiding me in a positive way instead of the negative. Positive reinforcement abates the fear. Positive words decrease fear. I can remember one of my previous bosses saying to me, "You are not good enough unless you have a degree".

It didn't matter that I had goodness and kindness in my heart. These are things that we are born with, inside us, our true being, kindness, and love. It's easy for someone with an open heart to be taken advantage of, as I have learnt over the years.

Through my learning, I am now aware of when my mother's energy is inside me. A past life like this can be cleared easily. My children suffered because of what I did and became due to my past childhood. Hopefully, this book gives insight and understanding of why we do what we do. Without knowing, we most certainly suffer. When we know and understand a new way of being, we can embrace it.

Fear can take you on a journey to the shadows and dark side. We don't want that. We need to be near the light side; pure innocent and full of unconditional love like a newborn.

My spiritual journey started after the NDE. I can now remove myself from my physical body, taking myself into the blissful place of unconditional love. I came to this lack of fear through my NDE and the subsequent research and travel that followed it. I tap into all sorts of knowledge in my journey to learn more about many things like, psychic ability, yoga, meditation, Ayurveda, light, and love.

Ten fear emotions you can find a positive word for:

- Hate - love
- Envy – generosity
- Anger – forgiveness
- Sad – happiness
- Nervous – confident
- Grief – gratitude
- Anxious – inner peace
- Rejection – acceptance
- Shame – honour
- Poor – abundant

Exercises

- What is your greatest fear?
- Think of that fear. Tell it you see it. Then say, "You are with me, but I do not choose you. I choose happiness (or whatever the opposite of fear is) instead." Try this mantra for a week. Get in tune and go deep. Do not allow your fearful to come, instead, allow your cheerful. Or say a mantra, "I am divinely guided always or I am light." Affirm by saying, "I AM," which brings in conscious awareness. "I have," dives into subconscious overriding and changing neural pathways in the brain(belief system). The subconscious is like a filing cabinet that keeps everything in a place. When we work through and tidy up our cabinet we can become powerful and strong. Throw away thoughts that do not serve you. Awareness helps people heal past emotional wounds. The idea is to change the way you feel and connect to the emotion. Replace it with kindness, or loving mantra, music, dance, whatever can change that moment of fear. Fear can be debilitating if it takes hold.

- Do you have a long-term fear (perhaps from your childhood)? If so, acknowledge it, face it and banish it. Do you have a photo that can trigger the fear, or teach you to dissipate that fear? This may take more than a week but keep trying to banish the fear. Write about how good you will feel once this long-held fear is out of your life. Think of something that brings joy to your heart. Let it fill the void once you remove the fear. When something is removed from our subconscious, we need to replace it with something else. Like clearing your filing cabinet, take an old folder out, throw it away and replace with something new.

Golden Gem for your Spiritual Treasure Chest

I was interviewed on The National Healing Show for UK Health Radio hosted by Catherine Carrigan *'Kerry Clancey What a Near Death Experience Can Teach You About How to Overcome Loneliness'*. It's nearly 50 minutes of me discussing my NDE and how to overcome another emotion; loneliness.

It's on YouTube at https://youtu.be/74hoBKFOz9o

CHAPTER 8

Thoughts Create Fantasy or Reality
Positive thinking really does manifest things

"Happiness depends on ourselves."

—Aristotle

Thoughts are very powerful. I mentioned previously that they are contained in our mind. The mind does not know fantasy from reality. One day near my home on the Gold Coast, I was sitting by the ocean looking at the booming surf, smelling the salt, with sunshine warming my skin. I was pondering things. I thought if I change my thoughts then many other things can change. It was two years before my NDE in 2009.

I had digested much information, yearning for something. I read many books, handouts, web pages, workshops, retreats and other resources. I listened to different theories from health professional throughout my working career with Queensland Health and NSW Police.

The one thing I never heard anyone say is, "Your thoughts are not real. They are just matter, and they don't matter. They are a belief or others, an expectaton of who, why and what you should be. What matters is that we have an awareness of what they do and what they are? Once we come to realise this, we can create, manifest and have the life we want and desire."

There is an abundance of everything on this planet, and we each have a purpose to live a happy life. Whether we are a spiritual teacher, medium, chef, doctor, receptionist, author, business owner, manager, it doesn't matter. We each have a purpose, and if we are not living our life with purpose, then we are disconnected from who we are. More importantly, we will not know what we are here to do.

Have you ever just daydreamed about having a job and doing what you love? Well, that means you need to do that. The only way to find your true purpose is to find what truly makes you happy. I could not see myself doing anything else but what I'm doing now. I love travelling, teaching and connecting with others. I especially enjoy making a difference to peoples lives. When I reflect on my life, I can see a pattern or trail that has led me to where I am today. It wasn't just the NDE. It was the fact that I became a different person when that happened. I found myself and my purpose. I became me. With that process I found my inner child, my light and my love.

Finding happiness is not about a thing, a country, a house, a car or a destination. Happiness is an ongoing path. Once we discover who we really are (emotional beings) we can bring happiness in a second, through meditation or by changing our thoughts.

When I was working for Queensland Health, I held a community workshop. I wanted to get my attendees to get in touch with their feeling. Showing them a picture of Mother Theresa, Hitler, a baby, and puppy, then a known serial killer, I wanted their reactions to each photo. How do you think they reacted? Each image impacted on their thoughts, be it either love, disgust, gushing, happiness or dread.

Dr. Emoto from the Emoto Peace Project also proved that words are consciousness and can change water. Writing 'love and peace' on a bottle of water can change its frequency. Plants do the same. They fear and feel love. Dr. Emoto showed images of dolphins to water, and it changed to beautiful crystals. Water is part of us. We are eighty percent water.

These types of images are another reason why I don't watch television, and I recommend you cease viewing it too. That way I am not involved in politics or negativity on social media. Remember what I said earlier, Mother Theresa is quoted as having said, "Invite me to an anti-war rally, and I will not come. Invite me to a peace rally, and I will come." They both mean the same thing but are worded very differently and have a dissimilar impact on our emotions. Anti and war are negative. Peace and love are positive and high vibrational frequency. We light up when we are emotionally connected to love and peace. Its gives out a sense of freedom.

Try this little exercise with a friend

1. Have them close their eyes and say, "Hitler", "Hate" or "Soul", "Kindness", "Love". Perhaps, ask them to think about a situation they didn't like and a situation they loved. Let them describe their feelings. Its important to feel the emotion. This allows connection to our inner world. What we think, we feel and what we feel we create.

2. Ask them to show you where they feel the emotion (feeling). Many people I have worked with place their hand on their heart when they feel love or kindness. You can also do this exercise as part of forgiveness. Think of someone or something that has hurt you in the past. Go to the feeling and acknowledge it, sit with it, then release it. You will feel a sense of calmness. This is healing past emotional pain. It sits within us until we release it and set it free.

3. Ask them to take a long slow breath into that emotion and exhale out slowly. After that, ask how they feel again. It's amazing how our breath can heal these negative feelings and release them from our bodies. Afterwards, look into the eyes of each other (raja yoga), and you will feel a soul connection. Emotions will arise, and you will feel something penetrating your heart. This is coming from the other person and is showing you how to connect. It is part of healing work I do and works the same as if you were being massaged by someone. A massage focuses on healing through the hands but also the power of the mind to push energy to the emotion of the heart. Then the healing begins.

I was writing this book on Christmas Day 2017. The rain poured down as I stepped outside my room looking at the rain drops falling into the pool. I was in beautiful, tranquil Ubud, Bali working at The Yoga Barn. The garden looked lush green with colourful flowers. I seemed to feel the plants in a way that communicated how good they were feeling. They loved the rain. It was like the plants were saying, "Thank you heaven for providing us with a drink of water." They seem to stand up, full of life.

Have you ever observed plants when it rains? They seem to stand taller and look more vibrant. It's as if they are saying, "Thank you for the rain it gives me strength." The magic that happens between the two is incredible, add some sunshine to the two, and it becomes like a family. One does not live without the other; it's a connection. Add a rainbow and moon, and we are living with the five elements, which connect with our five channels, senses. How fortunate are we to be connected to this? Our 6th sense is our divine connection.

I believe if we were more connected, we could do anything. Just like the plants, perhaps we can wish something upon ourselves to grow strong. Shifting into consciousness is the key to inner knowing and awakening.

Finding a positive vibe with your tribe

Through my spiritual journey, I have discovered that there are many pretentious people. Some give vulnerable people the wrong message about their spirituality and the meaning behind it. They draw on Hindu or Ancient Indian texts, Balinese text or scriptures to make them their own ideas and philosophies. They change their western name to Hindi Gods so that people follow them. It's okay if it's their thing and is set up like that to draw people to them; if it's genuine. I want to tell you this, so you are aware. Be cautious. As we become more conscious, we will awaken and enhance our psychic abilities. They will draw out the darkness in people. Our intuition will become more heightened than ever before. Crime rate will drop because we will know when someone is lying, cheating or doing wrong by others.

I do believe that the more people tapping into spirituality in some form, the better the shift in consciousness. That shift will cause inner peace and the planet will be at peace. If we all have inner peace the world becomes peaceful.

It's like saying we have peace over here and war over there, which one do we want? We have love over here and hate over there, which one do we want? Which one do we choose? We have like over here, dislike over here, which one do you want? Do you want the rainbow, or do you want the darkness? Colour in your life or shade? Do you want to feel light or do you want burdens on your shoulders? Do you want to feel lightness and love in your hearts as much as you can? This is why many of us search for spirituality.

The Universal Laws – how powerful they are

The law of attraction, the law of polarity and the laws of nature rule us. The law of attraction is whatever you think about you bring about. The law of polarity is that everything has an opposite, love-hate, peace-war, trust-distrust, confidence-fear. The laws of nature are cause and effect, such as global climate change due to our overuse of resources. This has seen our seas rising 6.7 inches this century due to global warming; effect and cause. However, if we look at divine Mother Nature, she can heal and purify. It is more about why we are consuming so much we don't need. If we minimised, we would have fewer things to worry about, and we would need less money.

The reverse is if you balance the laws of nature. If you take one plant out of the ground, replace it with another plant or two, so that we can replenish and rejuvenate. On a cellular level where we use these plants and herbs to replenish and detox by getting rid of the toxins and purifying the cells.

Using the law of attraction works by using your energy to create intention. Your goal maybe to create. Connect your energy to the people you want to attract. Put your focus and with the power of your imagination, practice drawing your energy around your body. Expand that energy out to the people who are perfect for you. Increase that by using the power of your imagination. Direct it into a room or a country or the planet. Using the ability of your samsara chakra, light yourself and those you want to attract. Your perfect people will show up for you at that moment. They will come into your imagination and then your physical life.

There are seven universal laws and principles which are governed by the universe governed by the universe. The universe is perfect in harmony due to these laws. Ancient, mystical, esoteric and secret knowledge, aging back thousands of years, tell it. Ancient Veda's (traditional ancient India), Ancient Egypt, to Ancient Greece, Ancient Indigenous Australia all have commonalities which connect to the universal laws. Mastering each of the seven laws will transform every area of your life, beyond imagination. "Imagination for Creation," said Kerry Clancey. Everything comes from thought, imagination of someone.

The science behind what I have discovered.

Learning about energy and vibrational frequency was a huge discovery. My NDE was an experience of an energy shift in my body, a spiritual shift taking me to where it all began, into the Light. I was part of that light. I believe that light is the Universe. We are all part of it. It is connected to different sounds, vibrations, and energy. Science has proven that we are all part of that energy and frequency.

Japanese water researcher, Dr. Masaru Emoto, did a test of students holding hands over samples of dirty water. He asked them all to pray with intent. The water went from murky to clear as crystal. These facts were verified. Their combined thoughts became what they envisioned; clear, drinkable water.

Testing words

Here's a fun test for you to try. Make two equal jars of rice. Mark them, so you know which is which. You could write 'hate' on one and 'love' on the other. Say to the jar marked 'hate', "Jar of rice, I hate you." Say to the jar of rice marked 'love', "Jar of rice, I love.

This is what happened when Dr Emoto did this experiment. The 'hate' jar grew mould through the rice. The 'love' jar rice stayed pure white. Proving that our words are indeed energy.

Ho'oponopono is an ancient Hawaiian practice based on forgiveness. It is believed to restore harmony within. Saying words, I'm sorry, please forgive me, thank you and I love you. Hawaiian therapist Dr Ihaleakal Hew Len used this technique to cure criminally insane inpatients. Without ever meeting them he was able to cure them through thoughts and word. Notice the words. They are all high vibration.

We must choose our words and thoughts carefully. Whatever we say is within us. We will hold that thought in our cells, tissue, muscles and physcial. If we gossip or say unkind words about someone, we will hold that inside us. Hate creates hate. We must work on trying not to do those things in our life. It's a bit like saying, "Karma". Be nice, or Karma will come back on you. There's something in that which science has also proven. Every human being is at a level of consciousness or unconscious. They either want to raise up to this level or they want stay unconscious. If it is not our way to judge, its our way to heal, uplift and rise up consciously.

Scientifically energy is everything. On a cellar level, in Sanskrit and many other ancient text, it's been written that our cells are connected to the Universe. Your thoughts go out to the Universe and come back to you. You feel sad, and somehow this makes you sadder or someone around you sad. You are kind, and without asking, someone is kind to you. Be aware your thoughts also create what is inside you. You will hold hate (low vibration), if you say you hate something or someone. I smile and my heart becomes full when I read or listen to someone who says "I AM the Universe" or I AM God...

Exercises

- Have you ever pictured something clearly in your mind and sometime later that thought has become something tangible?
- Do you find yourself having negative thoughts? Can you now find a way to turn that negative into a positive thought?
- Are you a positive or negative thinker? Can you write down ways to become more positive to create abundance in your life? That is, what are the golden gems for your spiritual treasure chest are for. Fill your chest with joy? What does Joy mean for you?

Golden Gem for your Spiritual Treasure Chest

The Golden Gem for this chapter is a mantra I want you to use daily, as you wake: A mantra is something you say over and over to change the vibrational energy within you. "Raise your vibration through meditation"

Take a deep breath in, sit quietly and say the below mantra.

"I am grateful to be alive, living a happy, joyous, prosperous, abundant life." Remember, using *I AM* to start your mantra will bring you into a conscious state.

CHAPTER 9

Emotions
Why do we feel them?

"If I feel depressed, I will sing. If I feel sad, I will laugh."
—Og Mandino

Emotions are a part of human life. They are with us for various reasons; you become redundant from your job (resentment), a loved one crossed over died (grief), you won the lottery (shock, joy), your car was involved in a crash (fear, shock, anger), you dived into cool water on a hot day (apprehension, exhilaration). We fear in chapter seven, but there are many more emotions.

How we respond to stress is very important. If we don't realise that we are feeling stressed we can manifest disease, including insomnia, diabetes, high blood pressure, skin conditions, including eczema among others.

The key is to appreciate our feelings, both good and not so good. This is what brings us back to balance. I believe and practice this. For example; if I were stressed with my work I would try and do something that made me feel good. This would change the stressful thought. Choosing a natural way to feel good is empowering and extremely good for our soul.

Another way is taking time to meditate. I thank my inner being for bringing the stressful thought into fruition. Once aware of the thought and what I am doing physically I can acknowledge it. Try this next time you are at work and feeling stressed about meeting deadlines. I'm pretty sure no one has perished because they haven't met a deadline. If you look at stressful situations in life, they eventually work out. Have you ever said to yourself, why did I worry as it all worked out? It always figured out for our higher good.

I tell my clients, if you're at work, socialising or in any situation where you feel a little wobbly with your thoughts go to the bathroom. No one will interrupt you there. It gives you minutes to relax, do meditation and breathe. Escaping is effective and simple to do. It brings you back to within and who you truly are.

Connection, not rejection, never reject your thoughts, or they will return with power. You cannot give them power if you are in your power within. Only we can hold the power inside us.

Emotions and why you feel them

Our emotions have a deep connection with what we think. They are why when we think something isn't good for us, it results in us feel bad. What happens is, our thoughts hold vibrational energy that we are all connected with, both good and bad (law of polarity). Apparently, there are 10 Universal Laws which operate in the outer universe. This was discovered by scientists and called natural laws. By staying in mindfulness of these laws and understanding they are related to self and to others, we keep to these laws. We need to know that in love, all life is given and loving all things. Knowing that 'love' is life.

I live by as many of these laws. The law of polarity is that everything has an opposite and cannot exist without out its opposite. Combining this with another universal law (law of attraction) we can all create of life of prosperity and abundance to stay healthy and happy. For example, if I was having a bad morning. I then meditate into, why am I feeling (emotion) this way? I would hold my awareness of what my thoughts were doing? When we master our thoughts, we master how we feel (emotions) both good and not good.

Monitoring our emotions is one way to discover how powerful our emotions (thoughts) can be. I remember working with a client for the UK, who was so distressed emotionally (she had just found out her husband was having an affair). I needed to change her thoughts, so she felt better. I decided to combine CBT with spiritual therapy and was able to pacify her emotions. She was able to take control of the stressful situation enough for her to be empowered to look at her emotions and situation in another way.

I have had many clients I have helped in such a way. Through my own emotional experiences, I find that when we are able to look at our thoughts and connect them, we not only feel better, but we can make improved life decisions. Being happier about what life brings us. We need emotions as they are part of our being. I have learnt we are emotional beings having a physical experience. When I first heard this, I thought, what does that mean? I couldn't find a clear explanation anywhere, which is why I love writing about this topic.

Emotions are attached to many experiences and attached to the way we live our life. For example: If I'm thinking (thought) something that is beautiful, I think about how my granddaughter and I play in the park together. We could just sit by the ocean and talk or go for a walk while she tells me little stories. She is one of my biggest teachers in writing about emotions. I'm always learning from her.

Children are filled with unconditional love. We were all born this way, and we all leave in the same way (read about it in chapter 1 my near-death experience). Remember how I said when she was three years old and I said to her, "You are so beautiful and cute."

She said to me, "You are too, Nan. You are cute and beautiful" My emotions opened. I could feel that connection of pure love and joy; unconditional love. It's where souls see souls before the conditioned thinking creeps in.

Even as I write about it, I can feel (emotion) in my heart and connecting with my inner being (true self). When I was at university and studying the psychology of the mind, there was lots of theory. There was no so much about how we feel or the connections we can have.

In class, I asked my lecturer, "Why would we use certain theories when we are all individually wired? Wouldn't we need a theory for each person in the world?" I thought maybe he just doesn't understand my understanding, which is okay. We only know what we know. Until we have an experience nothing else changes, hence, we think what we think, and we feel the way we feel (emotions).

Another explanation, when we, think about things that give us joy, happiness like our heart feels like it's going to explode out of our chest, it is because (science) we are connecting to our inner being (emotions) and our heart (soul). It projects out of our heart centre (chakra) (energy) and sends out a feeling of love from one person to another. I found books and movies that explain this more in depth are; *Change your thoughts change your life* by

Dr. Wayne Dyer and *The Theory of Everything* by Stephen W. Hawking, a physicist and is known for his work of cosmology and quantum gravity and who also discovered the context of the black hole (planet). He is one of my favourites and has many books, articles and the movie about him, 'The Theory of Everything' was released in 2014. This movie gave me lots of clarity and confirmation on how we are connected through thoughts, emotions and the universe.

EGO 'Edge Goodness Out'

Our thoughts are based on ego, and our minds cannot decipher a good thought from a not so good thought. Knowing this makes you think of your thoughts in a different way. To allow the connection with what you feel to flow and take control (empower). For you to change what you were thinking (ego) to create a better feeling (emotion); love. Yes, that is right, if we think loving thoughts and let ego out of the way instead of thinking loving thoughts of kindness, compassion and forgiveness. Don't let the ego (escalate good out). It's not what we want, and that's why when our emotions are out of balance, we tend to think thoughts not good for our health or wellbeing (soul or emotional). If we are need of confidence ego is good. Don't get me wrong, ego can also produce arrogance.

The best way I can describe this is by sitting quietly and closing your eyes, slowing down your breath, ask your inner self (inner being) is this thought good for me? Once you tap into your inner-being, then the answer comes. This comes from our in-tui-tion (into self) our spirit within (spirituality). Once you have this experience, you will understand that there is something inside us that is connected to our guidance system and emotions.

I was speaking to over one hundred medical and psychology students at a university on the Gold Coast. Having been asked by the faculty to speak about anxiety and depression, I decided not to do the usual PowerPoint presentation. This was something they would have expected. The only PowerPoint I did was my biography so that they understood who I was and my background.

I talked about feelings (emotions) and how we can change our emotions by doing an action. I invited them to do a little exercise on how we can change what we are thinking. If we could connect to what we were feeling, we could change the energy in the entire room. I asked for a volunteer to come up and share their career goal.

A female medical student kindly volunteered. I asked her to wait outside for a few minutes to work on what she was going to say. I then left her and went back inside to all the other students, asking them to allow her to speak for around two to three minutes. I wanted them all to then stand, cheer and clap. Standing back to watch, the energy in the room shifted. It was amazing.

I asked how the students felt. The medical student who had volunteered said she felt so happy inside. All students agreed they felt her happiness and felt the emotional connection of joy. I have similar exercises in my workshops, programs and use them from time to time with individual clients. It works so well to shift emotional energy that doesn't serve them.

I often say to people, "Why would you do that to your beautiful heart? It loves you, and by feeding it negative emotion, it puts stress, strain, and pressure on it. Our hearts give us so much, especially our heart chakra, which you might like to read about in Chapter 16. Love who you are, connection and affection; love and nurture your heart. This is self-love that starts within you.

You are the only one who can love who you are. Love your inner being, who you truly are. Feed your soul with positive emotional thoughts of love and joy. Then watch your heart sing to the tune of blissful joy. Yay!!

It will love you back. Love, love, love; it's an universal law. Just like, like attracts like, positive attracts positive. Have you ever wondered why you feel (emotion) good around some people and some you don't? This is because their emotional energy is not vibrating at the same level as you are.

A good example is when you walk into a room, and everyone is working hard doing whatever task they have been allocated. You walk in and say, hello to everyone. "My name is blah, blah, blah and it's lovely to meet you. You all look amazing." Watch what happens. They start smiling.

It's the same thing as when you're feeling great. You're really on top of your game, and someone comes to you, and you ask, "How are you? It's so good to see you?"

And they say, "I feel terrible. Life sucks and I hate my life." That will interfere with happy, vibrational energy you are carrying. It will deplete it. If you say, hello to someone who is vibrationally sending out happiness and love, then your energy will thrive and lift even higher. You will be in synchronicity and share high vibrational energy. You will align with similar ideals because you are vibrating at the same frequency. The law of polarity kicks in and alignment is flows.

Let's say, if I said to someone, "Hi, it's so good to see you and I love what you're wearing. Your hair looks great," or anything nice about who they are. Whatever is going on for them will shift, just as you have just shifted or plucked the negative energy they were carrying and replaced it with positive energy. This keeps us at a state of goodness, compassion, love, and kindness.

Sometimes as I walk, I notice how many people are not present. I say, hi or hello with a big smile. Most people smile back. This makes me feel good as I receive what I have given. See how this all works. Humans are emotional beings (physical experience).

Souls connect with souls. Recently I met someone who I now consider having deeply connected with on a soul level; emotional, spiritually and a relaxing sensual level (as he puts it). This chance meeting was divinely sent to me to have the experience of feeling love again.

I didn't realise immediately. I still had some unfinished emotional block within that was attached to my heart (chakra). Gradually, I allowed myself to be vulnerable, open and non-resistant. This allowed the energy between us to flow naturally. We now share a beautiful connection, which is teaching both of us.

It's like we are all healers and when we need healing the healer for the healer appears. Ironic, as it seems to be because he is a doctor and I am a healer. I say this with a heartfelt smile as he has really made me look inside my inner self and see what I need to tend to. I need to have this experience to share and help others heal. It's meant to be. It's amazing how words of kindness and love can change the way a person is feeling.

I am very mindful how I write to this book and how it may be interpreted. I do not want to project or trigger any unwanted feelings for anyone reading. I feel a sense of sharing all my knowledge. I try to make sure I keep it as simple as possible so that everyone is able to understand, who and what we are and where we come from.

Through my own experiences I realise, if I hold thoughts that are not good for me, then I have a feeling that is not nurturing me. When I don't experience good feelings, it means things are not going well for me. For example, one day I woke up for no apparent reason and didn't feel like doing anything. I couldn't work out why I was feeling this way. Instead of lying in bed wondering why I was feeling that way, I changed what I was feeling by thinking in another way. I did this by saying to myself, I know if I change the way I think emotionally then I can change how I am feeling.

As soon as I realised I was in control of my thoughts, my vibrational frequency changed and I became connected to something else outside my mind. This insight was coming from my internal guidance system (inner being) I bounced out of bed, did a dance of celebration and went for a walk on the beach. I instantly felt, empowered, vibrant and sustained as it felt like I was nourishing my soul. I was having insightful thoughts and changing my emotional state through awareness. Insightful thoughts and communicating to my inner being (soul) was so much better than the way my day had begun. How cool is this, I thought to myself, as I look at the Sun glimmering over the ocean. I raised my hands above my head and reached up and looked at the heavens. I get it, I have got it! The truth is "don't let it matter" mind is just matter, so don't let it matter I thought as I took a step forward noticing how my feet feel above the white sand. Feeling every grain of soft white sandy grain, between my toes. Wow!! This is empowering.

I have put it into practice many times. Not only with my own self-realisation, but with clients, friends, and family. I have become very aware of their emotional energy. I don't allow that to interfere with my energy, especially when my good emotional frequency is vibrating at a level of love and compassion.

When we connect with someone on a spiritual, emotional and physical level or (relaxed sensual or physical level), once you feel that, you will know it.

Questions to ask yourself, either in meditation or in a quiet moment

1. What are my thoughts doing? Am I letting my thoughts control me or am I aware what they are doing?
2. Is it helpful stressing about something that I can or cannot, change at this moment?
3. Is it life threatening?
4. What power am I manifesting inside me? Good or not so good?
5. Am I feeling worthy?

6. Am I with ease (self-care) or manifesting disease (you are not at ease)?
7. What can I think of to change this feeling for my inner good? What will bring goodness to me?

We do need a little ego to help get us to where we want to go. For example; if someone is an empath, they find it difficult to set boundaries, so they just go along with whatever a person says or does. They don't set healthy boundaries. Because consciousness is shifting quickly and awareness of who we truly are is being discovered, empaths no longer fear. The empathy needs confidence which is part of ego mind.

Empath's can set healthy boundaries for themselves. I have struggled with my empathy for many years. Pleasing others, giving over of myself, wanting people to love me, feeling I needed to please them or I was not worthy. Setting healthy limitations for myself by letting someone know when it doesn't feel good for me, is what I now do.

Possibly growing up around 'apaths' or people who are consumed with their own wants and needs can push principles onto others, making it difficult to embrace who you truly are. When I understood apaths narcissistic behaviour, I comprehended more about my upbringing. My family became easier for me to deal with. We cannot change someone's behaviour, it is up to them.

Alone in my room one night, I was looking at the image of Shiva on my bed covers. I felt relaxed as I tuned into *Hay House Radio*, a free app that I have on my phone. The wisdom of Doreen Virtue flowed to my ears. Doreen Virtue is an author of numerous books and Angel Oracle Cards. She spoke about how narcissists (apaths) cannot change unless they have plenty of therapy and are over 40 years old. They cannot feel what it would be like to sense someone else's emotions. They are so consumed by low vibration of ego, they carry arrogance and resentment. It's hard to carry love inside when we carry this.

An empath knows they are an empath because they can feel the energy of the apath, though they want to feel good. The apath always lays the blame for how they are feeling. They blame others and like to shame others. It's their way of lashing out Therefore, they are difficult to change. Mostly they put the fault to others and do not look to change their behaviours. It's a bit like someone telling you, "You must work hard, get a good job, earn a certain amount, own a certain car or do it this way." Empaths then become stressed about what to do. Apaths enjoy the company of other apaths and feed off each other; like someone with an addiction. They struggle because they don't know another way. Universal law; like attracts like. Misery attracts misery.

Always look for a word that that inspires you or makes your thoughts go from misery to mellow. Asking yourself questions over and over is self-enquiry and communication with your inner being (soul), your higher self or higher consciousness. This is where the truth of who you are is held. To access it you need to take time for yourself. Am I in my heart or am I in my head? This is simple yet effective and will change the way you feel. The heart does not procrastinate. It knows the right thing to do. Your inner guidance (GPS) always knows how you feel. When its not right your mind will feel heavy and weak, it feels burdened. Your inner guidance system feels like, inner peace, it feels good, it feels aligned and free.

By asking questions like what thoughts am I manifesting? Am I manifesting thoughts which are of no benefit to me or lack the integrity of who I am and what I want to create? Don't allow thoughts to rule you. To know what you want (life purpose) you need to know what you don't want. It's like the laws of the universe, opposites; negative and positive.

From Darwin's theory, Aristotle's rhetoric to Robert Plutchik's theory, there are plenty of lists of the main emotions. Here's a list I've compiled:

- Grief
- Happiness
- Fear
- Anger
- Sadness
- Surprise
- Disgust
- Trust
- Anticipation

Grief

Grief is probably the most confronting and difficult emotion to deal with.

One morning in a bustling café, a friend and I were discussing grief. I glanced away from my friend's face, noticing people and staff busy doing their own stuff. No one was showing or vibrating out joy. There was little happiness. More upsetting, it was Christmas Eve, a day of joyousness and goodwill.

The people were on holidays and yet there was no pleasure in the air. As I pulled myself back into our conversation about grief, it dawned on me, that I too was still carrying some grief. I continued to carry around loss; of myself (little of the 'old me' existed anymore). The me that used to be caught up in the world of climbing the corporate ladders so high I couldn't see the bottom rungs or the top. I was stuck in the middle. I'd achieved a university degree to become a social worker, but I no longer fit that version of me. I struggled with that corporate ladder like each rung was going to break away and I'd fall to the bottom any minute.

Becoming a Social Worker and helping others was what I thought my purpose was. I planned to make changes in my community, my country and have an impact on the world, teaching, peace, harmony, and happiness by helping those in need. Working for a Government system, run by people climbing the corporate ladder; nepotism, plagiarism, and bullying. Sadly, I soon found out, these were not the behaviours of people who want to make changes to better the world and aid people. It's interesting as I have never seen a peace and harmony policy put forward in any government system. Hopefully someone will read this and implement one. It would make a huge difference if there were peace and harmony policies in workplaces, schools, legal systems, government agencies etc. Peace and harmony policy would shift consciousness and create a place where everybody gets along together.

I took a sip of my coconut milk latte, pondering how life was controlled by expectations, beliefs, past principles, judgements and expectations of others. I said to my friend, "Grief is a feeling that we feel with loss. It is seriously one of the most painful emotions we can experience."

Each of us experiences grief differently. However, while listening to the radio recently, I remember hearing that the pain of grief lasts for the same time as conception to birth – nine to ten months. Then we work through it. I thought that was interesting because, who can say how long a person is to grieve. There is no time line in my opinion. It just is whatever it is for the person grieving.

Sometimes I feel my old self-returning. This is not easy because I choose the new me. The joyous spiritual me. I am confused when the old me emerges. My friend agreed that grief is an emotion that is confusing.

It comes and goes without warning. I say, "At least I'm living this path. Learning each day is a blessing, particularly since I did leave my body." I'm silent, in thought. I think to myself as I order banana bread 'who is the real authentic me?'

After losing the fear, guilt, shame and self-worth issues I have become independently selfless to the self. This means I no longer need others to fulfil me. I am full and whole exactly as I am. The guilt shame and self-worth that I put on myself are not true me. They are only other's perception of me and expectation of me. How do people live, thriving on forcing others to believe their beliefs? Their way or no way.

Becoming selfless for self wasn't easy at first. However, once I understood that if I were the best I could be within, filling my heart with love, that love would trickle out to others. By doing things that make me feel good, like meditation, yoga, socialising with respectable kind loving friends, swimming in the ocean, keep me within. These are what top me up so I can help the people I do.

I have clients at The Yoga Barn who have held onto grief briefly or for many years. In my days when I was a social worker and counsellor, I'd seen enough grief, and it affected me. Grief can consume, not only the people experiencing it first hand, but also those around them.

Once I met a couple who had come to me for grief counselling. They had lost a child in Bali. It was extremely distressing as they told their story. Many tears were shed, and the tissue box ran empty. The worst emotion to deal with is possibly the grief of losing a child. Most of us expect to go before our children.

The heartspace - Meditate not Procrastinate

Through meditation and breath work, I use a technique that requires only five or ten minutes.

For anyone enduring grief, this meditation will help by gaining a connection with their lost loved one. We breathe until we are close to a meditative state. I speak softly taking them into their heartspace. There I can help them connect to whoever has passed over. They will start to feel that deep connection of love, perhaps feel or see that person, but feel the love and light of them.

One lady came to see me, explaining that six years ago her daughter was killed in a car accident. Tragically, she was only eighteen years old.

The mother felt like she died when her daughter did. She heartbreakingly said, "I forget what she looks like because it's too painful." She dabbed at her tears and continued.

Her relationship with her husband had soured, mostly because she was unable to feel or love any more. The grief in her heart was palpable. My own heart ached for her. I spoke to her about spiritual things. I said, "We all have this ability to connect". I asked her to trust me.

We began my meditation technique. I took her into a state where she connected to her daughter. Once we finished the session, we were both crying. More tissues were found to blow our noses and wipe our tears.

She said in a wobbly voice, "It's the first time in six years I've been able to see my daughter. She was there. I could feel her. I could see her." Then she smiled for the first time in a long time. She couldn't wait to share the experience with her husband.

It is a beautiful thing to be able to do that for someone. It makes me grateful that I discovered this gift to be able to teach people about connection. I guess I understand it too, because of my experiences with grief. I have empathy for what they are going through, and I am aware that they can feel that and trust me to take them towards the Light and connection.

That mother had been holding massive grief within her. This was causing her much pain and would have eventually caused disease in her body. By connecting with her daughter, she was finally able to move on with her life. Her grief didn't disappear immediately; it became softer, more bearable through the meditation and soon after was replaced by calmness, gratefulness, nostalgia and then happiness.

There is something unique in the way that, we as human beings have this deep soul connection with each other. Which is, scientifically we are connected universally. What does that mean? On a heartspace level, if we look inside and don't see the physical person, we look deep into what is in the soul. You can find it through the eyes of your loved one, and you can find something amazing.

I asked a friend to gaze into the eyes of her husband for two minutes. Set the alarm. Don't touch, just stare at other's eyes. Sit in facing chairs. Play something soft in the background. See what happens. This is an energy connection. Your heart space (heart chakra) connecting. We all have the ability to do it.

Her husband is a bit of a joker, but he agreed to do it. Both smirking until they relaxed. She could see the kindness and love in his eyes mirrored in hers. A definite soul connection.

At Greens Ayurveda Study Centre in India, I had a deep connection with Dr. Asghar. He was speaking about serving humanity, caring for and doing kind things for others. It was like my heart was defibrillating. I didn't understand what I was feeling at the time. I know now that I was connecting with him on the same level. He was thinking and discussing something that I am very passionate about.

It is something we could mistake with being in love, but it is only connecting of the heart. It's a deep-level connection on the same energy vibration. It could be a past life connection. You may want that connection again to benefit you or someone else in some positive way. Perhaps you didn't finish what you were doing in that past life. I believe in my past life I had experiences with Buddha, Shiva and Lakshmi. I have a connection with Braham Kumaris. I know that for sure.

While travelling and meeting healers, I discovered more about connection. When people have a disconnection, they want connection, the connection of self and connection to others. They want community and love. They don't want to be put down and told to do what is expected of them by others but it is not their true path.

Many healers and healing artist have disconnected themselves. Some do not know or have awareness. Knowing this comes from within us. We all can heal ourselves within. Through our own self-love, awareness and inner guidance system we can connect with our inner being. This is our true being who feels wellbeing, joy, and love. This is our connection to self, to our true spirit and to the spirit inside us as well as the spirit world. This is what I believe should be taught in schools and be part of our education system. This is spirituality.

Happiness

Happiness is an emotion we all want to feel. We strive to be happy. Positive thoughts lead to further happiness. Connecting and understanding who you truly are will bring happiness and joy. Feeling into your body and quietly connecting to your inner being will not only relax you but will connect you to your heart and soul. Through breath we can relax, become calm and let go of stress and toxin which sit in our cells, tissue and muscles. We can dive deep into everything inside us connect with it and heal it.

When you feel who you are inside, you can feel the love; feel the joy. That's the best time to feel into what you want to create. As love flows, you go into who you truly are; a beautiful bright shining *light*. This is the lightness of the *light* flowing from the universe; connection.

Fear

Please see Chapter 7 – How I faced my own fears; where I have already discussed fear in depth. Fear paralysis us and stops us moving forward to our true selves and our life purpose.

Anger

Anger is a normal emotion, however, releasing anger in a healthy way is best. Why do we get angry? Shouldn't we all remain calm? It's easier said than done when something happens to stir your anger, but you do need to try to control it. Again, replace the angry thought with a positive thought like, 'forgiving' or 'calm'. Choose the light thought, or emotion, not the dark one. You can express anger in a healthy way. If you hold anger, it can manifest into bad things inside you, like a disease. Release it; 'let it go'.

Punching a boxing bag or pillow can help release rage. Holding your breath for 10 seconds, then exhale. Doing forward bends and yogic breathwork. Repeating it can also be beneficial. It calms the nervous system to make us feel better. We feel better because we return to our guidance system that lets us know we are ok and this is part of the process to let go. Like anything that you train for or stydy for the more you do it, the better you became, it's the same you're your spiritual path. I call it spiritual boot camp. These are healthy ways to release built up anger. As you transition into a calmer spiritual way of being, anger will come up and out. Anger will not show itself as often. You can also try 10 star jumps. It's great to do as it shift from mind to physical and connects with heart.

Learning that life 'just is', we create what we think, is the best way I can explain anger. It's not about blaming or shaming, it's about knowing that we come into this world knowing our purpose. We just need to reconnect with who we are.

If you are furious, you cannot access light because anger is a shadow emotion. Go for a walk in nature.

Life purpose of love. Letting go, just like the *Disney* character *Princess Elsa* from *Frozen* sings, "Let it go." "Shine bright like a diamond," is another from *Rihanna* or *The Beatles*, "Let it be". Like Katy Perry says "I am the eye of the tiger and your going to hear me roar".

Tap into everything around you; nature, ocean, music, fine restaurants, home-cooked foods, places to meditate, dancing, gardening, painting and spaces to connect with others. There are plentiful Spiritual Community Groups who practice yoga and meditation. Even Facebook and Instagram can be used in a loving, positive way to feel good. Yes ! Social media was introduced so that we can connect with each other globally and instantly. It is unfortunate that sometimes it is used as a way to manipulate, bully and put others down. This is not the spiritual way. If we look at social media, for example, there are many things are negative or make us feel less than we can really see where someone is at in their life. They are either authenic or manipulative. Use your inner power of your guidance system to give you answers through Social media. It's a good way to start your spiritual practice.

Spend minimal time on social media; however, do use it to tap into places and people who inspire you when you want to manifest. Finding a visual to use with your imagination is a great way to see what you want to create. This is a good way of connecting to feel it. Not only can you reach out, but you can give a positive comment. Passing on positivity always makes you feel good. Sometimes people post before realising what they are putting out to themselves and the planet. They are not conscious of it. Only put out what inspires you.

Be an inspirational action taker. In-spirit-at- I-on-al means 'in spirit of'; I am spirit. I am inspirational to myself and others. I use the spirit within me to inspire others.

Sadness

We've discussed grief which is a harsher emotion than sadness. Sadness can also be due to loss, but it doesn't make us feel disconnected the way grief does. We may cry when we are sad, but it doesn't consume us like grief. Think happy to replace the sad thought. What makes you happy? Find it.

Surprise

Don't we all like a good surprise? This book could be a pleasant surprise as you read the pages feeling the connections, I have been explaining to you. The surprise for me in NDE was that we are all physical and non-physical. Knowing this can change the way you live and feel about yourself. We are in a new paradigm, having a new understanding to reach super consciousness (higher self) through meditation, awareness, wisdom and knowledge. The higher self is *light* or enlightenment. We all hold the power within.

Disgust/Negativity

We've all been disgusted by some of the things people do; murder, rob, blackmail, rape and most recently, in the headlines bullying. We have every right to show the emotion of disgust when things like that happen, but if they don't serve our true self, replace them. Don't watch gory movies. Stop watching the negativity of the daily television news. Let's take bullying as an example; the words 'anti-bullying policy' is negative and will create more bullying.

If the words were 'peace and harmony policy' it would not only change the environment but would have a more positive. These words hold the highest vibrational frequency and when spoken have a positive impact on people and surroundings. I am yet to see a school with a peace and harmony policy. My clients who are lawyers or involved in writing political policy have been told by me that if they want their work to change start saying and writing things differently. Surely someone is able to create a peace and harmony policy.

Trust

As they say, trust must be gained, and that is true, though some trust blindingly and this can lead to being manipulated by the person you put your blind trust in. Better to trust yourself first. Remember trust in your inner being or inner knowing. If it feels right it's right. Many times in my life I have had people I have trusted do things that are not with integrity. I have found these people are part of the learning and letting go process.

Don't hold anger toward them as they don't know any better, so how can they do better. They too are stuck in an old paradigm way of being.

Manipulation is a type of belief that serves others but not in a good way. Manipulation is having someone believe that they know the best way for you. Some will even put fear into a person so they can influence that person. This is often used in war, allowing them to control people. If we trust that all our answers lie within us and not outside, we can heal to live a life of trust. Do not allow the fear of others to bother you. Trust and have faith, all will be good. Doing a five minute meditation before sleep, going over your day and releasing any negative thought from you day is very calming and a form of releasing negative patterns. Allow yourself this time every day. Knowing you have done your best is powerful. Trust your inner being (guidance system) or heart.

Anticipation

Did you anticipate that anticipation would be the last heading? You should have because it was the last on the list, but this isn't the kind of anticipation that is the emotion I'm talking about. Anticipation is hope, expectancy, and eagerness. It builds excitement if it is something you are looking forward to like a win, birth of a child, wedding or celebration.

Golden Gem for your Spiritual Treasure Chest

Everyday when you wake up, close your eyes and think of a bright light beaming into every cell, every tissue, every muscle, every bone, every organ, vein, capillary and into all parts of your skin. You will start to feel light as *light* enters your every being. As you release you relax.

CHAPTER 10

Holistic Healing Meditation
*Yoga therapy and Ayurveda using Sacred Heart
meditation to connect with your soul*

*"When you discover something that nourishes your soul and brings joy, care
enough to make room for it in your life."*

—Jean Shinoda Bolen

Yoga Therapy or Ayurvedic Yoga – a balanced way to exercise

In the history of Ayurveda, the ancient vedics, rishies and monks would meditate, and some would do yoga and then receive divine messages; receiving messages of how to heal, replenish and rejuvenate the body. I think that's why Ayurveda really resonated with me, its part traditional yoga and meditation. Once you've learnt these practices and mastered them, you will have an understanding that you can connect to the pure divine energy. You can connect with the universal divine energy that is your pure divine heart. The key to the light, the inner spirit of our soul. The mantra, saying a word or statement over and over repetitively to penetrate the depth of unconscious mind and raise vibration. Healing affirmations work in a similar way. For example, it is said Om is the sound of the universe. Saying words (mantra) with love and peace is also a sound of the universe.

When practising traditional yoga techniques, you will feel connection and light. This allows you to be present 'in the now', mindful of your past (thoughts) and your future (thoughts). You become the observer of your thoughts and feelings. A connection inside you that is calm and peaceful will fill you. This is a divine presence. Once you tap into it, you can ask your inner being questions? You might say, "I like this house. Is it good for me to buy it?", "Should I take this job?" or "What is my next step?" You will receive guidance. Traditional yoga is done with ease and grace. It is slow and transformative. Integrating the mind, body and spirit. Some like physical yoga. This is a personal choice, however, it will not take you into balance of mind, body, spirit. This is because we push ourselves to become something else and not at peace. Peace is for all and not just for some. Being comfortable with who we are and what we are is "Perfectiom".

Here's how: Intuitively you will become woken up, awake and awakened using your inner guidance system to navigate your inner systems (IGS).

Step one - Sit in a comfortable position, making sure your surroundings are quiet and that you will not be disturbed for the next 20-30 minutes. Gently close your eyes, relax your body, being mindful of your shoulders and neck, relax them. With a client, I would send healing energy to their shoulder and neck by placing one hand on their neck or back to release the pressure. It's a very effective way to get the person to relax. Once you feel relaxed into your breath, take the breath into your heart by using visualisation and imagination. Feel the breath flowing into your heart chakra located in the centre of your chest, you should feel a connection into your heart. If not, say to your heart while taking a breath, "You are beautiful, and I love you." This is also effective. Do this for five minutes or whatever feels good for you.

As you breathe in, visualise the colour green from Mother Earth. The breath that Mother Earth gives to you is streaming into your body with ease and grace. Allow yourself to drop into deep consciousness, then super-consciousness will take over. Once your muscles are relaxed your cells and tissue become relaxed, and that's when the magic happens. Listen to some angelic music or music of high frequency hertz or binaural beats as you meditate. These potent sound frequencies are part of what the universe dances to.

Your cells relax to receive healing energy and make divine connection. Both masculine and feminine energy can be received. You will learn whether you are in male or female energy, as both need to be balanced to receive.

Shavasana or corpse pose, which means (corpse posture) in Sanskrit, is usually done at the end of the practice. However, when I studied yoga therapy in India, it was done after every yoga pose (Asana) to integrate and connect with mind and body. This allowed the breath (prana, life force energy to flow). Lie flat on your back with heels spread as wide as the yoga mat and arms a little away from your body with your palms facing up. Slowly and gently breathe (prana) bringing awareness to the breath, body, and mind. You should feel relaxed and calm after this asana.

Your body will flow, taking you to where you need to be with every asana. Yoga should not be difficult or emphasise on the physical. When the mind softens, the body softens, and that's when transformation happens. You will be surprised at the difference to the flow once you know how to balance the mind, body, and spirit.

Traditional Indian Healing Therapies – 'Holistic Healing Meditation – Yoga Therapy & Ayurveda'

In the workshops I do, students discover the science and philosophy behind meditation, yoga and Ayurvedic medicine. They then learn how to implement these three practices into daily life to revitalise, rejuvenate and replenish the body.

Although the practice of meditation is associated with a sense of peacefulness and physical relaxation, meditation also provides cognitive and psychological benefits that persist throughout the day. Yoga therapy is a holistic treatment for many diseases which do not require medication.

The Six Yoga Therapy Principles

1. Cleansing the body (Ayurveda)
2. Diet (Ayurvedic)
3. Exercise (Yoga Therapy)
4. Breathing (Sacred Heart Healing Meditation)
5. Relaxation (Breathing Meditation)
6. Positive thinking (Meditation & Relaxation)

Ayurvedic Medicine

Over the centuries traditional Ayurvedic medicine has been particularly renowned and effective for the treatment of many diseases. It is a natural way to heal our bodies. When the body is imbalanced, we are unable to do our normal daily functions. This can have a negative impact on our immune system and quality of life. By keeping the three doshas balanced we can improve our life and longevity. Ayurveda is balancing the mind body and spirit.

My own Ayurvedic Yoga Therapy

I developed this sequence of yoga therapy. Though I partly learnt yoga in Australia, Bali and India, I found that I wanted to do things differently. I tried various diverse types of training to develop the sequence into my own. It is my connection with meditation, yoga, and Ayurveda. I believe it is a beneficial way for students to learn. Learning of our chakra's and its wisdom is part of the yogic world.

Ayurvedic Yoga Therapy Sequence

Yoga is a science of life
Yoga stops the functions of the mind, then
communicates with super consciousness
Traditional yoga should be comfortable, steady and with flow...
Yoga Therapy is for the elimination of common diseases
Yoga Therapy is not different from yoga and is modified or
structured according to the intensity of the disease
Holistic treatments for psychosomatic diseases without medication.

Yoga Therapy Principles

1. Spiritual Counselling
2. Proper Cleansing & Clearing
3. Proper Exercise
4. Proper Breathing
5. Proper relaxation
6. Positive Thinking
7. Healing Affirmations

Breath

Breath is the bridge between body and mind, if something is happening in the mind, the breath will be affected, that is why it's important to observe the breath, observe the mind and observe the body when we are sad, the breath slows; when we are angry, the breath increases. For example, when a Mother gives birth or someone having an anxiety attack.

Yoga is a universal science and understanding of the three minds, super consciousness- understanding of self and all living beings and knowing that we are all connected (universal unity):

To love
To Share
To Serve
Lord Shiva is the Father of Yoga, in Hinduism
The Universal Energy
Shiva means consciousness
Shiva means energy
So, hum means I am that
I am – consciousness
I have – subconscious (belief of others)

I always ask if there is anyone who has any health issues, we should be aware of such as high blood pressure, back injury, strains or other injuries. This is to ensure that those people do restrained yoga to suit their health issues. Adjustment is part of yoga as it's a unique individual practice that serves person to person. The main causes of these illnesses are stress. When we remove stresses from our life, we feel better. With yoga therapy, we can eliminate stress and come into a place of solace. You become you. There is always an emotional attachment to physical pain, once this is released, then we begin to feel better. For example, if we have a heavy workload, we will feel stress or tension in our upper back, neck and shoulders. Release this tension and the stress will release. Through yoga therapy and meditation, the mind becomes peaceful and the body becomes relaxed, hence, stress is released and eliminated. Knowing and understanding yogic and meditation principles is the best way to learn about Mind, Body and Spiritual Self.

Aranas

Arana's open the energy centres which are channels, or the chakras are the send of the energy which is sent through the austral tubes (nadis) or marma's. Chakras hold wisdom

Pineal Gland

Pineal gland (in the middle of the forehead above the eyebrows) is the only spiritual gland in the body.
Pineal gland is connected to the moon and is said to be the feminine aspect (Shakti) energy. We have both masculine and feminine within us when balanced life becomes light and clear.
Pineal gland is the command centre and balances the body mind and spirit.
As a command centre, it can navigate many things. It's the GPS of our inner-guidance system
When you close your eyes and look up you can activate your pineal gland, visualise it. You may see a vision of an eye. This is the 3rd eye chakra Over time a third eye appears. Many of the clients I work with have this experience and see colours. The pineal gland is purple or violet. However, many other colours may appear including a bright light.
Pineal gland is responsible for keeping our bodies healthy and is also for creating intention and receiving divine insight.
The spiritual soul within us is impersonal which means it is connected to the universe,
for example, Mother earth, sun, moon, stars, planets, water, the earth (ground) 'It's everywhere'.
Every Asana is designed to open our channels, chakras, and marma's.

Prana

Pranayama is a process of respiration or breath; almost mystical. It is connected to the brain, receptors, and emotions all over the body. The rhythms of deep breathing can activate the physical body and trigger the homeostasis, guiding the mind and its GPS to into a meditative state and active intuition.

This is sometimes called Theta state, where we can relax with breath and relax our nervous system. It teaches us to deactivate the stress hormone to be in a more relaxed state of consciousness. By inhaling, receptors in the body are activated when there is too much carbon dioxide in the lungs. They send signals to the brain to stimulate the diaphragm. The diaphragm is a large muscle which separates the digestive organs for the lungs. When we exhale the blood has oxygenated, the receptors stop triggering the brain and the chest area relaxes the muscles.

Just like yogic breathing, long, slow and deep; promotes a greater exchange of prana. When practising asana, the yogi should maintain a deep even flow of breath into the base of the lungs to prevent the build-up of lactic acid in the muscles and tissue. Slow deep breathing cultivates expulsions of built-up toxins and stresses in the body.

Bringing new air into the body will refresh and rejuvenate. It also helps to still and balance the mind, bringing a sense of calm and inner peace. Prana means life force energy (air or oxygen) and are subtle forces expanding spiritual growth. It is channelled through energy centres in the body, including, nadis, marma's, meridians, purifying them and bringing the mind to a point controlling thoughts and retaining the energy life force.

Using prana to cleanse and clear the internal body will expand energy and enhance meditative state. There are various meditations, including singing, kirtan, chanting, humming; also breath regulators.

Lifeforce energy can be lost in many ways, too much talking, multi-tasking, fast movements, over exercising and stress. Ayurveda talks about this and how you can overstimulate and go against your constitution (dosha), causing imbalances within.

For kapha types, dynamic prana breathing cleanses the lungs. Mucous is released and gives a sense of invigoration. Out of balances produces weight gain.

For pitta types, being mindful, expanding the breath that creates a feeling of freedom and openness or cools the breath with retention will calm the fire within. Out of balance produces anger.

For vata types, use a calming and restorative breath by laying and doing abdominal breathing. It allows vata to use their natural tendency for etheric, vibrational qualities. Setting an intention and knowing how to use energy is helpful. Using oil to massage the navel ribcage and feet will help with ojas to assist with channelling prana through the body. Mental instability is part of vata imbalance and disturbs energy flow. Thoughts are energy. Out of balance produces anxiety and memory loss.

Mind Body and Spirit

Yoga therapy and meditation stops the function of the mind
then communicates with super consciousness (higher self).
By opening the channels and nadis, we allow the life
force energy to flow through our bodies.
This life force energy is directed from our energy centres
(chakra's) through the power of our breath.
The energy centre is like a vortex that pushes the energy
through the nadis, keeping our energy centres balanced.
The crown is not a chakra it is the coordinator of the chakras. It's a white lotus
with 1,000 lotus petals - (higher consciousness). It's the soft spot which we
are born with. We have 114 chakras, 72000 'nadis' or energy channels, along
which vital energy or 'prana' moves. The seven chakras are the centres in our
bodies which energy flows through when blocked it can lead to disease in our
bodies. It's important to understand what each chakra represents and what we
can do to keep our energy centres flowing freely. With ease to prevent dis-ease.

Prayer

Prayer will boost your immune system and is what fights for us. Mental Prayer helps sets the intention behind the prayer, i.e. (putting energy into our food).

1. Prayer for respect to the forms who cultivate the food for us (Mother Earth).
2. Prayers for food, give thanks to all the plants which are giving the energy to nourish our bodies.
3. Respect the person who makes the food for us.
4. Praying for food is equal to love and affection, it fills our bodies with love (makes us feel good).
5. Minimise talk while eating (gratitude to food). Conscious eating.
6. Eat food with awareness. Conscious eating
7. Yoga says, eat anything you wish with awareness.
8. Gratitude love and affection to all.
9. Avoid snacking, i.e. biscuits, ice-cream, baked or oily foods (acidity).
10. Eat between 8am - 9am, 12 - 1pm and 5- 7pm.

11. Eat vegetarian food- yogic food, the goodness of god food. Minimise meat intake if possible.

12. Plants (Mother Earth) provide our food for healing and connect on a Universal level. Without prana or plants, we would not survive. The prana comes from the Sun, Universe and Mother Earth. They all work together to nourish and support us. Without them, there would not be life or life force energy.

13. Vegetables contain antioxidants. Phyto-chemicals are in vegetables and good for cells, skin and, our immune system.

14. Banana skin is full of serotonin if it's organic and is washed. If you can eat it it's very good for you.

15. Pomegranates are good to prevent breast cancer and prostate cancer. They also are good for three Ayurvedic Doshas.

16. Certain vegetables can cure some diseases. Freshly squeezed lemon in warm water will alkalize the body.

Our blood is alkaline in nature, and we should eat as many alkaline foods as possible to keep our bodies healthy. 100% alkaline is not possible in the world as it is today. 75% is excellent 50% good, and 25% is acidic. Acidic foods are processed foods and low prana.

5 min Meditation and Prayer

Prayer improves concentration and relieves stress.
Goodness (God) Universe we or Divine is the pure state of consciousness.
The purpose of meditation yoga is to see pure consciousness (super consciousness).
Meditation is inter-related to yoga and Ayurveda.
Subconscious and unconscious are states of no
awareness – consciousness is awareness.
Dreaming state is when all things bad are thrown
out. You are neither asleep or awake.
Cognitive mind is rational, logical and problem-solving.
Effective mind is emotions.
Psychomotor mind is the movement of the mind, i.e. good behaviours.

I will not teach you yoga exercise techniques in this book. Otherwise, this would be a very thick book. There are plenty of teachers and books on the subject. What I will teach you is that yoga and meditation go together in creating a meditative state that leads to heightened spirituality and includes Ayurveda. I use the above sequences and you can too, with whatever yoga you have been taught. There are many gentle yoga techniques you can use which are taken from the ancient yogic philosophy. Go gently with your body when doing yoga, this is the way of yoga.

Yoga Therapy for Constipation

Sit in a position with legs out in front. Drink one to two cups of warm water. Take a deep breath and do a side twist. Have the hand at the back of your spine and the other reaching across your hip. Hold the pose for about 20-30 seconds. Release. Take a deep breath in and repeat that. Then have a glass of warm water.

What is Yoga in Today's Modern World

Be mindful that not all yoga is ancient 'yoga'. With the ever-increasing marketing of brands, yoga has lost some of its original essence and spirituality. The best yoga to practice, I believe, is traditional Ashtanga or Hatha. There are many variations today that have fancy western names like hot yoga (Bikram) or modern yoga, fly high yoga even goat yoga, but I prefer sticking to the traditional kind of Indian Hatha.

Exercise

- How can you incorporate regular yoga practice into your life?
- Why do you think prayer is such an important part of yoga?
- Find a quiet spot of your own to practice your yoga. Where would that perfect place be; a beach, backyard, by a flowing creek, under a tree, in a gym, at a retreat or just in your bedroom?

Light Magic Bonus

Go to my website for my favourite yoga exercise that helps me towards meditation and finding the light.

At www.kerrythehealer.com/yoga-exercises you can also download my Yoga Slideshow to enhance your own yoga practice recommendations *and Instruction of Yoga Practice.*

CHAPTER 11

Ayurveda
Ancient Wisdom from India

"There is no respect for others without humility in one's self."
—Henri Frederic Amiel

Ayurveda Study

While studying and learning about Ayurveda, I learnt about our constitution and how from the moment of conception, whichever, parent's constitution was highest is what we are born with. I thought how amazing this was and wanted to learn more. At times, I wondered why I was so drawn to Ayurveda and how it was going to influence my life. It turned out that it was part of each one of us and is connected to my NDE. Ayurveda is about cleansing, cleaning and clearing toxins, negative emotions and replenishing and rejuvenating the cells to reach a higher state of self. Connecting with mind body and spiritual side of us.

We vibrate on a frequency connected with the five elements. These are connected to our five senses, which are channels connected to Mother Earth, Fire, Air, Water, Universe. Mother Earth provides us with healing medicine through plants and herbs. She also purifies toxins, the carbon oxide we release, then purifies it and sends it as oxygen, life-force energy or prana. This is our life force. You will learn more about this in chapter nine.

I had discovered something remarkable that needed to be shared in Western World. I know I am not the first to do this, but perhaps I am the first to share it with knowledge of NDE combined with an ongoing thirst for spiritual and scientific knowledge. With the help of brilliant yogis and teachers, I have embraced Ayurveda.

Ayurveda Explained

Ayurveda is an ancient traditional Indian medicine, or life science, linked with Mother Nature by integrating plants, herbs, supplements, diet, exercise, massage and lifestyle for health and wellbeing. For over 5,000 years Ayurveda has been practised in India though it is spreading rapidly throughout the world, as people begin to seek a holistic lifestyle. The word Ayurveda comes from the Sanskrit (the equivalent language to Latin in India); ayur (life) and veda (knowledge).

Ayurvedic philosophy indicates that everything in the universe is made up of five elements; fire, air, water, earth, and space.

- Air represents all that is gaseous
- Earth represents matter that is solid,
- Water represents all liquids are represented by water,
- Fire represents any matter that can transform
- Space represents all that

Ayurveda (Ayurvedic medicine) is documented in the sacred historical texts, the knowledge, or the Vedas. It has evolved over the years and is now integrated with other traditional practices, including meditation and yoga. Holistically, Ayurveda looks at the whole person then applies healing medicines to rejuvenate and purify the body.

Modern scientists now prove that there is evidence of a mind-body-spiritual connection. It's the same belief that the sages of India developed thousands of years ago. Linking mind, body and spirit in a balanced way helps people to realise their full potential and to stay fit, healthy, rejuvenated and joyfully connected.

A skilled Ayurvedic doctor can do an assessment by taking a pulse reading that will give information about your constitution (prakruti). Their knowledge and intuition will ascertain what elements are balanced, what is out of balance and what you need to do. This practice is similar to Tibetan or Chinese medicine. Working with a qualified Ayurvedic doctor is a valuable and effective way to stay in wellness. They also understand the chakra system and energy.

Three Systems of Ayurveda

The three systems of Ayurveda are, of course; mind, body, and spirit. The guiding principles are:

- Mind and body are inseparably connected
- The power to heal and transform the body through the mind

Freedom from illness depends on our knowledge and awareness to balance the body. It's not as complicated as it sounds. I have mastered it and so can you. For example, when you meditate, you effortlessly enter a state of expanded awareness. This inner quiet refresh the mind and restore balance. Since the mind and body are inseparable, the body is naturally balanced through the practice of meditation. As you meditate, your heart rate and breath slow. Your body decreases the production of 'stress' hormones such as cortisol and adrenaline. You increase the production of neurotransmitters that enhance wellbeing; including serotonin, dopamine, oxytocin, and endorphins.

Meditation is just one of the many powerful tools the ancient Ayurvedic physicians prescribed for balancing mind and body. Ayurveda also offers many other practices for expanding self-awareness and cultivating your state of balance. Ayurveda's personalised approach to health and knowing your mind-body type allows you to make optimal choices about diet, exercise, supplements, and all other aspects of your lifestyle. As always balance is the key, but you need to know your body and mind to turn that key.

Key points on Ayurvedic approaches to a healthy life

- Find out your mind and body type
- Eat a balanced diet
- Strengthen your digestive system
- Sleep to nourish your body
- Exercise to balance your body
- Understand your emotions

I will go into these points further in subsequent chapters but briefly:

Find out your mind and body type

Discover your mind and body type to understand yourself better. We all have a dominant constitution. You'll be aware that you are an emotional being who responds to different things in your own unique way. You have three dosha's that govern your mind and body; Vata, Pitta, Kapha (you'll discover more about these in the next chapter). By learning more about your mind and body you'll be able to balance your dosha's to experience good health and wellbeing.

Eat a balanced diet

Being mindful of what we consume is extremely important to your body. Certain dosha's need different foods to rejuvenate cells and reduce toxins for a disease-free body. Your digestive fire needs to be strong. Ayurveda teaches how to treat your body like a temple. It will guide you to the best-balanced diet for your body type.

It's not just about eating clean, fresh food. It's also about hot food, cold food, how they are cooked, how they digest, what are their additives, how they are absorbed, how they relate to the balance of your doshas.

Strengthen your digestive system

As with a balanced diet, you can strengthen your digestive system by pushing toxins out and nourishing cells, but your digestive system can also be strengthened, combining yoga and meditation. Ayurveda teaches good health is dependent upon our capability to fully metabolize the nutritional, emotional, and sensory information that we ingest. Once again, it's about balance.

When our digestive energy, known as agni (fire), is robust, we create healthy tissues, eliminate waste products efficiently and produce a subtle essence called ojas. Ojas or our vitality is the source of perception, physical strength, and immunity. On the other hand, if our agni is weakened, digestion is incomplete and lead to an accumulation of toxic residue known as ama. Amacan obstructs the flow of energy, information, and nourishment. Build up of Amacan lead to disease.

Sleep to nourish your body

It goes without saying that we need sleep. Roughly eight-hour sleep revives our body for a full day. Though it's not the amount of sleep we get but the quality of the sleep that revitalises the body by rejuvenating cells and resting our mind. If our doshas are imbalanced, such as too much Vata, our sleep may be disrupted. Meditation helps too, but sleep is also an important part of optimal health. With improper sleep, you may eat more (and not the healthy stuff), have a foggy brain, become irritable. Good sleep will lift your emotions making you feel positive. It will give you more energy and build creativity. It releases hormones and encourages tissue growth which fights disease. Time for a snooze?

Exercise to balance your body

I suggest yoga as the best exercise to balance your body. It blends with the Ayurveda methodologies. If yoga isn't your thing, you could take long walks, surf, go for a gentle jog, dance, whatever makes you happy. Some doshas require different exercise to find the best exercise for your dosha. Incorporate whatever makes you feel good physically with yoga and you will find inner peace.

The reason yoga is a wonderful exercise is that yoga is the science of self-realisation and balances with Ayurveda, the science of health. Both guide you towards sattvic (having a serene, harmonious, balanced mind or attitude) states of consciousness. In the ancient yoga texts, poor health is clearly described as one of the major impediments to self-realisation. Ayurveda can work in partnership with Yoga to support the self-realisation process and help you towards the light.

Understand your emotions

Emotions and thoughts create our reality. As I said before, fear creates fear, joy creates joy. If you cannot understand your emotions how will you ever be able to change bad thoughts, old pattern or paradigms, into good ones? Don't ignore or suppress your emotions. Bottling things up always leads to a cork popping. Like a pressure cooker, self destructive and explosive. Acknowledge whatever emotion you have been feeling, understand it, transform it (if it's negative) and release it.

Chapter 7 explained how to overcome fear. In the same way, you overcome fear by admitting that fear; you can do the same with all your emotions. If you wake up to a sunny day with kookaburras cheerfully cackling in the branches of a gum tree, smile, enjoy the raucous laughter and be grateful for another sunlit day. Days began recognising a positive emotion usually gets better and better.

Since my NDE and further studies to link my spirituality with science, I have found much of Ayurveda teaching makes so much sense. We should be taught it in schools, where children (like with language) can harness what is already in them. Wouldn't it be wonderful if once we left school and became adults, we were mostly spiritual and could find the Light? There would be much peace and harmony in the world.

While studying in India with Professor Padmanabhan, his teaching taught me that my subconscious mind and conscious mind are both very powerful. He said I could override my subconscious with 'I have' affirmations or by sayings and 'I am'. These bring me into consciousness and super consciousness (higher self).

It's odd, when travelling I used to see the 'I am' statement written and used often. I never understood why? It was a great awareness for me when I realised the power of these affirmations. Feeling and confirming affirmation is powerful. It creates those magical moments I have written about in this book. By affirming who you are with feeling, sends the mind into a state of non-resistance, allowing the thought to flow harmoniously; hence, magic to flow.

I now use this as part of my daily practice. I also use an image of a filing cabinet image. This metaphor is used with my clients. I ask them to imagine their subconscious as a filing cabinet. Inside that cabinet are files from every year they have lived. Contained in each file are their thoughts, beliefs, and values; their subconscious. This is everything from birth to now. I ask them to tidy up the filing cabinet by going into the files (thoughts) and taking out the ones that don't serve them. Replace them with an 'I am' or 'I have'. This works extremely well for people who have anxiety or depression. Thoughts are energy. They can make us feel depleted of energy if we continually have negative ones.

I also use the analogy of pretend you are running a 10-kilometre marathon. You need to train. You would not just go run a marathon without training. You would start with perhaps 1 km and ease into it. Just like your thoughts, in the beginning, your mind will tell you things like 'this is silly' or 'why are you doing this?'It's just your subconscious at work.

I have learnt that positive repetitive daily thought has an impact on how my day is going to be and what people or situations I attract. Like attracts like. Love attracts love.

We can use the power of our mind to heal our own body by using our light, love and unique but universal energy. The light is attainable to us all, and I will show you the way.

Exercises

- What is the daily mantra you could use to improve your life?
- Do you eat a balanced diet? What could you do to improve your eating habits? Think of one thing you could change today that would improve your diet, for example, eliminate sugar or even reduce sugar.
- Emotions and thoughts create your reality. What negative thought can you change to positive thoughts? Listen to your thoughts with feeling, ask yourself, how do I feel when I think this thought?

Golden Gems for your Spiritual Treasure Chest

I have created a free mantra for you.

I am one with the universe.

I am oneness with self.

I am the lightest.

I am the light of my soul

I am bliss

I am beautiful

I am love.

Namah Ha.

Namaha is a Sanskrit word and means not me. Or I am not that. Om Namaha Shivaya is one of the most beloved Hindu mantras. It is a respectful mantra showing acknowledgement and honour to Lord Shiva. Chanting this mantra helps to still the mind. Traditionally it's sung 108 times with Om gam ganapataye namaha. When I was a studying yoga teacher, I chanted this every morning at 6am with other students and sang it 108 times. I loved it!

CHAPTER 12

Heal with The Three Doshas
Vata, Pitta, Kapha

"No matter how much it gets abused, the body can restore balance.
The first rule is to stop interfering with nature."

—Deepak Chopra

I first discovered my Doshas when I was doing my 'Yoga Teacher Training' in Bali. I had never heard of a Doshas, let alone Ayurveda before I became involved with Yoga. At the beginning learning about body, mind, and spirit, was challenging. I had to overcome, my beliefs, my ego, and shift into who I really was.

Learning about my Doshas inspired me to learn more. I wanted to discover how my Doshas gave meaning to the connection; to who I was. When I first heard the word 'Pitta' I thought it was bread. It is so much more...

It's my constitution, part of who I am. If it's out of balance then I am unbalanced, so is my mind, my body, and my spirit. What it means is, if I have an imbalance in my digestives system, it will be like a domino effect. It will cause problems with my immune system and guidance system. All my systems will be affected.

On another level, going to India to explore Ayurveda has given me an understanding of who I truly am, the real internal me, the guru within me. I discovered why I am still here on Earth. The day I arrived at Greens Ayurveda, was memorable. Meeting the Ayurveda doctors was significant and special. I could see that their passion was to teach me all that they knew about my Doshas (yes, Doshas meaning plural). I need to manage all three and keep a balance. Otherwise, I will become, anxious, stressed and put on weight. I am Pitta/Vata. Later in this chapter, I will help you discover which Doshas dominate you.

Doctor Asghar has been very supportive. He has imparted his knowledge and wisdom about Ayurveda and let me share some of our workshops with you. He taught me that without our Doshas being in balance the body's inner intelligence is disrupted, often leading to disease.

Explaining the Doshas

Vata Dosha ~ Body energy that controls motion; circulation, breathing, blinking and your heartbeat. Elements of space and air. Vata is the supreme of the three doshas. Pitta and Kapha Cannot move without Vata.

- Unbalanced ~ Fear, depression and anxiety.
- Balanced ~Inspiration, creativity, and vitality.

Pitta Dosha ~ Body energy that controls metabolism, nutrition absorption, digestion and temperature. Elements of fire and some water.

- Unbalanced ~Antagonism and ulcers.
- Balanced ~Serenity and astuteness.

Kapha Dosha ~ Body energy that controls growth maintains the immune system and provides water to the body areas. It helps cells form muscle, fat, tissue and bone. Elements of water with some earth.

- Unbalanced: Jealousy and self-doubt.
- Balanced: Forgiving and loving.

We all have three Doshas, with one or two being dominant (as with mine, Pitta/Vata). Different Dosha amount regulate our likes and dislike giving us our personality characteristics.

The five elements of water, air, fire, earth, and space govern our bodies. Not one dominates continuously as they coexist harmoniously. It forces and manages a relationship of the elements of nature, remembering that we are all a part of everything and everything is a part of us. We are energy. The dosha's represent understated energy which is balanced and united. The forces combine contrary forces such as Kapha being earth and water. Pitta fire and water. Three doshas include living things like wildlife, plants, fruits, insects and they can be classified using similar principles.

Our bodies are controlled by the doshas, in the ways explained in points above. Vata controls motion, Pitta controls metabolism and absorption, and Kapha controls growth. You can see that each have a vital part of sustaining body health. Ayurveda medicine tries to balance doshas by changing diets, exercise and lifestyle to suit.

The food we eat will be transformed into the most basic form for our entire body to have nutrients that can be absorbed sufficiently. The combination of all doshas is needed to help with body, mind, and spirit.

There are usually two dominate doshas characteristics. You may be a Pitta/Kapha, Kapha/Pitta, Pitta/Vata, Vata/Pitta, Kapha/Vata or Vata/Kapha. You may have one dominant dosha, and you can also have equal combination of all three. You are born with these dominance, but they will be fluctuating fluidly throughout your life. In a natural state of balance, the doshas provide strength to our bodies. This stops diseases forming.

Imbalances cause ill-health. If you are fighting a disease, your doshas are unbalanced. The body's loss of haemostatic causes the body to lose heat through this imbalance. You can understand why balanced doshas are so important. I'll go further and explain how the disease is caused by dosha imbalances.

Disease through unbalanced Doshas – how to fight it

As I've explained; disrupting the balance of our Doshas can create disease, illness and even depression.

If you have poor dietary habits, smoke (toxins), live a stressful life, don't exercise enough, live in a terrible climate or have other bad habits, you will have an accumulation of toxins in your body. There is no need to deny yourself everything. Moderation is the key. Use your self-control, but there are, of course, some things better avoided altogether. Just remember to practice moderation within your body type. Constant denial can be almost as unhealthy as indulgencing too often. It can also lead to bigger binges of whatever it is you crave. I will often enjoy a few treats like chocolate or the occasional glass of wine but am always mindful of regulating them.

My advice is to discover your doshas by using the chart below. Once you know your dosha, you will be able to balance your diet, exercise, sleep, work, and life balance to suit your body type. Ultimately, this knowledge may lead you to mind, body, and spirit joining in your quest to find the light here on Earth.

Knowing and understanding that we are both physical (body) and nonphysical (spiritual) is the first step to spirituality and enlightenment. The knowing is the key to a happier healthier life. *I AM LOVE! I AM LIGHT!*

Vata Dosha ~ Overall Characteristics

- Tall and slender
- Dry skin and hardly sweats
- Excitable, energetic, joyous and fun personality
- Short bursts of high energy
- Fast learner of new knowledge
- Creative
- No daily routine or schedule
- Often have cold feet or hands
- Moody, impulsive with fragmented thoughts
- Stress creates fear

Healthy Tips for a Vata body and mind

In Ayurvedic medicine, we teach the dosha body Vata to stay healthy by advising these general tips: Dairy food is usually good for Vata, as are nuts, blueberries, most fruits and grains such as rice. Foods should be cooked but only eaten warm (not hot) and be easy to digest. Find nourishing rather than sweet and fatty.

Don't eat large meals. Try using a small plate and include lots of raw or cooked vegetables, fruit, wheat bread, cheese, milk, soybeans, and easily digestible food. They should be warm or light. Avoid cold and dry foods like red meat and beans.

You need to get yourself into regular habits like planning your day (try a diary) and sleeping regularly. Set your clock to wake up at the same time and go to bed at the same time daily. Make it a habit.

For exercise, I suggest a moderate exercise for you, Vata. Things like walking, swimming, Tai chi, Pilates, low-impact aerobics, golf, and yoga. Running, weightlifting and HIIT are too intense for you. Have regular massages, take yoga classes and often read for your thirst for knowledge. Swedish massage will calm you and is a good option. Using sesame oil to massage your feet and toes is also recommended as a weekly ritual to keep you grounded and tranquil.

As you grasp things swiftly, you may also forget them just as quickly. Again, I suggest a diary or journal. You don't have to keep it in book-form, it can be on your mobile phone if you wish. Though a book journal can be meditative and good for you. Since you are also creative, you may create something substantial in a journal or use that creativity in the arts of some kind. Try and remain focused.

You don't have much self-assurance and lack resolve. You are most often active or restless. You need to stop dithering and face your fears. The way to do this is to always have a routine that keeps you on track.

Warning signs of an out-of-balance Vata

- Extra dry skin and hair
- Aching joints
- Arthritis
- Feeling cold
- Nervousness
- Confusion
- Constipation or flatulence
- Emphysema (not just caused by smoking)
- Tics and twitches
- Anxious
- Panic attacks
- Losing weight
- Uncertain

Pitta Dosha ~ Overall Characteristics

- Strong, well-built medium size body
- Athletic

- Fair or ruddy skin that can become sunburnt
- Often have freckles
- Inpatient and ill-tempered
- Entrepreneurial leader or good manager but can be controlling
- Good concentration, focused thinking and orderly
- Self-assured and competitive
- Materialistic
- Ambitious
- Likes a good challenge
- A romantic
- When stressed can become angry and demanding
- Uncomfortable in the heat of summer
- Heat can tire you, and you'll sweat
- Good digestion and appetite

Healthy Tips for a Pitta body and mind

Ayurvedic medicine suggests keeping a Vata body in balance by using these general tips: It's fundamental, because of Pitta's heat, to remain cool by keeping hydrated always. Avoid too much exposure to the sun by keeping in the shade. You'll find you usually gravitate to the shady areas and don't like to sunbake.

Though you may love spicy foods, such as chilli, salsa, peppers, and tomato, balance them with non-spicy foods, and avoid adding salt. Don't overindulge in fried or takeaway foods. Sorry to say it, but you are the dosha that is most likely to be affected by vices like smoking, alcohol, sugar, and caffeine. As I said, it's all about moderation.

The best foods for Pitta are fresh salads with dark greens like spinach, rocket, and kale (yes, the superfoods). Sweet and water filled fruit and vegetables; watermelon, cucumber, avocado, mango, berries, pears, and cherries. Eat white meat like chicken and fish but avoid red meats. Dairy foods like cottage cheese, cheddar, and milk are good for Pitta.

As for sport and exercise, you work well in a team like touch football and netball where you are a part, rather than the only competitor. You are too competitive for solo sports like golf or tennis. You should enjoy stand-up paddle boarding (also great for the core) and other water sports.

Gentle massage using pressure points and tapping are good for a Pitta body. Don't use hot oils, try cooling essential oils and aromatherapy instead.

Pittas people need to avoid conflicts or may anger easily. Try to use self-control and endeavour to be kind. Be honest and do not exaggerate about your wealth or abilities. Don't let your competitiveness get in the way of your intelligence.

Warning signs of an out-of-balance Pitta

- Irritability
- Aggression
- Jealousy
- Hatred
- Obsessive and compulsive
- Rashes
- Acne
- Boils
- Heartburn or acid reflux
- Diarrhea
- Colitis
- Bad metabolism
- Ulcers
- Dry, sore eyes
- A sore throat
- Fever
- Insomnia

Kapha Dosha ~ Overall Characteristics

- Heavy build, robust and sturdy
- May be overweight
- Big kind eyes
- Soft, radiant skin and hair
- Voice may be low and soft with slow speech
- Very easy going
- Undemanding

- Calm
- Relaxed and unhurried
- Good stamina
- Compassionate and affectionate
- Self-sufficient
- Gentle
- Good memory but slow to learn
- Possessive
- Hates dampness and cold
- Often pacifying others

Healthy Tips for Kapha body and soul

In Ayurveda, we are taught that Kapha is the most harmonious of the Doshas, but that means when out of balance they can become depressed. Because they are prone to sluggish digestion, this can lead to weight gain and depression. It is best for Kapha to keep active to avoid these things.

You can enjoy spicy foods (unlike Pitta) if they are warm and light. Try flavoured herbal teas, such as liquorice and ginger. Limit dairy, rice, wheat, and eggs. Keep away from sugar and oily foods.

Kapha's exercise regimen should include long walks or hiking, HIIT, football, volleyball, bicycling and rowing. Mix it up so that your body is being surprised by the exercise. It's not just your daily routine that needs variety.

Warm massage oil with a deep tissue massage is best for helping you transfer retained fluids. Spicy essential oils with aromatherapy are also good for Kapha.

Kapha people tend to be warm-hearted and laid back. They are extremely forgiving because they like harmony. Because they are reserved and contemplative, sometimes they can prefer their own company but don't withdraw too much, or it will lead to depression. Get outside your comfort zone and explore new things. Change is good for you, to avoid getting in a rut. Vary your routine (I know you don't want to but just try it). Don't be so possessive either because when you tend to do so, it can lead to envy and jealousy.

Warning signs of an out-of-balance Kapha

- Sluggish digestion;
- Depression
- Possessiveness
- Feeling too cold or damp
- Headaches
- Respiratory issues
- Asthma
- Atherosclerosis
- Coughs and colds
- Sinus
- Flu
- Allergies
- Diabetes
- Water retention
- Jealousy

Now that you've figured out what your dosha is you can use the above strategies to keep in balance. In the next chapter, I have included some herbal remedies and recipes to help you with your personal doshas. There are plenty of books that go further with the doshas, but for the sake of *Heal to Live*, the quest is ways to find the *light* while here on Earth. I want to get you there, so keep reading to find out how.

Exercises

- Fill out the chart on the next page discover your dosha. What is your dosha? What are the main qualities of that dosha that make it yours?
- Is there something that you think may be out of balance with your dosha? How could you correct it?
- Do you enjoy regular massages (you should)? What would be the best massage and sports for your dosha type?

Golden Gems for your Spiritual Treasure Chest

I have a bigger, colourful version of the dosha chart on my website. You can download a copy by clicking the link that will be placed at www.kerrythehealer.com/dosha_chart.

The quiz below will help you figure out your Dosha.

What's Your Dosha

OBSERVATIONS	♡	VATA	♡	PITTA	♡	KAPHA
Body Size	♡	Thin build	♡	Medium build	♡	Large build
Body weight	♡	Low	♡	Medium	♡	Heavy side
Weight change	♡	Trouble gaining	♡	Can gain but lose quickly	♡	Gains weight easily, hard to lose
Skin type	♡	Thin, dry	♡	Smooth, combination skin	♡	Thick, oily
Skin texture	♡	Cold, roughness, light colour	♡	Warm, reddish, freckles	♡	Cool, pale
Hair	♡	Dry, brittle, scarce, gets knotted	♡	Straight, oily, prone to hair loss	♡	Thick, curly, oily, wavy, luxuriant
Hair colour	♡	Brown, black	♡	Blond, grey, red	♡	Dark black, dark brown
Teeth	♡	Big, roomy, stick out, thin gums	♡	Medium size, soft, tender gums	♡	Healthy, white, strong gums
Nose	♡	Uneven shape, deviated septum	♡	Long, Pointed, red nose tip	♡	Short, rounded, button nose
Eyes	♡	Small, sunken, dry, active, frequent blinking	♡	Sharp, sensitive to light	♡	Big, calm

Eye colour	♡	Black, brown	♡	Bright grey, green, yellow/red	♡	Blue
Nails	♡	Dry, rough, easily broken	♡	Sharp, flexible, long, reddish tint	♡	Thick, smooth, shiny surface
Lip	♡	Dry, cracked	♡	Often inflamed	♡	Smooth, large
Lip colour	♡	Black or brown tint	♡	Red or yellowish	♡	Pale
Chin	♡	Thin and angular	♡	Tapered	♡	Rounded, big
Cheeks	♡	Sunken, lines or wrinkles	♡	Flat and smooth	♡	Big or round
Neck	♡	Long, thin	♡	Medium	♡	Wide
Chest	♡	Small, flat	♡	Moderate	♡	Broad chested
Belly	♡	Small, flat	♡	Moderate	♡	Large, defined
Belly button	♡	Small, regular	♡	Oval, superficial	♡	Big, deep, round
Hips	♡	Small or thin	♡	Moderate	♡	Big
Joints	♡	Cracking noise	♡	Moderate	♡	Large, lubricated
Appetite	♡	Irregular in frequency and magnitude	♡	Strong, cannot skip meals	♡	Steady, regular, skips meals
Taste preference	♡	Sweet, sour, salty	♡	Sweet, bitter, astringent	♡	Bitter, pungent, astringent
Thirst	♡	Variable	♡	Need water regularly	♡	Sparse need for water
Digestion	♡	Irregular	♡	Quick	♡	Slow
When there is indigestion	♡	Tendency to constipation, forms gas	♡	Causes burning, heat burn, reflux	♡	Forms mucous
Elimination	♡	Dry	♡	Loose	♡	Thick, sluggish
Physical activity	♡	Always active	♡	Moderate	♡	Slow, measured

Mental activity	♡	Always active	♡	Moderate	♡	Calm
Personality	♡	Vivacious, talkative, social, outgoing	♡	Likes to be in control, intense, ambitious	♡	Reserved, laid back, concerned
Emotional response when stressed	♡	Anxiety, fear	♡	Anger, jealousy	♡	Greedy, possessive, withdrawn
Faith or beliefs	♡	Variable	♡	Dedicated, strong	♡	Consistent
Intellectual response	♡	Quick, not detailed	♡	Accurate, timely	♡	Paced but exact
Memory	♡	Good short term, quick to forget	♡	Medium but accurate	♡	Slow to remember but then sustained
Career, life preference	♡	Creative arts, designing	♡	Science or engineering	♡	Management, human relations, care giving
Environment	♡	Easily feels cold	♡	Intolerant of heat	♡	Uncomfortable in humidity
Sleep	♡	Short, broken up	♡	Moderate and sound	♡	Deep and long
Dreams	♡	Multiple and quick, fearful	♡	Fiery, often about conflicts	♡	Slow, romantic
Speech	♡	Rapid, hither thither	♡	Precise, articulate	♡	Slow, monotonous
Financial	♡	Buy on impulse	♡	Spends money on luxuries	♡	Good at saving money
TOTAL	☐	VATA	☐	PITTA	☐	KAPHA

CHAPTER 13

Dosha Diets
Using doshas to balance health

"The greatest wealth is health."
—Virgil

Diet is such a misused word today. Diet is about creating eating habits that are good for you. It's not about fads, quirks, starvation, and denial. Again, it's about balance, and the best way to achieve that is through Ayurveda principles.

I believe learning about your constituting, and Ayurvedic principles will give you the insight and knowledge to understand when your body is out of balance and then correct it. Learning to feel into your body and knowing how it works on a cellular level. The physiology of our bodies will help with tuning into your inner guidance system. Our bodies are constantly changing on a cellular level putting our doshas off balance or in balance. Stick to the lifestyle, diet, and foods suited for your dosha body type, and you can sustain good health.

Food for Vata

Lifestyle and Diet:

- Vata is cold, light, irregular, dry, and always changing. To balance Vata, make choices that bring warmth, stability, and consistency to your life.

- Try to get to bed before 10 pm, awaken by 6 am
- Avoid becoming chilled. Wear adequate clothing appropriate for the season and keep your head covered when the weather is cold.
- Perform a daily self-abhyanga massage using warmer, heavier oils like sesame or any medicated oils
- Light exercise that enhances balance and flexibility is best for a Vata body type. Take care not to push yourself too far and exceed the limits of your energy.
- Yoga, pranayama is advisable
- Favour soothing, calming music.

Dietetics

- Foods that are warm, moist, oily, smooth, and nourishing – can help to balance excess Vata.
- The warm quality can be emphasised by eating foods that are warm in temperature (it is best to avoid foods with a cooling energetic, cold and frozen foods or drinks, carbonated drinks, large quantities of raw fruits and vegetables, and even leftovers that have been kept in the refrigerator or freezer. The cold quality is inherently increased in these foods, even if they are served hot.)
- Vata's dryness is offset by eating cooked rather than raw foods, by cooking and garnishing foods with generous amounts of high-quality oils or ghee, and by staying hydrated.
- Vata's lightness with sustenance – eating foods that offer solid, stabilising sources of energy and deep nourishment to the physical body (very heavy foods like deep-fried choices can easily overtax Vata's delicate digestion. Eating too much in one sitting can also be overly heavy, so it's important not to overeat.)
- Raw fruits and vegetables are sometimes called roughage; their fibrous structure gives them a very rough quality. Therefore, Vata does well to resist large quantities of raw vegetables and fruits. Eating foods and preparations that are smooth in texture – things like bananas, rice pudding, hot cereal, hot spiced milk, puréed soups, and the like – can really help to soothe Vata's roughness.
- Vata is pacified by the sweet, sour, and salty tastes
- The sweet taste is the foundation of a Vata pacifying diet. It is the predominant taste in most Vata foods. Sweet foods tend to be

grounding, nourishing, strength building, and satisfying (does not require us to eat large amounts of refined sugar or sugary sweet foods).

- Favour sour additions like a squeeze of lemon or lime juice, a splash of vinegar, a slice of cheese.
- Salt stimulates the appetite and digestion, helps retain moisture, supports proper elimination, and improves the flavour of many foods.
- Diet pattern should be regular with regular interval (5 meals per day)

Breakfast: Breakfast is a critical meal when Vata is elevated. After an overnight fast, Vata needs real nourishment, and a hearty breakfast is generally very stabilising.

Buttered toast, oatmeal, rice pudding, cream of rice, and cream of wheat, add warming spices like cinnamon, nutmeg, ginger, cloves, and cardamom. Milk, almonds, dates.

Lunch: Lunch is the main meal of the day, meaning it's the largest and the most nourishing of the three.

Hearty grains steamed and sautéed vegetables, appropriate bread, soups, and stews, split mung dal with basmati rice, sautéed okra with shredded coconut and naam.

Dinner: Dinner is ideally a bit smaller and lighter than lunch. But to soothe Vata, it needs to offer adequate nourishment. Soups, stews, carrots, beets.

Specific Vata foods

Fruits:

- Fruits that pacify Vata will generally be sweet and nourishing. While some raw fruit is appropriate, cooked or stewed fruits are easier to digest and offer additional warmth, moisture, and sweetness – which make them even more beneficial for Vata.
- Favour: apples (cooked), bananas (ripe, not green), berries, coconut, dates (fresh, cooked or soaked), cherries, figs (fresh, cooked or soaked), grapes, Kiwi fruit, pineapple, lemon, mango, orange, papaya, melons, peaches, lime, plums.

Vegetables:

- Vegetables that pacify Vata will generally be sweet, moist, and cooked. Avoid exceptionally dry, rough, and cold vegetables, including most raw vegetables. If you must have raw veggies, a salad, or any of the Vata-aggravating vegetables, keep the quantities small and eat them at mid-day, when digestive strength is at its peak. A thorough cooking or a well-spiced, oily dressing will help to offset some of the dry, rough qualities of these foods.
- Favour: asparagus, avocado, beets, carrots-cooked, cilantro, garlic, okra, sweet potatoes cucumber, green beans, onion- cooked, pumpkin, spinach.

Grains:

- Grains that pacify Vata are generally sweet, nourishing, easily digested, and well cooked. Mushy grains and puddings (things like oatmeal, cream of wheat and rice pudding) exemplify the smooth quality and, when sweetened and spiced, are often delicious comfort foods. Avoid grains that are exceptionally light, dry, or rough, or especially dense and heavy.
- Favour: wheat, rice (all types), oats-cooked, amaranth.

Legumes:

- Vata can enjoy a narrow selection of legumes, provided they are well-cooked and well-spiced. The beans that work best for Vata are a little less dense, rough, and dry, than other legumes. They tend to cook relatively quickly, are easily digested, and offer grounded, nourishing quality. Many other beans are simply too dry, rough, and hard for Vata's delicate digestion.
- Favour: mung dal, split peas, mung beans, lentils-red, tur dal, uraddal.

Dairy products:

- Dairy products are generally quite balancing for Vata, but it's good to avoid highly processed preparations (like powdered milk), and especially cold dairy products. For example, boiled cow's milk (ideally a non-homogenized variety) spiced with cinnamon and nutmeg, sweetened if desired, and served hot, is a tonic for Vata, whereas cold cow's milk may be too difficult for many to digest. As a rule, dairy milk (cow's milk, goat's milk, sheep's milk, etc.) should be taken at least one hour before or after any other food. For this reason, avoid drinking milk with meals.

- Favour: butter, buttermilk, cheese, cottage cheese, cow's milk, ghee, goat's milk, yogurt (fresh).

Nuts & Seeds:

- In moderation, all nuts and most seeds are pacifying to Vata. They are oily, nutritious, and they offer a power-packed combination of proteins and fats that are highly beneficial to Vata. That said, nuts and seeds are quite heavy and should be eaten in small quantities so as not to overwhelm Vata's fickle digestive capacity.
- Favour: almonds, cashews, coconut, hazelnut, walnuts, pistachios, pumpkin seeds, sunflower seeds, sesame seeds.

Meats:

- Vata does well with eggs and a variety of different meats if you choose to eat them. If you do eat meat, the meats to favour are those that are nourishing, sweet, moist, and relatively easy to digest. Meats to avoid tend to be either too light or dry or too heavy, for Vata.
- Favour: beef, chicken (especially dark), eggs, fish (fresh and salt water), seafood, sardines, salmon, turkey (dark).

Oils:

- Most oils are beneficial for Vata, provided they are high-quality oils. Sesame oil, almond oil, coconut oil, olive oil, and ghee are among the best choices.
- Favour: almond oil, avocado oil, castor oil, coconut oil, ghee, mustard oil, olive oil, safflower oil, sesame oil, sunflower oil.

Sweeteners:

- Most sweeteners are good for Vata, but it's generally best to avoid large quantities of refined sugar. Favour sweeteners in their most natural state over anything highly processed.
- Favour: date sugar, fructose, fruit juice concentrates, honey (raw), jaggary, molasses, rice syrup.

Spices:

- Most spices are wonderful for Vata, if none of your dishes are fiery hot (due to excessive use of cayenne pepper, chilli peppers and the like).
- Favour: Ajwan, basil, bay leaf, black pepper, cinnamon, cardamom, cloves, coriander, cumin, dill, fennel, garlic, ginger, hing, mint, mustard seeds, nutmeg, oregano, paprika, parsley, saffron, turmeric.

Food for Pitta

Lifestyle and Diet:

- Pitta is hot, sharp, sour, pungent, and penetrating. To balance Pitta, we need to make choices that are cooling, sweet and stabilising.
- Be certain not to skip meals and do not wait until you are famished to eat. Favour foods that are sweet, bitter and astringent. Favour cooling foods such as cucumbers, sweet fruits, and melons.
- Perform a daily oil massage using cooler oils such as coconut or olive.
- Favour aromas that are cooling and sweet. Sandalwood, rose, jasmine, mint, lavender, fennel, and chamomile are recommended.
- Laugh many times each day.
- Keep cool physically and mentally, Apply an attitude of moderation in all things.
- In hot climates or seasons take cool baths, stay out of the sun in the hottest part of the day, wear loose light-coloured cotton clothing (especially white and pastel shades like pale blue), take enough fluids, wear a hat.

Dietetics:

- Pitta is oily, sharp, hot, light, spreading, and liquid, so eating foods that neutralise these qualities – foods that are dry, mild, cooling, grounding, stabilising, and dense – serve to balance excess Pitta.
- The cool quality can be emphasised by eating foods that are cool in temperature or that have a cooling energetic – and by using cooling spices generously. It is best to avoid fiery hot dishes, foods with a sharply warming energetic, alcohol, and caffeine; these influences can increase heat.
- While the heavy quality is the true antithesis to Pitta's lightness-eating foods that offer solid, stabilising sources of energy and adequate nourishment to the physical body. Highly processed foods such as canned foods, ready-made meals, and pastries often lack prana (vital life force), are excessively heavy, and should be avoided.
- Pitta's liquid nature and a tendency toward excess oil make drying or astringent foods like beans, potatoes, corn, millet, oats, pasta, popcorn, and most vegetables very appropriate.
- Sharp flavours like pineapple, pickles, vinegar, and sharp aged cheeses are better replaced with milder, gentler tastes, like those found in apples, cucumbers, lime juice, and soft cheeses. Caffeine, nicotine, and hard alcohol are too sharp and penetrating for Pitta. Substitute more stable and sustainable sources of energy.
- Pitta is pacified by the sweet, bitter, and astringent tastes and aggravated by the pungent, sour and salty tastes.
- The sweet taste is cooling and heavy but also anti-inflammatory. It pacifies heat, satisfies thirst, benefits the skin and hair, and tends to be grounding, nourishing, strength building and satisfying.
- The bitter taste is exceptionally cooling but also drying. (Bitters cleanse the pallet and improve the sense of taste. They tone the skin and muscles, benefit the blood, relieve burning and itching sensations, satisfy thirst, and balance the appetite, support digestion, and help to absorb moisture, sweat, and excess Pitta.
- The astringent taste is basically a flavour of dryness; the astringent taste is heavy, cold, and dry. Pitta benefits from the compressing, absorbing, union-promoting nature of the astringent taste.

Diet pattern:

- As most people with Pitta digestion know, Pitta's sharp appetite can lead to a general intolerance for skipping meals.
- Pitta does well to stick to a regular eating schedule and to eat at least three-square meals each day.
- Eating at consistent times from one day to the next further helps to balance an overactive digestive fire.

Breakfast: Breakfast is usually not to be skipped when Pitta is elevated. Oatmeal made with hot milk, almonds, ghee, egg omelette etc.

Lunch: It is the largest and the most nourishing meal. Grains, beans, and vegetables are great building blocks for lunch. Sautéed purple cabbage and a green salad, add vegetables like carrots, celery, and onion to your soup. Sauté the cabbage in ghee with cumin, coriander, turmeric, lime juice.

Dinner: Dinner is ideally a bit smaller and lighter than lunch, but it also needs to sustain Pitta's active metabolism. A simple but nourishing meal- mung dhal, basmati rice, asparagus, kidney bean curry, sautéed green beans (cooked with cilantro and coconut) and quinoa or flatbread.

Specific Pitta foods

Fruits:

- Fruits that pacify Pitta will generally be sweet and somewhat astringent. Dried fruits are typically also acceptable, but are best in small quantities, fruits and fruit juices are best enjoyed alone – 30 minutes before, and ideally at least 1 hour after, any other food.
- Favour: apples (sweet), apricots (sweet), berries (sweet), cherries (sweet), coconut, dates, figs, grapes (red, purple, black), mangos (ripe), oranges (sweet), papaya, pineapple (sweet), plums (sweet).

Vegetables:

- Vegetables that pacify Pitta will generally be somewhat sweet and either bitter, astringent or both. Many vegetables include some combination of these tastes; experimenting with a wide variety of vegetables is a great way to pacifying Pitta. Pitta can usually digest raw vegetables better than Vata and Kapha, but midday is often the best time of day to have them because digestive strength is at its peak.

- Favour: asparagus, beets (cooked), bell peppers, bitter melon, broccoli, cabbage, carrots (cooked), cauliflower, cucumber, green beans, celery, cilantro, mushrooms, okra, onions (cooked), potatoes, radishes (cooked), peas, sweet potatoes, zucchini.

Grains:

- Grains that pacify Pitta are cooling, sweet, dry, and grounding. Many of the grains that benefit Pitta are rather dry; this helps to offset Pitta's oily nature. Avoiding grains that are heating (like buckwheat, corn, millet, brown rice, and yeasted bread).
- Favour: barley, cereal (dry), couscous, oats, rice (basmati, white, wild), wheat, wheat bran.

Legumes:

- Legumes are generally astringent in taste and are therefore largely Pitta pacifying.
- Favour: chickpeas, black beans, kidney beans, lentils, mungdal, mung beans, lima beans, split peas, soybeans, white beans.

Diary:

- Dairy products tend to be grounding, nourishing, and cooling.
- Favour: butter (unsalted), cheese, cow's milk, ghee, yogurt, cottage cheese, goat's milk, goat's cheese.

Nuts & Seeds:

- Nuts and seeds tend to be extremely oily and are usually heating, so most of them are not terrifically balancing for Pitta. Some nuts are acceptable in small quantities.
- Favour: almonds (soaked and peeled), flax seeds, popcorn (buttered, without salt), pumpkin seeds, sunflower seeds.

Meats & Eggs:

- Pitta does best with animal foods that taste sweet, are relatively dry (like rabbit) and that is either mildly heating or cooling in nature.
- Favour: buffalo, chicken (white), eggs (white only), fish (freshwater), rabbit, turkey (white).

Oils:

- Pitta does well with a moderate amount of oil.
- Favour: coconut oil, flax seed oil, ghee, sunflower oil.

Sweeteners:

- Most sweeteners are well tolerated by Pitta; naturally occurring sweet tastes are far more balancing than sugary sweets, so even the appropriate sweeteners should be used in moderation.
- Favour: date sugar, fructose, fruit juice concentrates, rice syrup.

Spices:

- Most spices are heating by nature and therefore have the potential to aggravate Pitta. The spices to favour are only mildly heating, help to maintain a balanced digestive fire without provoking Pitta, and, in some cases, are actively cooling.
- Favour: cardamom, cilantro, coriander, fennel, mint, cinnamon (small amounts), cumin, dill, basil (fresh), saffron (less amount).

Food for Kapha

Lifestyle and Diet:

- Kapha is inherently cold, heavy, and dense; the key to balancing Kapha is stimulation.
- Follow a regular daily routine, ideally awakening before 6 am each morning. Avoid taking naps during the day.

- Stay warm and avoid dampness. Kapha is particularly sensitive to cold, damp conditions and benefits from heat.
- Perform a daily garshan (dry massage) on your body to stimulate circulation.
- Get regular exercise – preferably every day. This is the best way to avoid stagnation and the accumulation of toxins in the body.

Dietetics:

- Kapha is heavy, cool, oily, and smooth, so eating foods that neutralise these qualities – foods that are light, warm, dry, and rough – can help to balance excess Kapha.
- Favour light and airy over dense & heavy property.
- Fruits and vegetables are typically wonderfully light, so a diet that is fresh fruits and vegetables, preferably cooked, is a great start.
- Eating too much in one sitting also leads to excess heaviness, so it's important not to overeat.

Specific Kapha foods

Fruits:

- Fruits that pacify Kapha will generally be astringent and only mildly sweet. Dried fruits are acceptable, on occasion, but should only be enjoyed in small quantities because they are so dense and concentrated.
- Favour: apples, apricots, figs (dry), strawberries, prunes, raisins, grapes (red, purple, black), pomegranates, lemons, limes, peaches, pears.
- Fruits to avoid are those that are exceptionally sweet, heavy, dense, or watery – like bananas, coconut, dates, melons, pineapple, or plums.

Vegetables:

- Vegetables that pacify Kapha will generally be pungent, bitter, and astringent. Most vegetables include some combination of these tastes, so vegetables are an important centrepiece of any effective

Kapha-balancing diet. Cooked vegetables are generally easier to digest than raw ones, so it's best to have raw veggies, salads, and Kapha-aggravating vegetables in small quantities and at mid-day when digestive strength is at its peak.

- Favour: artichoke, asparagus, beets, broccoli, chilies, cauliflower, cilantro, celery, cabbage, carrots, bell pepper, bitter melon, Brussels sprouts, corn, Daikon radish eggplant, garlic, green beans, Jerusalem artichokes, kale, leafy greens, lettuce, mustard greens, okra, peas, onions(uncooked), peppers, potatoes white, radishes, spinach, tomatoes (cooked).

Grains:

- Grains that pacify Kapha are light, dry, and rough. In general, grains tend to be staples in our diets because they are somewhat heavy and nourishing. Reducing grain consumption overall can be a huge benefit. Avoid grains that are exceptionally heavy, moist or dense (like wheat, flours, bread, cooked oats, and pasta) as much as possible, and eat smaller quantities of appropriate grains.
- Favour: Amaranth, barley, buckwheat, corn, couscous, oat bran, oats (dry), rice (basmati, wild), wheat bran.

Legumes:

- Legumes are generally astringent, which is one of the tastes that balance Kapha. Kapha can enjoy a wide variety of legumes, but they should generally be well-cooked and well-spiced to make them more digestible.
- Favour: black beans, chickpeas, lentils, lima beans, mung beans, pinto beans, split peas, tur dal, soy meats.

Dairy products:

- Dairy products are best minimised when trying to reduce Kapha because they tend to be heavy, unctuous, and can increase mucus production. Goat's milk and goat's milk products are the best options for Kapha because they are lighter

- Favour: buttermilk, goat's milk (skim), yogurt (fresh and diluted), goat's cheese (unsalted)

Nuts & seeds:

- Nuts and seeds tend to be heavy, dense, and oily and are generally not terrifically balancing for Kapha. But there are a few types of nuts and seeds that are acceptable in small quantities.
- Favour: almonds (soaked and peeled), flax seeds, popcorn (without salt or butter), pumpkin seeds, sunflower seeds.

Meats & Eggs:

- Kapha does best with animal foods that are light and relatively dry (like chicken or freshwater fish). Eating less meat all around is generally beneficial.
- Favour: chicken (white), eggs, fish (freshwater), rabbit, turkey (white).

Oils:

- Most oils are a bit heavy and, well, oily for Kapha. However, in very small quantities, the oils in the favoured column are acceptable.
- Favour: almond oil, corn oil, flax seed oil, sunflower oil.

Sweeteners:

- Sweet taste is not particularly supportive of Kapha, most sweeteners are better avoided. Honey on the other hand – which is dry, light, and heating – is the one exception, when used in small quantities. (Should be raw honey).

Herbal Uses to Balance Doshas

Ayurveda treatment remedies have been using what nature provided us, herbs and medicinal plants for thousands of years. I am particularly interested in the magic of some of these wonderful herbs and plants. It's amazing what our bodies can do once given the right ingredients to balance out the doshas.

Vata Herbs

Triphala: detoxification & rejuvenation for constipation and for a clean digestive tract.

Boswellia: this tree resin from Africa and Asia is inflammatory and great in joint conditions such as arthritis.

Guggul: tree resin secreted by the mukul myrrh tree is for arthritis, haemorrhoids, and urinary tract infections. It can also be used for weight loss and acne.

Ashwagandha: Indian ginseng is used to give energy and vitality. Good for restful sleep and alleviating stress. It can also improve fertility.

Chyawanprashwill: an extract fortified with herbs, extracts, and minerals that are high in vitamin C. It supports a fragile immune system (especially from disease) by rejuvenating and revitalising.

Pitta Herbs:

Gymnema (Gymnema Sylvestre): is a herb native to the tropical forests of southern and central India and Sri Lanka. Also, called cowplant; a sweet leaf extract for metabolic imbalance relating to sugar.

Picrorrhiza: one of the oldest medicinal plants from the Nepalese Himalayas used to strengthen the liver.

Phyllanthus (Phyllanthus genus): supplement made from flowering plants can help with cleansing the liver and prevent the formation of liver stones, which also aids in metabolism.

Kapha Herbs

Ashwagandha: Indian ginseng is used to give energy and vitality. Good for restful sleep and alleviating stress. It can also improve fertility. Best for Kapha's energy levels.

Gymnema (Gymnema Sylvestre): is a herb native to the tropical forests of southern and central India and Sri Lanka. Also, called cowplant; a sweet leaf extract for metabolic imbalance relating to sugar. For Kapha, it's used to reduce sugar cravings.

Picrorrhiza: one of the oldest medicinal plants from the Nepalese Himalayas used to strengthen the liver.

Phyllanthus (Phyllanthus genus): supplement made from flowering plants can help with cleansing the liver and prevent the formation of liver stones, which also aids in metabolism.

Follow the guidelines above by implementing these foods and herbs into your diet for well-balanced health. I'd like to thank Greens Ayurveda Study Centre, India for the use of notes from workshops I give on the Doshas along with Dr. Asghar. You can find out more about Greens at www.greensayurveda.com.

Exercise

- Make a list of the foods of your dosha body type that you like to eat?
- Make a list of the foods of your dosha body type that you would rather avoid but know would be good for you if you incorporated them in your diet.
- Are there any foods on these lists that you believe your body may be lacking? Try to include them in your diet from now on and see if they improve your health.

CHAPTER 14

Meditation and Yoga - Prana isn't just breath
It's life force energy

"When you own your own breath, no one can steal your peace."
—author unknown

"Meditate. Let the heart of the light engulf you."
—Gurumayi Chidvilasananda

Just breathe, take a second and notice your breath. This is your life force. Your life-force energy that Mother Nature provides for us. I didn't really understand what life-force energy was until I studied Ayurveda and yoga in India.

It was there I learnt that prana life-force energy is oxygen or air. It all means the same thing. It was an awesome discovery when I understood that plants purify our exhaled air (carbon monoxide) or toxins which are stress or blocked energy, then Mother Nature (plants) purify it. They release our 'life-force energy' or oxygen. This life-force energy purifies and rejuvenates our cells. Science has proven that plants, like water, have consciousness. Another amazing thing that Mother Earth provides. Wow!!

If God (Universe) is the father, then Mother Earth is the mother. We are all connected as one, through these elements. This is also mentioned in Aboriginal (Indigenous Australian) culture. They honour Mother Earth, the moon, sun, and universe. Through Dreamtime, Aboriginal people connect with universal energies and receive insight from above.

Ayurveda principles are a part of yoga and meditation. In this chapter, I will explain in simple terms how they work.

We take in prana, life-force energy. Our body is then rejuvenated, putting our bodies and mind into a state of relaxation. Then we can connect with our true being, our inner wisdom. As I mentioned earlier, when we calm the mind, we make space for the goodness to come in. Through breath, we calm the mind and a natural space forms. We can fill that space with new, relaxed, inspiring thoughts. Meditation is connecting to breathe in a way that we are empowered through breath and not mind.

It was while on my journey through Bali and India that I learnt what prana really meant. Prana is a Sanskrit word that means life force energy or life breath, (air or oxygen) our life force is what keeps us alive and helps us heal. For anyone thinking about studying yoga or meditation you will learn basic knowledge; how 'prana' 'breath' and how we are connected to it, and that it connects us to everything on this planet. When the 'penny dropped' for me I thought to myself, it's never really been explained in a way that I understand. Now I understand. Hopefully, when you read this, it will make more sense to you too.

Prana (oxygen, air, breath) is everywhere and is part of us as universal force energy, which rejuvenates and replenishes our cells. It helps to remove, move and shift toxins from our body. Prana breath also relaxes our muscles and body, which allows us to find a state of peace. When we exhale prana from the body, it is toxic (carbon monoxide) and is released from our bodies out into the universe.

Mother Nature (plants) take in the toxins (carbon oxide) and replenishes, cleanses and purifies the toxic breath, which turns it into prana (life force energy) keeping us alive. This prana breath is used to shift toxins out of the body while doing asanas (yoga postures). When we inhale, we take in life calmness. Calming our body and mind is a very important part of balancing mind body and spirit (spirituality). Without prana (air) we would not survive.

While studying in India, one of my teachers explained how our life force (air) runs down our spine If our spine were severed no more life force could get through. He also went on to explain that when we die, it's our breath, our disconnection to life-force that stops, which is our last breath. I always thought that our heart was the last piece of us that let's go and stops when we die. I wanted to discover as much information as I could because I found it so interesting. I wanted to know if science supported the theory; I found that it did.

Use Prana in your Daily Life

I practice prana in my daily life. If I'm overwhelmed or anxious about something, I close my eyes (meditation) and connect with my breath (prana). This brings my awareness to my breath. It allows me to feel my breath (prana) filling my body. Once I do this mediation, I feel my body letting go, allowing the anxiety or toxic thought to be released from my body.

When I'm working at The Yoga Barn doing this meditation with clients, I ask them to feel into their bodies and notice the feelings. It is not long (2-3mintutes) before they feel the lightness and calmness running through their body by using prana breath. As I said, prana is also found in all plants (Mother Nature) or Mother Earth, providing purified air to breathe. It's also in food that nourishes our cells and bodies. Research confirms that plants feel and think on a cellular level. We have a deep connection to plants (in fact everything). Some tests have shown that if we speak positive affirmations or words to plants, they thrive, just like humans. It's like the test undertaken by Dr. Emoto with the interesting findings with water and rice (that I mentioned in Chapter 8).

Prana helps balance our mind. Meditation calms the mind (breath) and asanas (yoga) balance the mind. Yoga means union. It is the combination and connection with mind and body; physical and thoughts. As we practice these ancient Indian techniques we are led into our spirit within; our spirituality.

Many words mean the same thing, and I am hoping this is helpful to those who read this book. We are all here to experience happiness, joy, and love. I believe we are here to co-create; so we teach, share and love each other. It's what we are all born to do.

Mudra symbolic hand gesture

Think about little babies; having so much innocence. They carry no judgements or baggage. Babies are free to express and be who they want to be. If you observe a baby breathing, you will see that they breathe the same as a yogic breath technique; slow, calm and deep with ribs rising.

It's amazing, we can learn so much from babies and children. Babies and small children do many asanas and mudras. Mudra is a Sanskrit word and means a symbolic hand gesture that has the power of producing joy and happiness.

It has been scientifically proven that regular practice of mudras, not only contribute to one's overall good health but can be used as a preventive measure. I enjoy witnessing babies and young children as they do asanas and mudras naturally. This knowledge gives me feelings of love, joy, and happiness, as I observe them. It is another example of connection.

There is love, joy, and happiness inside all of us. Place your hand in front of your heart in prayer. This position will boost your immune system as you connect with your heart. Close your eyes, and you can connect with your heart chakra. Start to feel your heart fill with love and peace.

Science now supports mudras as part of healing the body process. In these techniques, you can feel a connection and start to feel a sense of inner being. It's when the magic happens because that's when you start to connect to your soul.

We all can do this, to connect with our soul. Our soul knows the answers to everything we need to know. I have tried this hundred of times with myself and clients. If I need an answer to a life question or where I need to access something, I connect with my soul and listen. It is one way to receive answers, by connecting to your true being. The soul knows what the physical you have not figured out yet.

Saying Three Oms

Saying three 'oms' or "om shanti" is another way to connect with your soul and the universe. When you chant 'om' it connects to the divine intelligence that is within all of us; everyone has this. There is an excellent video that NASA released. They recorded the sound of the sun and found that it makes a sound that sounds much like 'om'. I thought WOW! I'm sure you think that is extraordinary too.

After my near-death experience, I felt a deep inner connection to the sun. Some mornings I would get up at 4.30 am and watch the sun come up. It made me feel good. I know now that the sun is referred to as masculine energy within us.

At times I would see the moon and sun together. This was very powerful for me. Still to this day, whenever I see the sun or moon, I feel a shift inside me; a deeply beautiful connection. I sometimes feel this in people I meet. It's what I call a soul connection, where two people are connected by energy. That energy is on the same level, meaning vibrational energy. It's a bit like two souls coming together and saying, "Hi. I really like you. Want to hang out and see what happens?" This can be two females or two males, male and female, person and pet, wild animal and man; any connection of souls.

When we connect to our higher self, we can access our higher intelligence. This gives us every answer to anything we need answers to. It also gives us the ability to access our guidance system which is connected to all systems throughout our bodies.

- Masculine energy (Sun) Male.
- Feminine energy(Moon) Female.

We are made up of both these energies. If Masculine Males were removed from the planet, the Female energy would not survive and become extinct and vice versa. We need both to balance, the planet and each other or we would not evolve.

A simple technique I use daily.

Find a quiet spot to sit or lie down. Place one hand on your heart and the other on your lower tummy and just breathe. Be aware of what your breath is doing as you inhale and exhale. Feel what is going on inside you. Feel the breath coming into your nostrils and down into the back of your throat. Slowly move your breath into your amazing lungs and into your beautiful heart.

You may feel tingles in your toes or other parts of your body. You could experience colour. You might sense a lightness, calmness coming over your body. Whatever you experience is right for you at this moment. Gently and slowly keep the focus on your breath. Using the power of your breath push into any pain or discomfort. You will feel the blocked energy release from your body. This is how we shift energy in and out. Release emotion, physical blockages, and pain from the body.

Never try to force meditation; it's a good idea to find time for yourself to practice.

The Power of Raja Yoga Meditation

Imagine being aware of each thought and reaction that comes to mind - and then ruling it. Within a nanosecond, you claim the power to act on the idea or ditch it.

Consider the negative traits in your personality that you wish would not play out: the thoughts of self-doubt, sabotage, low self-regard, guilt, worry etc. At your will, they will never again be spoken by you or affect your relationships at home, at work or on the sports field.

Some might baulk at being so 'in control' of themselves. But if you really 'get' soul, you can 'get in control' of yourself. Just yourself. Other people's lives and games are their own.

You are only responsible for yourself. Our mums and dads did what they did - sometimes well, sometimes not - but that time has passed, and you are now the independent soul, who can choose how to live.

With Raja Yoga meditation you can throw off the old patterns of influence and recreate yourself to be how you want to be. That is the power of Raja Yoga.

This ancient meditation practice harnesses your natural powers and trains your mind to be your friend. You are not your mind; you are not your body. You have a mind, and you have a body. These 'tools' sometimes work well and at other times may need calm and exercise to get back to a healthy path.

We all make mistakes. We all waste resources. We misuse our words, our energy and our time until we pause and think deeply about what matters in our life. When we hold on tightly to our views, the mind shrinks and smothers any power to love. In that state, the soul can't breathe new energy into a situation - and everyone loses.

But when we sit quietly, cancelling all mindsets, and allow ourselves to know the deep peace of the soul; miraculous changes can happen for the better. People will understand you. Clearly, new doors will open, friends will call, and that stiff neck will relax!

Raja Yoga teaches us to step back and observe life, take a calm breath, cool our reactions, and step forward in the way we choose - independent of others urging us to think or act as they wish.

- Raja Yoga sets you free.
- Raja Yoga releases the power to respond with love.

The Eight Principles of Raja Yoga

We will concern ourselves mainly with Raja Yoga, a system which has been found to be most applicable to the mental and physical conditions in which we live. Raja Yoga, also known as Ashtanga Yoga has eight principles. These are:

1. Yama: non-killing, truthfulness, non-stealing, continence;
2. Niyama: cleanliness, contentment, mortification, study, and self-surrender to good;
3. Asana: posture;
4. Pranayama: control of vital body forces;
5. Pratyahara: introspection;
6. Dharana: concentration;
7. Dhyana: meditation;
8. Samadhi: super-consciousness/higher self

Hatha Yoga deals entirely with the body. The sole aim of that school of yoga is to make the body physically strong. For a strong body, however, you can achieve almost the same effects as those given by Hatha Yoga by enrolling in a gymnasium course at any muscle-building establishment. The exercises of Hatha Yoga are difficult and demand years of steady endeavour. Through this system, it is claimed that a yogi can establish perfect control over every part of his body. The heart can be made to stop or go at his bidding and can control the flow of blood and the sensations of his nervous system.

The result of this part of yoga is to make people stronger and to prolong their lives; good health is its one goal. From the Raja Yogi, if you perfect yourself in Hatha Yoga, you are merely a healthy animal. This system does not lead to spiritual growth or give you the help to meet your need for relaxation, which is found in Raja Yoga. However, certain aspects of Hatha Yoga have become part of the regime of Raja Yoga. These include some of its exercises, dietary aspects, and disease preventives, which provide the physical state of wellbeing which enables the proper pursuit of Yoga.

Yama Principles

In classical yogic doctrine, there are five Yama principles:

1. Ahiṃsā: do not harm;
2. Satya: be truthful; speak your truth, be honest about how you feel.
3. Asteya: do not steal; this includes someone's time. Always honour people who want to see you. They are letting you know they want to be with you and show up for you. Honour that.
4. Brahmacārya: chastity, fidelity or sexual restraint;
5. Aparigraha: do not overindulge, do not over-possess;

Niyama or Discipline

Like Yama, Niyama also means restraint, but it's the other side of the polarity.

While Yamas are the aspects you should avoid or restrain yourself from, Niyamas are the aspects of yourself you should cultivate more into your life.

There are five principles:

1. Shaucha: Purity (e.g. of mind, speech, and body)
2. Santosh: Contentment (e.g. acceptance of others and our circumstances)
3. Tapas: Asceticism (e.g. perseverance, austerity)
4. Svadhyaya: Study (e.g. of scriptures, of self, introspection)
5. Ishvara Pranidhana: devotion to God (e.g. contemplation of the Divine)

In my quest to find an Ayurvedic training centre to learn meditation and yoga, I didn't find the best places for a conducive learning experience immediately. My first experience in India at one of the Ayurvedic training centres was not enjoyable. There I was treated with disdain as the only foreigner. Non-Indian people were expected to be doctors, not people who genuinely wanted to learn. They seemed aggressive and were continually invading personal space.

I regularly wrote in a journal during my stay at one such establishment. They had absolutely no awareness of my privacy, reading my journal and touching my clothes. This made me feel vulnerable as if they were trying to control me.

Due to the stress of the experience and bad hygiene, I developed an abscess on my leg. To my disgust, there was no better care at the nearby hospital. I had to dress and look after the wound myself.

Of course, soon after I left. Something inside me said that I had this experience as part of my life purpose. There is always light in the shadow, we just need to look for it. It taught me to trust my intuition. Before I left Bali, I had an unsettling feeling inside me. Every time I met with the Ayurvedic doctor, it was like something inside me said, "This is not right. This person is not what he seems." It turned out he wasn't.

I use this experience as a highlighter as it enhances not only my spirituality but my intuition becoming an internal navigator of all good things. I meditated for a whole day, while in that state. The idea to keep searching online for something better came to me. I found three suitable centres to consider. Back then I was channelling Buddha, or I say he channelled me first with a smile, I was asking internally for answers as I connected with the ascendant master for spiritual guidance. It was given.

I found Ayurveda. The teachings at Ayurveda centres in India are ancient, so you are always being taught something deep and meaningful. Learning from Mother Earth, herbs and plant medicine, healing through the hands, plus prayer to the ascendant masters and gods. A good Ayurvedic practitioner will do a prayer before they put their hands on your body which is an amazing experience.

Meeting Brahma Kumaris Sisters

I went from a bad situation to a lovely one by tuning in to what I needed. A bad or negative situation or thought can be easily transformed into a positive one.

I found myself staying with the Brahma Kumaris a very joyful experience. Treating Sister Sama, a woman (BK Sister) who had fibromyalgia. Fibromyalgia is a chronic disease associated with pain in the trigger points. It can be debilitating, leading to pain, fatigue, headaches, depression, and anxiety. As I did the healing on her, she talked of angel visions that she had. It was beautiful. Her sister and the Ayurveda doctor came in and saw it too.

When the Brahma Kumaris asked me to stay in their ashram, I was honoured to be shown their ancient text. Brahma means god in Ancient Hindi scriptures and Sanskrit. The gods in Bali and India have that same connection that began in 1930 and is now in 110 countries. They understood that I knew about the ancient Sanskrit because of my visions of them. I also had visions of gods and deities during my meditations.

I saw the Hindu god, Lakshmi, during one meditation. Lakshmi provides wealth, prosperity, health and abundance. She came to me and placed gold coins all around me. I did not know who she was, but an Indian friend listened to my description and found her in the Indian texts. He said, "She's Lakshmi."

I was surprised, to say the least. "What does she want me to do?" I asked. It was all new, but I wanted to discover what it all meant. I tried to remain calm. Through their teaching, the Brahma Kumari grounded me. They helped me to understand that I must be a healer. Teaching that should include guiding people back to their spirituality; to find themselves.

Through meditation, you can achieve this. I am able to find the light regularly seeing the ascended masters to gain my own guidance to help others.

Another breakthrough in my spiritual healing journey was when I learnt how to do Reiki. This was through my friend Punu Wasu, who is a Reiki grandmaster (he has a doctorate). During reiki training, he attuned me (my eyes closed). My heart was green at the start, then it exploded into a rainbow of colour; a beautiful feeling and vision. I realised that if I could combine Reiki with my channelling and crystals, I would be able to heal my clients further. I am now a Grand Master of Reiki and use this as part of my daily practice with clients.

As this book was being written, I was invited to the Brahma Kumari's global conference at Mount Abu in India. This International Conference was held from 23rd to 27th February 2018. The theme being 'God's Plan - Yoga for World Peace, Health and Happiness', was an opportunity to connect. I spoke about world peace. Also, Shiva and Vishnu, who are in my channelling and visions and part of Brahma Kumari, were used in my talk, because of the goodness of the teachings through them.

I would recommend for anyone who is starting on their spiritual path to learn Raja Yoga meditation. Visiting the Brahma Kumari ashrams is a magical experience with so much to offer both spiritual and meditations. Some other ashrams charge exorbitated amounts. I advise you to be aware.

Find your internal connection to lead you to the right place. You can be ripped off if you are not cautious, so please do your research first. You should not have to pay lots of money for a spiritual experience or to learn ancient traditional yoga.

Trusting your thoughts each day

Every morning you decide on what you want for the day. Once you achieve those goals, move to the next ones. Declutter your mind of thought by giving yourself loving thoughts of your mind, soul and physical body. This is what will make you happy and get you ready for the day. When you reach a point of inspiration you are on your path. Wait for the inspiration then act. This is divine connection coming through you, inspiring you and supporting you.

Gifting yourself the present of meditation and prana breath first thing in the morning is like taking a shower, brushing your teeth or doing your hair. Habits that make you feel better will make you feel good. The result is; you become happier and more joyous. This is the bliss, the state of wellbeing.

Many things can make feel good. The key is to find and do as many as you can, as often as you can. This keeps the happy momentum going. It may be listening to your favourite song, walking in the sunshine, patting your dog or something else. You cannot sit and meditate all day. You need to find simple things to keep your happiness alive and ongoing. You want it to last as long as you can all day, most days.

As mentioned, even in a work situation, you can excuse yourself to go to the bathroom or lunch room for a few minutes and sit in silence. It gives your mind a chance to settle and your breath to calm. You can connect to your true loving self. You may need to make a list of things you can think of to change the way you think so that you feel better and can cope with any situation. This is something we all can do. You need to commit to it.

Instead of ten minutes scrolling through Facebook, quieten your mind. Fill it with loving, kind thoughts about yourself. Feed your heart nourishing thoughts. This is the recipe for a happier life filled with joy. My NDE taught me to disconnect from negative people, thoughts and things. Go to where you are truly happy within yourself.

Exercise

Try these mantras:

- I believe and I receive.
- I receive all good to come my way today.
- I am connected to source energy, the universe and God (all mean the same).
- I am in alignment with my true self.

CHAPTER 15

Living in Harmony
Create your own blissful life

"Let your breath come to you and flow through you, this is bliss"
—*Kerry Clancey*

Understanding how we are vibrational beings and manifest by our emotions is important. Our emotions are our guidance system, our connection to (Divine) source energy and divine connection. All we need to do is make sure our vibrational frequency is in alignment with our soul connection. This knows our soul contract or soul purpose; life purpose.

You learn to tap into your vibrational being through thought, as thoughts are connected to your feelings (emotions). I say to my clients, "If in one hand I gave you a choice, being the left contained a negative and fearful thought and the right was a happy, positive thought, then which one would you choose?" They all choose the right one with all the happy, positive thoughts.

However, you will not be aware if you are doing this daily. You may be caught up with life and what it is offering. Instead of bringing awareness into your day. If you look at what your thoughts are doing, they are not real unless you want them to be real. They are just there doing a job of thinking.

Don't give power away because you think you should, when we give our power away, we are not in our own power. It's important to understand this as once we understand our lives will change dramatically.

Learn to change thought. Learn to love yourself by changing one unhappy thought to a happy one. Believe me, you will start attracting new friends, new love, new workplace, and new money. It's a universal law, and it works. Why not try it?

Even while you are reading this, you are manifesting and overriding your subconscious with good, loving, kind thoughts. It is even stronger when you use 'I am' affirmations or statements. Telling yourself for a couple of weeks, daily, "I am a wonderful person" or "I am a good person" is something you may doubt sometimes. Using affirmations to heal internal data (I call them healing affirmations) I developed a handbook which I give to clients with healing affirmations. It really helps to stay focused with your thoughts. It's simple, yet effective.

Keep at it. Try not to doubt it. If you don't believe it, then you will not manifest it. Instead of feeling wonderful or good, you may feel terrible instead. Sometimes it is because thoughts were put there by someone or something else. They were not put there by you, so it's difficult for you to connect with them.

The way to connect is in meditation. Try it in front of a mirror (your soul) or whenever you're sitting in a place of goodness or joy (perhaps under your favourite tree). Keep telling yourself enough times, and you will be what you are telling yourself you are. It's like; if someone tells someone, they are not a good person it may hurt them. If they believed in themselves, it wouldn't affect them.

What matters is that you believe in yourself and who you really are. You will then become the light on earth. You will feel lighter, brighter and blissful. It is amazing how it works. Set yourself a one-day target of how many thoughts you can turn into love and lightness? How many people can you tell you love them, or send a loving message to, or compliment them? It will come back to you as something nice: this is a universal law.

Once you align emotions, such as love, joy, harmony, peace, and goodness you can connect with divine inner being. Remember divine inner being is connected to the universe (divine, creator or God). You then receive the next steps in your life. For example, meditating on the breath, by being aware of our breath just as it is. We don't try to breathe. It is automatic, and we just do it. How amazing are we? We are breath, we are the life force, we are light. Try, for five to ten minutes per day, breathing gently into your lower abdomen and starting to feel your inner connection. It will make you feel light and relaxed. You may even feel sensations going through your body. Perhaps you'll have visions of what makes you feel good. Your inner being will guide you through this once you start communicating with your inner self. Use the power of your imagination to connect to self. It's been said, "Use your imagination for creation." Your have the power within to begin and transform. Take your power back.

Your emotions are manifesting as you are doing this. You are manifesting your emotions, your thoughts will change and feel happiness inside. Its feels like relaxation, it feels like lightness, it feels like your about to fall off to sleep. This is you, the real inner self. It clarifies what is going on within you. How much are you allowing yourself to be in the moment? Ask yourself, "What is going on for me right now? "What do I think?" If your thoughts are taking you outside yourself and into your head, return to your breath and start over again.

The inner source connection within you is your emotional being (within you) or nonphysical. It's an emotional experience that you don't want to leave once you feel it. It feels like your everything, your joy, your seeking of love and worthiness. It is your true you.

There is a 'feeling place' that exists when we meditate. You can feel wellness and joy, but also work out what you want. If your happiness relies on another person or thing, then you are disconnected from who you really are. What regular meditation does is, it helps you realise that you can seek happiness without relying on others or material things. You can realise your happiness is within you. You'll be able to create joy, love, and happiness in yourself. You will understand who you are what you are here to do or be. Once you can regulate your emotions, then you control what you create and manifest.

Be You

You are capable of anything; believe it. Become the emotional you. Refuse to put up with anything that doesn't make you feel good.

This year I sat in Yoga Barn café, beholding the beauty of the surroundings. There were lush, colourful gardens with roosters crowing, water running, birds chirping and soft chatter of the guests. The staffs were exceedingly friendly, more like family than workers. Their bright, infectious smiles and politeness gave me a warm connection in my heart. It felt pure and unpretentious. I took a sip of my coconut milk coffee, glancing over my mug at the wonders of the amazing space. I felt blessed to be able to visit. I was living in the moment and having gratitude for it.

The Yoga Barn reminds me of several other places in the world that give me a sense of inner peace and harmony. When I started connecting with my NDE, my thoughts took on a new meaning. I felt more connected. I understood about co-creation; the connection to each other. Unfortunately, many people don't feel that connection. I want to change that.

There is void (or non-existence) without an inner and outer connection. Try to think about being present. You can't always be present, but if you focus on yourself and your wellbeing, you'll get close. Sometimes you'll be out of comfort zone and need to connect with others when you would rather withdraw. Always use the intuitive side (intu-i-tion) into I. This means inner self or inner guidance. The self knows everything. All the answers lie within us.

I have this desire where I want to meditate, sleep or eat by myself. I like my own company. You may too. I feel it's easier than pushing through and connecting (or meeting new people). Some people want you to give them all your knowledge. I am okay with that but at the right time. I choose to honour who I am and sometimes need to be alone to self-care. Setting self-boundaries is the key to looking after one's self.

Allowing yourself to be present with your thoughts and feelings is becoming aware of your connection with others. You need to ask, "Am I present or am I focused on me?"

There is a time for your own wellbeing, but you also need a connection. People need connection and love. Sometimes by not connecting, you miss opportunities. There needs to be a balance.

Ask yourself other questions, like, "What do I need to do?" "What is that person saying?" "Does that sit well with me?" "Do I want to run off and meditate?" I think we can all apply too much self-care or not enough. The key is to balance everything in life.

Even in the spiritual community, it can be psychologically competitive. Some spiritual healers and yogis become competitive with their practices. They want to claim that they have the most knowledge or have done the most healing. Maybe they think they've completed more yoga teacher trainings than another teachers. They may judge others by saying things like, "This will be good for you because you need to lose weight", or "If you don't follow this routine, you're not a good yogi", or "I have been to many different countries and studied this and that, so trust me". Phew! A true yogi understands that wherever we are is PERFECT!

Truthfully, they don't need these to enhance their spiritual practice, nor do you. Once you know your inner being and how it functions, both good and not good, you have the tools. You'll have the wisdom and insight to do anything as part of your spiritual practice.

There are, unfortunately, many people who are, 'spiritual cowboys and cowgirls'. They confuse people who connect with them because they are not connecting with who they truly are on a spiritual level, themselves. If they did, they would understand that spirituality is not about how many certificates you hold, or how many years you worked at a certain place, or how many countries you have visited and studied at. It's about your inner journey. It cannot be bought, stamped on a certificate, studied at university or given in a rank system.

Spirituality is about oneness, self, inner being, wellbeing, and connection. The opposite is non-spirituality.

Find your spiritual family

Finding my spiritual family was one of the most amazing experiences. I worked out which vibrational frequency and emotions I wanted to be at. After that, it was easy to know and understand which spiritual family I chose to be in. There is a saying that I read on Facebook many years ago, you vibe with your tribe. This is so true, and if the people you choose to be around are of high vibration, then you will become that. If they are not, then you will become that.

My spiritual family is extremely broad. They are people all over the world and come in different shapes and sizes. All are kind and loving people who enjoy living in peace and want to make this world a better place. These people are the spiritual warriors, the lightworkers, individuals who see the light in every living being. They are you and me.

My spiritual family has taken me to many places and countries. They have taught me to find myself; who I truly am. I asked myself what sort of people I wanted in my life. I found a common thread or alignment as to why I came together with them. I ask my inner-self and the universe to let the right people appear to take me to the next level. People will come into your life when you ask for them and need them for whatever you are manifesting.

Soul Ego and Soul Spirit

A big experience I learnt was knowing the difference between Soul Ego and Soul Spirit. One is the mind, and the other is inner being (heart) soul. Soul Ego is based on the intention of lack, fear or bad feelings. It is the belief of that's how it should be without feeling into it first. It is the energy of the ego. Thoughts (mind) is the ego.

Soul Spirit is when you feel expanded or inspired. This is in the spirit of self. In spiritual terms, it is who you really are; your spirit. We are spiritual beings, having a human experience. You are both and once you wake up to this knowing you awaken. Once awakened you will see and no longer seek. Your heart and soul are one and the same and deeply connected. When you feel your heart, it will fill with love. Spirit consciousness is impersonal, it nonphysical and non-materialistic. Soul is the knower, the knowledge or the insight the soul contracts. It understands and knows why we are here and what our life purpose is.

One of my soul spirit purposes is to write this book. I enjoy sharing it with you and others because I intend to help, heal and teach as many people as I can while on this planet. Starting with my family, I will continue my spiritual path and help those who come before me for assistance and guidance. I hope this book is a step in achieving that life purpose.

I see countless suffering, but I know they could be leading a happy, blissful life. They just need to change a few small things. If they made thoughts their priority, they could mend. To heal with love, they must come out of thought and into the heart. This is where the bliss and happiness are the joy and kindness of living. Using the power of breath to slow the mind, to make space for the new. This is healing within.

Using thought will change you forever. As the awareness grows, unhappiness goes. Sadness leaves for as long as you want it to leave until the next thing happens that makes you sad. There are so many ideals and beliefs put on us. Like; go to university, get a good paying job, if you get a government job then your set for life, and so on. Have status, be a thing, buy a big house, you are not worthless if you don't achieve these things. Who has the right to use this to control another human beings' life? Sure, if you desire a big house and you manifest it with ease you are on your path. If you believe you need to work hard to achieve then you are off path and have taken a wrong turn or reversed. Life is meant to be easy and with ease, not dis-ease.

Asking, how do you feel when you do that thing or what is it you feel you want to be or do is more in alignment with true self than anything else.

Saying other negative things are just that, another person perspective. These are someone's opinion, belief or perception. It's not who you are. Find who you are by connecting through your heart. Your heart is you, it is developed before your mind. Your heart tells all the cells where to go and what to do, well before the brain is formed. We each have a higher intelligence inside us. To tap into it, we must believe, meditate, trust and have faith.

Soul language is like any language. Changing it is not always easy, however, once we do, things start to change and manifest for us. Manifesting is magical once we start it.

As I mention in chapter eight about using 'I am' and I have statements' you are speaking to your inner being, your soul. Soul says, "Where have you been?" Heart says, "You found me."

Saying affirmations or statements in meditation is very powerful. It sets your intention to create and manifest whatever you wish to attract.

Say things like:

- I am healthy and fit and have vitality.
- I have source energy running through my body that reflects my soul and its essence.

Set soul based and heartfelt intentions; love intentions. Learn from people who are active, with a being of higher consciousness. They work the same way as affirmations.

People from all areas of the globe need to come together. When this occurs something amazing will happen. It's a gift, a gift to receive and a gift to give. It's always you first to be in a place to give, then you can receive and so on. Learn to fill your heart cup first. The little bits that trickle over are for everyone else.

Connecting with our inner being and awakening to our spirit or spirituality is something everyone has the potential to do. By meditation and using our breath, life force energy, our prana, we can go into cosmic energy and life force energy inside us.

You can connect with universal spirit and join with whoever we want to. Until you are in a place of love and peace, you cannot connect to the energy life force. I do so in meditation. Why can't you? I have connected with Buddha, Jesus, Lakshmi, Shiva, Archangel Michael, and countless others. Some I don't know who they are. They just come to help heal.

There are evidence and data to give us information about spirituality, vibrational frequency and who we are. There are many testimonials and statements from people who have crossed over and come back. I find common threads in their testimonials. They are authentic. Listening to Abraham Hicks or Anita Moorjani are some of my favourite things to do, especially when I feel disconnected from source energy, pulled away from my vortex into a low energy dimension.

Some people need acceptance, attention or just want to be seen and heard. I'm not judging. It's an observation that they do, and they are not aligned with who they truly are yet. They have not found their inner happiness. Some people need someone to fulfil them. If they only knew that their joy is within them. Searching for it in other people or things will only lead to disappointment. Stress often means that the needs of that person have not been met. The person feels that their stress is the problem of someone else, not themselves.

In my experience with clients, the ones who feel they are not being heard by the person they are relying on to fulfil them are the most exhausting. They are in a place of, 'I want to transition, but I cannot do it without you'. They need someone to take care of things if they can't do it. This is not how we align with the true spirit of self. We align by continuing forward.

The highs and lows the ups and downs, the low vibe and high vibe, are all here to take us there; where we need to be. It's like daily cleansing and clearing until it becomes a habit.

Daily enquiry is useful, giving the opportunity to reflect. Once you reflect, you can clear unwanted energy and shift into a peaceful state. "You cannot hold the emotion of others or self." Make this your daily ritual. It's like sweeping your floor every day, routine habit. Give your mind a little sweep. Keeping things clean and tidy gets you ready for the next thing.

Prayer

One of the best things I recommend is prayer. Prayer is good for our immune system. It is like talking to our soul our spirit within; the state of prayer. Set a time of intent to prayer. Think of love or things you love and desire. Imagine those things and send vibrational source energy. By doing this manifesting is easier. Use the intelligence of your imagination for creation. This is how we manifest. It is how we use the law of attraction.

Symbols

Symbols are used as a visual so that our mind has something to focus on. By having a vision of something our mind then believes it is happening. Just like if you believe every time you pray to Buddha's symbol, then good things will come to you and hence you pray to Buddha's statue or picture more often to produce that abundance. Using a candle, sitting, staring at the candle you will start to see colours. Before long, you will notice the candle, and it's like you become the candle and nothing else. The candle is *light*, and so are you.

Vision Boards

Vision boards or holding a vision is how we create what we want to manifest or want. Our mind will believe that whatever we feed it, just like fertiliser, water, and sunshine on a plant. See it, and you will believe it. If you want a new vehicle put a picture of the car you want on your vision board, then everyday visualise it as you have it already. See yourself driving it. What colour do you see as you put the key in the door to get in it? What does that feel like, a nice firm steering wheel? Do you see lots of bright gadgets on the dash? Does it smell of new leather? Do whatever it takes to keep yourself focused, reminding you of who you really are. You can manifest whatever your heart desires.

Journaling

Journaling is a really good way to keep yourself in check with your emotions. It is the best way to get to what you really want because it sets out what you don't want to attract. As you go on your meditation journey, journal your experiences. Keep writing about it and connecting with your emotions. As you practise your meditation you will notice, it becomes easier and freer as you move into a state and place of goodness, freedom, and love. This is the moment of joy, of finding the light, the place you want to be in. Focus on what you really want. Look back on what you have written in your journal and what you have achieved through your meditation and manifestations. Only look back from time to time and keep your focus on moving forward (not backwards). Stay present as much as possible and journal the things that give you joy and that which you wish to create. I often sit quietly and day dream. This is a good way to check in with your feelings and when you reach a place of calm and goodness then create you vision. To create something we want we need to be in a place of love, joy and calm.

Try not to reflect too much on the past, its merely there to remind you of how far you have come. Living in the past doesn't serve your higher good. Worrying about the future does not serve your higher good. Living in the moment and in a state of creating, meditating and manifesting is for your higher good.

Expansion is a word being thrown out there in the modern world. To me expansion means growing, learning and manifesting. It is knowing that 'in the moment' you can change a thought, a thing a, vibration. You can change whatever it is you need or want to create.

Say; my life is light, my life is rich, my life is abundant, my life is filled with joy and happiness. My life is abundant and prosperous, and I am free. Once you say, these things set the image in your mind. Remember, the mind doesn't know truth from fantasy. Try playing at being happy or daydream about things that make you feel good? Think them and make sure they are good thoughts. You don't want anything that doesn't feel nice. Daydream your best fantasy and get busy with your creations any desires.

I discovered some of this chapter through my journey with Brahma Kumaris (Global 'spiritual organisation).

Exercise

Try these ideas to manifest the things you want in your life, be it spiritual, monetary, friendships, career goals, anything:

- Symbols – do you pray to a symbol? Is it Jesus, Buddha, Ganesh, Shiva or what? Why? Does it make you feel good?
- Vision boards – create a vision board by cutting out pictures, quotes, and places, from magazines that you would like to see in your life.

- Journal – write about your meditation and yoga journey. How do you feel about your progress?
- Talk about it to those who understand how it all works and manifest it. Try this with friends; talk about what you want to manifest as if you already have it. If you can't find anyone you trust just talk to yourself. I know this may sound a bit strange, but if you have faith and believe in yourself and love yourself, then this will not be hard to do. What have you got to lose?

Golden Gems for your Spiritual Treasure Chest

Do what makes you feel joy, your happy place, adding to your life force energy. Do something you want to get up for every day.

Do a short five-minute meditation, connecting with your breath and heart. Fall into your body.

Here is another video for your spiritual treasure chest:
http://www.kerrythehealer.com/sacredheart

CHAPTER 16

Chakra Balancing
The body's energy

"To keep the body in good health is a duty... Otherwise, we shall not be able to keep our mind strong and clear."

—Buddha

For thousands of years chakras have been known as the seven (or more) vital energy centres in the body. Every cell in our body dances with universal energy like a cobweb weaving into everything within. If unbalanced it is blocked preventing the web to continue, effecting physical, spiritual, emotional and mental wellbeing. We come into the world with our nonphysical side, connected to the auric field which surrounds us.

Chakras are a vortex of energy that sits in a couple of centimetres from the spine. In Sanskrit, it means 'wheel' or 'vortex'. They are the energy centres where the life force energy flows. The life force energy is the oxygen that mother earth produces. She takes in the toxins – the carbon monoxide, pollutions and purifies the air and sends it out as oxygen. In the yoga world, it's called 'prana', life-force energy or in the spiritual world. When breathed in it goes into the chakra, like a whirlpool of energy being sucked into your body. Allow this energy to rejuvenate and replenish every cell, muscle tissue, vein, fascia, in your body. The more you put into your meditation, the more you will enhance the life force energy and allow it to enter your body.

Connecting Asanas to Chakras

There are seven main chakras (Ayurveda), and they are the energy centres in our bodies in which energy flows through. Lactic energy in our seven charkas can often lead to illness. It is important to understand what each chakra represents and what we can do to keep this energy flowing freely. Asanas are connected to our chakras and breath. By breathing into each asana, we can release toxic buildups and keep our chakras balanced, hence flowing with the prana (life force energy). When we move our body a certain way (asana) and connect with our breath through inhaling and exhaling we connect the physical and emotional side of us. We are then ready to meditate and connect to our spiritual side.

This prevents many illnesses or stiffness throughout our bodies. It's an important part of yoga and meditation...

When I teach yoga therapy or Ayurvedic yoga, I like to teach certain techniques to give meaning and understanding as to why we need to keep our life force energy flowing and our bodies moving to release toxins through chakras and nadis in our body.

There are seven main ones, but there's about 114 chakras, seventy thousand 'nadis' or channels in which prana moves. This is scientific. The main ones starts from the base of our spine to the top of our crown. That energy is then pushed through a nadi tube and then pushed through the body.

If they get blocked, they cause pain and stress (mental) in the body. Marma points are psychic centres which hold ancient wisdom and a linked to our channels and meridians through the body If blocked energy cannot run freely through the body.

It's a bit like the famous Chinese medicine and the meridians; another name for nadi.

In theory, we breathe in the purified air, oxygen, prana or life force energy. What we exhale is the toxins, carbon monoxide, pollutions etc. Hence when we do meditation, and we slow down our breath. We inhale prana, exhaling toxins, inhale, exhale, inhale, exhale and we're releasing.

In some forms of Yoga, Hatha especially or Yin Yoga, when you move into an asana (posture) you are breathing the life force energy into the body. As you move into that posture you may, or may not feel discomfort, but as you exhale, the toxin that is in that particular asana, joint, muscle or whatever will release. You will feel the energy discharging from your body as you exhale. That's how it works.

I've practised it numerous times myself. If you try a yoga posture and you think you can't accomplish it, try it again. Take a deep breath in, releasing it at the end of the posture. I know you will feel the difference through the body and be able to do that a little bit more each time.

Vibrational energy works, the vortex and our thoughts. Thinking we are something else will create a negative and not good way of thoughts, over time that is what we are going to attract and become. Greed is such a low vibration. The old paradigm is to work hard, make lots of money, retire and then enjoy your retirement. Mmm, this does not resinate with me as it once did. I have learnt that day to day things change, as my thoughts change so do my actions and those around me and who and what I attract changes.

Superconsciousness and connecting with the universe and spirit world happened to me at The Yoga Barn, with a group of people who were open to bringing more energy. It was such a beautiful experience for everyone. Like when I wrote about Dr. Emoto and the combined energies, the prayer and combined minds wanted the same outcome.

In Bali, when I went with the priests and priestesses at Lake Batur, all temples were built around the lake. Because there was so much prayer, it is filled with holy water. So much belief! Set the intention, and that is what you create. The law of attraction and the power within us to do that.

Chakras Explained

- Are interconnected by Nadis
- Symbolically represented by lotus flowers with a particular number of petals
- Lotus represents 3 stages
- Energy centres that contain wisdom of life

How to stimulate the Chakras

- Visualising symbols and pathways in the psychic path.
- Sensations
- Awareness
- Guided meditations (Yoga nidra and pranavidya)

Kundalini Shakthi

- Static (potential energy) and Dynamic (kinetic)
- Kundalini is the dormant, static serpent (coiled) energy at Muladhara
- Union in yoga is achieved by raising the Kundalini and ultimately joining (yoga) with Siva.

Awakening Kundalini

- Hatha Yoga
- Raja Yoga
- Bhakti Yoga
- Mantra Yoga
- Tantra Yoga
- Jnana Yoga
- Guru Kripa
- Asana, pranayama, and mudras
- Concentration and training of the mind
- By devotion and self-surrender to God
- Mantras
- Tantric rituals
- Acquiring true knowledge
- By blessing from Divine Persons

Pineal gland

- Lower animals it is atrophied photoreceptor
- Secretes happy hormones; i.e. melatonin and serotonin
- Astral tubes

Nadis

- 72,000 in number
- Ida, Pingala, and Sushumna the most important (Tripura Sundari)

Ida Pingala and Sushumna

Ida

- Moon (active at night)
- Feminine
- Passive (introvert)
- Tranquillizing (induces sleep)
- Cools the body
- Parasympathetic nerves

Pingala

- Sun
- Masculine
- Active
- Stimulating
- Promotes digestion(fire)
- Generates heat
- Sympathetic

Different bodies (Koshas) according to Yoga

- Annamaya Kosha   The physical body
- Pranamaya Kosha   The energy body
- Manomaya Kosha   Mental body
- Vijnamaya Kosha   Intellectual body
- Anandamaya Kosha   Bliss body

The colours of chakras

Chakras, psychic centres are within our bodies and help regulate all process from organ function and systems, immune system, nervous system, emotional system, and adrenal system.

Although there is a lot of information out there around chakra, the one thing I remember when studying in India was there are seven chakras.

The crown is the supreme divine energy portal, which is the connection between us and the universe.

Chakra has colours, for example, the root chakra which is situated at the base of the spine is crimson (blood red) which is where we feel grounded and have the inner knowing that we are connected to everything. Using the colours of the rainbow creates a healing effect on our bodies.

Sacral Chakra is Orange, being the orange sun. This is our creative side. It represents movement, desire, pleasure and flow. It is our power centre and align the spine.

Solar plexus is yellow like a bright moon, and this is our creative side, which taps into our feminine side. It's where we get our ideas or intuition. Our trust in this guidance system is very important if we want to stay balanced in life.

Green (Mother Nature) natural green is our heart. It's our love for self and others, it's our truth of who we are and truth to our self. It's our communication to others and self.

Blue (Ocean blue) and is the colour of prana (see chapter 14). This chakra and heart chakra are deeply connected. Sometimes in meditation or yoga, you may find your throat will get dry and you may cough. That means to notice what is happening inside or what you are thinking, what emotion you are experiencing.

There is a successful chakra meditation I do which I have received much positive feedback. I really want to share it in this book. I was taught this meditation by a professor of yoga and psychology in India.

Every cell and tissue, muscle in our body is connected to chakras, nadis, meridians, channels.

These are all stimulated and activated through sound (hearing), the other four senses and breath (air).

- Emotional wellbeing
- Physical wellbeing
- Spiritual (universal) wellbeing
- Mental wellbeing

Our chakras can become blocked through an emotional upset, such as conflict, loss, or accident. Fear, anxiety, and stress are common **causes** of **chakra** malfunction. When blocks accumulate in the energy field, it causes a disruption in the flow of energy (life force) through the body. It can cause disease in the body as the energy which lies within us is no longer flowing and is at dis-ease.

Keeping your energy flowing with ease is a very important part of being happy, enjoying life and fulfilling life purpose. If we disconnect or don't understand these energy centres and how our body's energy functions internally then we cannot release what is lying dormant and we can become sick and disconnected from self.

We can lose our sense of self and feel lethargic as the energy cannot function with ease throughout our body. Letting go and allowing is the key. Through meditation, we can open and release blockages which lie in our energy field and release them. De-stressing, de-cluttering the mind and body will bring the spiritual energy back in the flow, then you will glow. All chakras are connected to our internal organs.

Crown chakra

This chakra integrates all major chakra (Seven) and their individual qualities. This is a spiritual connection and can reach enlightenment for a short time. The crown chakra is connected to your higher self; to everything on earth and to divine energy. This energy created everything on earth, including you.

The Third Eye chakra

The third eye is related to vision and intuition. It's responsible for the perception of movements of energy and subtle dimensions. This chakra is also related to psychic abilities, clairaudience, and clairvoyance. When opened it allows access to mystical states of mind, body, and spirit.

Throat chakra

The throat chakra is in the base of the throat. It provides energy to the thyroid gland, governing hunger, thirst, ear, nose eyes and throat. Throat chakra is also related to the bronchial passage and the lungs, esophagus, vocal cords and speech.

Heart chakra

The heart chakra is near the heart organ. Located in the centre of our chest. It is associated with unconditional love and kindness, meaning unhurt, unstuck and unbeaten. It is associated with calm, serenity, without violence, and in peace.

Solar plexus chakra

The solar plexus is situated above the navel and is joined with ego. This is the personal power, self-belief, and self-worth. It can become active by doing something that you're fearful of. The function of the solar plexus is the body's nervous system. It keeps the organs functioning.

The sacral chakra

The sacral chakra is part of our psychological and behavioural functions. Our emotions and feelings, relationships, relating to others and self, our expression of sexuality, sensual pleasure, feeling within and external worlds, fantasies, and creativity.

This chakra is the centre of our feelings and sexual desires. It is the driving force for our enjoyment in life. A foundation of wellbeing and wellness. Listening, seeing, tasting, hearing and touching are all related to this chakra. It responds to stress by making changes in the metabolism.

Root chakra

The root chakra is closely related to feminine energy. It controls the lower part of the body, including lower back, pelvis, lower spine, kidneys, and bladder.

Without knowing and understanding we are made of life force energy. This energy is affected by the way we think and feel. Without understanding it, we cannot clear the blockages. Our Doshas, chakras, and all our systems are driven by the energy and given and received. Once we have the wisdom that our body is connected to everything and everyone, we can manage in a way that is healthy and aligned with who we are.

Knowing that blocks come from our everyday living and cause stressful thoughts and feeling, can be unblocked. Use daily clearing through meditation, prayer, yoga, Ayurveda and learning about these principles and how they govern us is the key to a healthy, healing and balanced life.

I have included these chakra massage steps to share with you the process of a deep chakra massage. Here is an example of Open Chakra Balancing Massage which integrates deep-tissue massage, foot reflexology and energy enhancing therapy, including utilization of essential oils, breathing exercises, aromatic steam towels, scalp massage etc. This massage is over 2 hours in a serene, spiritual and private environment focuses on energizing the seven chakras in the body towards balancing the mind, body and spirit in a holistic healing and wellness context. At the end of the chakra treatment, relaxing meditation enhancing peace and joy is practiced.

The Seven Chakras

Chakras control specific parts of the body, energizing particular organs; bringing harmony within the body. If any of the seven chakras are blocked, energy cannot flow freely. A 'closed' or 'imbalanced' chakra is indicative of a health and well-being issue; whereas an 'open' or 'balanced' chakra represents balanced health and wellbeing. Thus, an open chakra, for example, indicates our wellness with high energy and feeling positive, whereas a blocked chakra indicates low energy and less concentration.

Chakras are the energy centres in our body. These are seven chakras, located in a channel encompassing the spine and stretching from the tailbone to the crown of the head. This channel is called the sushumna nadi. The energy, namely Kundalini, flows back and forth from the first chakra at the sacrum, up the spine and out the seventh chakra at the crown of the head.

Muladhara Chakra at the root of the spine at the sacrum is the foundation of the entire system. It relates to our basic needs and our sense of security and survival and is affected by stress and worry. Blocked root chakra makes us insecure, scared and anxious.

Swadhisthana Chakra just below the navel is the seat of nourishment and vitality enhancing pleasure of learning, exploring and experiencing. This chakra stands for sexuality feeling, wellbeing and pressure. Blocked sacral chakra relates to feeling guilty, numb and lacking emotions.

Manipura Chakra located in the solar plexus above the navel is the center of our identity, confidence and drive of life and living. This chakra stands for confidence and power. When this chakra is blocked we feel insecure, frustrated and fearful of being rejected

Anahata Chakra is located in our heart centre relates to love, compassion, sympathy, empathy, and relationships. Complicated relationships, tragedy and loneliness often block our heart chakra.

Visuddhi Chakra is located in the neck behind the throat, is the centre of expression, creativity and communication. Blocked throat chakra is usually with problems of self-expression, deception & manipulative communication.

Ajna Chakra, the third eye chakra found between the eyebrows is the centre of imagination, intuition and perception. Blocked third eye chakra is usually related to poor concentration, remembering things, suffering from nightmares and lack of clarity.

Sahasrara Chakra located at the crown of the head relates to wisdom, spirituality and enlightenment. Blocked crown chakra relates of indecisiveness, meaningless existence and depression

Exercise

- How would you stimulate your chakras?
- If chakras are a vortex of energy how do you think they affect your bodily energy?
- Have you ever enjoyed a chakra healing? How do you think it would benefit you?

Golden Gem for your Spiritual Treasure Chest

These illustrations on the next two pages are my gift to you. They can also be found in colour on my website.

CROWN - LEVEL OF CONSCIOUSNESS - ENLIGHTENMENT

- Represents infinity, top of the head
- Supreme light, cosmic expansion, Psychic and Spiritual connection, divinity, nirvana. Its beyond separation

THIRD EYE - LORD SHIVA

- Between the eyebrows in the centre of the fore head. This is the command centre to our wisdom, higher self, intuition, oneness, where sharp ideas are received- pineal gland. We reach enlightenment in this energy.

THROAT - GODDESS SARASWATI

- Goddess of light, knowledge and learning. Communication to self and others. Speaking ones truth, self-expression through breath. Aligns mind and heart.

HEART - HANUMAN

- Unconditional love for self and others. Love, compassion, forgiveness and acceptance. Fun, playful and joy. Releasing and balancing stress

NAVEL - KINGS AND QUEENS

- Solar plexus
- The jewel within, willpower, inner strength, desire, purpose, gut instinct, digestive Fire

SACRAL - GODDESS LAKSHMI

- Sacred Space
- Reproductive organs, masculine and feminine, positive and negative energy, Sacred place inside us. Where we produce things, manifest health and wealth. Where our creativity and passion lies.

ROOT - DEITY GANESH

- Stability, feeling secure, grounding. Spiritual ascension for stable base. Foundation of stability with Mother Earth.

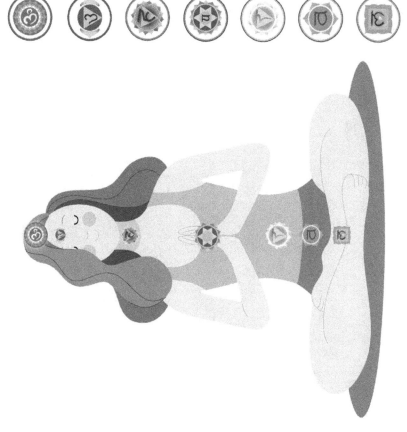

CROWN - LEVEL OF CONSCIOUSNESS - ENLIGHTENMENT

- Represents infinity, top of the head
- Supreme light, cosmic expansion. Psychic and Spiritual connection, divinity, nirvana. Its beyond separation

THIRD EYE - LORD SHIVA

- Between the eyebrows in the centre of the fore head . This is the command centre to our wisdom, higher self, intuition, oneness, where sharp ideas are received - pineal gland. We reach enlightenment in this energy.

THROAT - GODDESS SARASWATI

- Goddess of light, knowledge and learning. Communication to self and others. Speaking one's truth, self-expression through breath. Aligns mind and heart.

HEART - HANUMAN

- Unconditional love for self and others. Love, compassion, forgiveness and acceptance. Fun, playful and joy. Releasing and balancing stress

NAVEL - KINGS AND QUEENS

- Solar plexus
- The jewel within, willpower, inner strength, desire, purpose, gut instinct, digestive Fire

SACRAL - GODESS LAKSHMI

- Sacred Space
- Reproductive organs, masculine and feminine, positive and negative energy. Sacred place inside us. Where we produce things, manifest health and wealth. Where our creatvtery and passion lies.

ROOT - DEITY GANESH

- Stability, feeling secure, grounding. Spiritual ascension for stable base. Foundation of stability with Mother Earth.

CHAPTER 17

Intuition
Another spiritual experience

"Go into you, be in tune, this is intu-i-tion."
—Kerry Clancey

We can develop our intuition and learn how to listen to our inner guidance system. The feeling inside us (inner voice) and embrace the knowing and power of knowing who we are. This is empowering, knowing we have an inner power we can access at any time. This is our psychic intuitive self. Go INTU-I-TION (into you) or self. Go into your inner world.

Our gut feeling; trust it! Our intuition (gut or inner voice) is very powerful some of which is connected to receptors just like the brain to help us and guide us to where we need to be (IGS). Don't mistake your gut feeling as something which may need healing. We may need to assess why our energy is being depleted. You will know if its your intuition or something or someone that is making you feel uneasy. Ask you inner world. Is this right for me? If your energy feels depleted then you know what it is. Documents these experiences in a journal or phone, these are great to reflect on. As you learn your triggers you will enhance your intuition. Trust what you receive, don't second guess or procrastinate. If it feels good go for, it your first instinct is to pick the red ball and you change to the blue ball for example then you didn't trust. You send a message that you don't believe. This will block your intuition. Learn from it and keep moving forward as you develop, your intuition (IGS) will thrive.

If you feel queasy or your chest muscles feel tight, it could be your intuition. Feeling unwell around someone may be your intuition. You may be picking up on their vibrational energy. They may be experiencing low vibration. Developing your intuition is learning how to feel the energy and when its low and when its high. Be mindful of how you feel around certain people or places. Is your energy low or high. If its low then you may need to do certain things to bring your energy up. Go to your spiritual treasure chest and take out a golden gem.

Others can block our intuition if we allow it or not in tune with it. I look for feelings of joy, fun, love, peace comfort and freedom. If my intuition (GPS) is aligning I am usually smiling and singing. This is my guage. It's important to uplift our energy. The more positive energy you have coming into you life the quicker you heal. Your energy effects those around you just as those around you will effect you with their energy. Anyone who is in a position of healing, healers, massage therapist, physiotherapist etc pick up on others energy. If this is not released then this can have a detrimental effect on those they are in contact with. They may not realize they are intuitive and that their energy is being depleted by giving. Its so important for all of us to take care of ourselves first and make sure our energy (cup) if full. Once we do this we can then give to others. You are able to uplift others. Imagine yourself being a mobile phone, you need recharging every day or keep your charge up or you would go flat.

We may be intuitive and not know it. Monitor you energy levels. Do things that give you joy or make you feel good. This might be walking in nature, you feel good. When I am with my dog or cat, or funny movies, or out with certain friends, meditating and having fun. Look at what raises your energy. What raises your vibration. Everyone around us if effectived by energy. We are all energy beings. Taking notes and journaling what makes us feel good and what doesn't is a good way to check where we are at with our intuition. We cannot receive divine universal message when we are energetically low. We are disconnected from life force energy when we are in low vibration.

Your intuition can help you improve your digestive system. Our five senses are connected to the five Elements (Ayurveda). These five senses play a part in how we feel. If we understand the elements of life we can become more in tune with our intuition. When we feel good, then those around us feel good also.

When we are seeking guidance from our IGS or internal world, (intuition) switches on and we become excited, free, feeling inspired or inspirational, we may feel joyful. This is intuition.

A great way to understand your intuition is to think of someone then the phone rings. Or they pop up on Social Media. Or you were thinking of them recently, and they call you or you run into them. You may glance at your umbrella before you walk out the door. You don't give it attention, then it rains an hour later but the umbrella is still at home.

We have a built-in guidance system that operates through our digestive system, and it has an inner knowing when something isn't right, or a person may not be right for you. It also lets us know when something is right for us and what we need to do to take the next step. Never second guess this feeling.

Work on understanding the subtle energy. Meditation through breath and using your imagination are golden gems to connect with soul/spirit. Once you do this everything else aligns; chakras, third eye (insight) intuition and soul. They all align and connect with who you truly are. Intuition is 'flash insight' or the moment when you go 'ah ha'. It feels like clarity.

Just a short meditation daily will enhance and help engage with your intuition. It's a way of connecting with self and separating from others and go intu-i-tion.

When I first left Australia my intuition was guiding me. However, I didn't realise that's what it was. My inner guidance spoke, and I listened. I let go of what if? The fear was released. Should and could; all disconnect us from our intuition. I trusted what I was feeling and listened to my insight. Intuition brought me to where I am today. By letting go, releasing thoughts of fear I became who I was born to be.

Trusting our intuition is like trusting our GPS to get us to where we want to go. When we align with our intuition momentum starts. We become aligned with who we are and what we are here to accomplish.

Insight (third eye), Heart (inner spirit) and Intuition (lower tummy or digestive system). Through breath we align with our truth of who we are, joining all three. We can come into a place of inner peace when we let go of thought and feeling of low vibration. Allowing is empowering. Imagination, Meditation and Creation, more golden gems for your Spiritual Treasure Chest.

The power of sound is universal. Sound healing combined with meditation is like mixing two ingredients to come up with the perfect recipe for healing. They go hand in hand. The more healing modalities used in a session, the better the outcome for the healing session or client. If the teacher understands these principals then they are able to help heal others and remove their emotional blocks and painful patterns through hertz and vibrational sound, crystals, reiki, channeling, intuitive guidance and more. I think a great healer will always uplift the client/student if a few sessions. Not keep them coming back, this is not empowering or helpful for the person.

I meet numerous beautiful people on my journey and spiritual path. They were looking for answers and feeling lost within. Sound and gongs are part of the path to finding spiritual truth and connection. Sound, no matter where it comes from, is therapeutic to the soul and healing for the body. Holistic approach is one way to keep you vibrational energy flowing and uplifted.

Using your imagination or visualization is a great way to heal any negative blocks which may cause low vibration. Meditate in the vibration, your imagination is part of your intuition. It is true, your six sense, your connection with the universe. Set your intention to create your future. Send out love to all around those who are in your life. This will increase your energy. Use mindful meditation when walking in nature or by the ocean.

Sound waves travel through our body. Our cells awaken and smile inside as they rejuvenate and replenish. Scientifically, it is said that sound has a frequency that our cells resonate with. This frequency also comes from the sound of the planets. Ancient Ayurveda states our cells are connected to the universe. Our cells contain 95% water and as I mentioned before, Dr Emoto's research proved water has consciousness.

Becoming a Master of Gong and Sound in India gave me the understanding and knowledge of how important sound healing is as part of a healing journey.

Working at Pyramids of Chi as a Gong Master gave me an opportunity to expand, learn and develop my knowledge and wisdom of sound. Plenty of people are discovering sound healing. This modality of healing is a highly recommended to open up channels, cells and allow intuition to flow.

CHAPTER 18

Science v Spirituality
A search for the truth

"There are no facts, only interpretations."
—Friedrich Nietzsche

Bringing spirituality and science together. In an ideal world, if science, spirituality and western medicine all came together, there would be abundant healing done. People would have more understanding of their ability to heal themselves. I recently listened to a scientist and a spiritual healer who agreed with the placebo effect and how we can heal. All emotional, physical and psychological are linked.

We are all searching for the meaning of life. Scientist try to find it in laboratories. Spiritualist find it in churches, mosques or in the calm of nature. Most are now agreeing that both are irrevocably linked. People are coming to places like Bali as they are seeking confirmation and healing. They want knowledge and emotional healing.

Some people have a supplementary understanding of their ability to heal themselves. There is so much evidence that supports placebo; with evidence supporting there is very little difference between placebo and other medicines.

It's the same with symbols, idols, signs, mantras, music, meditation and yoga. If we are told it can heal us, then we will. Many people have healed through meditation, without exercise or assistance, only using their mind to heal. Just by saying every day, "My body is healing," and visualising the healing taking place. All emotional, physical and psychological are linked. Wouldn't you like to understand how?

I trust my link with science and spirituality through my studies and my inner being. I own a home, though I no longer have a deep connection to it. I no longer have enough time to settle in one place. I'm not displaced, I just travel by following my divine guidance. It sends me to where I should be at any given time.

For example; I was in Perth and ready to board my flight to Bali. The volcano Mount Agung had erupted again, and flights were being cancelled. I knew this but went to the airport. I was turned away, as were many other, and told I could not leave for a fortnight. I boarded a bus and while travelling recorded bits and pieces for this book, to send to my ghostwriter. I pondered why I should stay in Perth for two weeks. People on the bus were annoyed, showing anger, but I was calm. Something told me to go back to my house on the Gold Coast.

I returned. I'm sure my divine guidance told me to. Soon after I had another meeting about this book, that I wouldn't have been able to have if I hadn't returned, instead of waiting for my flight. I hadn't felt the need to write and was becoming stagnant. I thanked the energy of Mount Agung changing where I needed to be.

Trusting this process is what I have learnt. I put my faith into my soul divine connection, my source energy my universal connection. The universe always has my best interest at heart and when I want something, I align it with the thought. The thought is loving and joyful. This what the universe hears. It is what is sent back; what we receive.

I often look up at the clouds and talk to the universe. I say, "I know you are looking after me, guiding me, assisting me and helping me to where I need to be." For moments I take in the essence of a beautiful cloud, thanking it for coming into my path and reminding me who I truly am.

My message in 'Heal to Live' is for everyone to know this universal connection. I want you to have joy, love, peace, and kindness inside you. If you hold onto grief, anger, resentment, guilt, shame, anything negative, then the universe cannot hear your message of wanting love or whatever you desire.

The power of intent for self and others is the key to lightness (the light). Staying in a place of love, joy etc. will allow life-force divine-source energy to flow through you and back to the universe. The key is to believe it to receive it. Meditate and communicate; allow yourself to let go and flow. Fill your heart with love from above.

Be playful, be joyful. Let your heart and inner child sing to the tune of vibrational love energy. Through laughter, music, song art, sound healing, community, a person, a pet, the sky, the stars, moon, sun; do whatever it takes to open your heart channel (chakra). Feel the joy flow through you and to you when you do this. It's magical and *light*.

You'll know the wonderful feelings you have while listening to your favourite love song, playing with a small child or baby, watching a romantic love story, dreaming a nice dream. These good feelings belong to your heart and make it a place of love and joy. Do whatever it takes to have joyousness. Do things that give you a loving alignment with source energy. Hold onto your vibrational frequency of high energy. This is a way to find happiness. It is the key to abundant, joyful living and unlocking the door to life and the light.

There is plenty on social media, online, TV and in books about science and spirituality catching up with each other. They are joining, almost like a marriage. I would like to think I am in some way a bridge between the two, like the celebrant joining them.

I watched a movie about Stephen Hawking's life, many years ago. I thought why is this not out there in mainstream or don't people know? I was confused about it. Why would anyone, who had knowledge of this not share it? We would have knowledge of our planet, why we are here and how we are all connected. It would stop racism, judgement and if anything, alleviate war, poverty and many diseases. It would mean world peace.

The more I researched it, the more I found that this knowledge was like winning the jackpot. Why did so few people know this? There are many reasons why? Though I decided not to contemplate it too deeply and instead find ways to use it to help people and enlighten them too.

From that idea, this book formed. I needed to write an inspiring book with enough influence to help people. It would guide them into awareness. The rest would be up to them.

Consciousness is an enormous part of awareness. Our own insight and knowledge should be shared if we are to live a life on purpose. Not only that, it helps us to discover who we really are. We can uncover our true potential. Anyone can meditate, connect with the inner being and channel the spirit world. Most people just don't understand how to harness their powers.

Divine as a child

Though I had a non-religious background, I always had a deep knowing that I was linked to something. The name was Divine Universal Energy, but I believed it as the universe; something we are all connected. Living in the light of love, bliss, joy, and inner peace is the way I often exist. It's hard to describe how beautiful it is to those who are yet to experience it. It's a place you don't want to leave.

Someone said, "Don't talk about near death, finding the light and how blissful you found it. People will want to suicide."

I said, "No they won't because I'll help them find the state of bliss they can reach in our physical world." You don't need to die to experience the light. You need to heal to live a joyful life.

I said, "I feel like I'm in heaven," because I was enjoying the ocean's deep blue and the crash boom of waves on the white sandy beach. Using a word like 'heaven' conveys beauty and joy. There is a feeling behind each word. Look up at the clouds and feel connected. You'll possibly think it looks heavenly. Gaze at the azure sky and the pictures and shapes in the clouds; feel the connection. Heaven?

As you now know, I encountered lots of abuse as a child, including being sexually abused. Such traumatic events are often relived in dreams and visions later in life. At the time I was terrified and called to Divine for help. I asked him why the abuse was happening to me. I often talked to him, not understanding why I needed to do so, or why I had the determination. It seemed that, even then, I understood there was something that I could connect with if I put my thoughts and feelings out there. I thought these people hurt me all the time. I'd then ask, "What are my lessons from it?"

I often communicated this way. There were days I wondered how I would endure it. I believe I attracted that, so I could heal and then heal others. Eventually, the universe showed me (through my NDE) that it was available to me. It told me that I had work to do. This was when I realised, I had to experience this to help others. I signed up for this when I came into this world, even being chosen, by my parents.

No one explained the NDE and what I felt after it to me. I didn't need to be told when I discovered myself that I was the light. I was the universe; I was it. When I was above looking down at the medical staff, they told me to write a book about it. Did they? I can't remember, but I was told, maybe by the universe, that I had to do it.

As with my anaphylactic shock, subsequent NDE, then being brought back to life with two shots of adrenaline on February 15th, 2011, my life was never the same. After sharing my experience with one of the medical staff that day, her life will never be the same after witnessing it. She now shares how I left my body, had no control over it and returned when she is lecturing university students.

Well if she was teaching about it, since it was my experience, I needed to share it too, in this book. You to discover the same blissfulness I felt by learning meditation and connecting with your inner being; your true self.

When, during my NDE, I showed my three children how excited I was I could not feel their pain. All I felt was the bliss of the wonderful experience, letting them know it was fun and beautiful and not to worry about me. All the pain, the emotion, grief, suffering, judgement, guilt, shame, and anger no longer existed. My heart was so full of love. The love we all have but lose somewhere along the way in our lives.

You came in as a newborn, and you will go out in the same way. You will let go of all negativity, heaviness in our human experiences and we become light. But remember you don't have to die like I did. You can find it now. Call in the wonderful divine energy and spirit guides. Let them stream their love into you. Connect with past love ones like I did. That is how I learnt you can only get there if your heart is open. A closed heart cannot receive divine love.

You are supposed to live that bliss here in the present moment. Live in the love light, bliss, kindness, compassion by trying the principles in this book. The more you do it, the more people around you will do it. Saying it and speaking it makes you feel so good and you'll want to share the experience.

When I sang at that world peace event in Bali with Baba Ji from India, I enjoyed it, even though I was out of my comfort zone. It was so much fun singing about world peace, something I felt deeply about. The overwhelming connection with over five-hundred people will forever be etched in my heart.

A similar thing happened in India on meeting the Brahma Kumaris, when I could feel angels in the room. It was also such a beautiful but overwhelming spiritual thing. To connect with souls and see angels you need to still your thoughts. Thinking causes judgement. If you only feel them and you will find their heart and soul.

Like when people find connection with self, universe, devine God or join a spiritual event/program, they find a connection to something. After the NDE I know there is something I'm connected to. It's the placement of love, non-judgement, and happiness. I'm connected to my source (me) and the universe. The reverse of that is when I feel resentment, shame and guilt I am then disconnected to who I truly am.

What does it mean to find your happiness? It's tapping into your heart space and soul. Separate the two by taking your breath into your thoughts. Let your breath control your thoughts not the other way around. Tap into your inner being. Find your life purpose and what you are here to experience.

What about the Science side of things and Universal laws?

Plant medicines are used from the deities who received the answers from their meditation and prayers. Science now knows plants have feelings. Identical plants; one good word, one bad. One died, and one thrived. The same with humans. Tell them they are worthless they will be. Give them love messages instead. We all need to connect the dots. Therefore, my life is this way. Don't get confused with frog medicine or Ayahuasca for they are what I call spiritual drugs. The answers always lie within and not through external sources.

The law of polarity states a loving, kind person will attract loving and kind. This is deeply on a cellular level. Some put on a persona that isn't really what is deep inside. They can become abusive. I realised I was attracting that, through what I was putting out there.

Life has turned around since I began meditation, yoga and prayer. I find they keep me aligned with who I am. Allowing me to connect and tap into the universal laws, including the laws of attraction. Sometimes I need more self-care (self-love), and sometimes I just need to be alone and meditate. A day away from socialising, working, minimal connection and focus on my own thoughts, environment etc.

Science is discovering wonderful things about the connection of our minds, energy frequency and the law of attraction. I have discovered many well-respected findings during my studies. You may want to study some of these yourself. Such as:

- Steven Hawkins, the brilliant mathematician, and theologists. His ideas are clear to me and make sense when you hear or read them.
- Dr. Bob Proctor, renowned speaker, and motivational coach. He was a contributor to the law of attraction bestseller, The Secret.
- Oprah Winfrey, media personality and philanthropist, talks about the little voice inside us. When she nearly lost her television show because of bad business; a little voice inside told her that she was okay. It guided her as to what to do and into her next step.
- Wayne Dyer, self-help author, motivational speaker, Doctor and philosopher talks about the day he went to his father's grave and forgave him. He held resentment to his father since he was a boy. He had a vision of his father. All the anger and judgement were lifted, he was able to go into a place of forgiveness, find peace and enter into love, to then love his father again. He wrote, *The power of words – who are we*. Want to live a life of happiness, joy compassion. The people we hold anger resentment guilt and shame must be replaced. Bring it to the surface.
- Anita Moorjani, a motivational speaker, bestselling author *Dying to be Me*, who had an NDE. She had a body full of cancer and tumours. Her family were called to the bedside and were told that she was not going to make it. She had an NDE; her soul left. A relative told her to come back, so she did. A few weeks later she was cancer free. Amazing! She understands what I have been through. Moorjani also described the feeling of the bliss of leaving her body. She too let go of judgement fear, negative emotions. Physically we have those emotions, but spiritually we don't. NDE is pure bliss and nothing else. It is beautiful and who we truly are.
- Esther and Jerry Hicks, motivational speakers, bestselling authors, and travellers. Esther channels Abraham. She is a congruent to give messages to the people who came before her. She believes beings are energy vibrational beings. She talks about the words we choose and of course, the law of attraction. I really enjoy listening to her many videos as I feel deeply connected to the work her and Anita are doing.

CHAPTER 19

The Best Diet
For Ayurvedic living

"Without proper diet medicine is of no use.
With proper diet, medicine is of no need."
—Ancient Indian Proverb

"Go within and let the healing begin,"
—Kerry Clancey

I believe learning about your constitution and Ayurvedic principles will give you the insight and knowledge to understand when our bodies are out of balance and when they are in balance. Learning to feel into your body and knowing how it works on a cellular level. The physiology of our bodies will help with tuning into your inner guidance system.

Vata Dosha - Energy that controls bodily functions associated with motion, including blood circulation, breathing, blinking, and your heartbeat.

In balance: There are creativity and vitality.

Out of balance: Can produce fear and anxiety. Is connected to Air and Universe

Pitta Dosha - Energy that controls the body's metabolic systems, including digestion, absorption, nutrition, and your body's temperature.

In balance: Leads to contentment and intelligence. Is connected to Fire and Water

Out of balance: Can cause ulcers and anger.

Kapha Dosha - Energy that controls growth in the body. It supplies water to all body parts, moisturises the skin, and maintains the immune system. Also connected with water and earth.

In balance: Expressed as love and forgiveness.

Out of balance: Can lead to insecurity and envy.

Each person has all three Doshas, but usually one or two dominate. Various Dosha proportions determine one's physiological and personality traits, as well as general likes and dislikes. For example, Vata types will prefer hot weather to cold and Kapha types are more likely to crave spicy foods than other types. Pitta like sweet tastes.

Knowing what our bodies feel, think and connect with can keep our body balanced and at ease. Feeding our minds good wholesome thoughts, feeding our body decent nutritious food and feeding our spirit, the nourishing goodness of love and kindness it desires are the keys to good health.

I often ask my clients about their hearts and say, "Why would you not want to nourish your heart with beautiful, loving thoughts and kind words?" The words we speak lie within us. No one would speak about others unkindly if they held love inside them. It's impossible for depression, stress to survive in a body full of love.

"Why do we allow others the benefit of taking that from us? "Love what's within and let the healing begin."

Mother Earth's nourishment of plant medicines is a huge part of our healing. This knowledge is in many countries. Most practices are similar when it comes to healing our bodies with plants and herbs. Ayurveda has many recipes. Anyone can access them online or in cookbooks.

When it comes to stress, environment, and food, people are often looking for a quick fix. The answer lays with Mother Earth or Mother Nature. We need to protect her by not putting chemicals or toxins, including plastic, into her. Would you throw rubbish at your own mother? No. Then why would you throw rubbish at Mother Nature? She provides all our nourishment including our air or oxygen. She gives and gives unconditionally and asks for nothing from us. We need to all think about taking responsibility for her. It's not up to one country, one person or one place; it's a global responsibility.

Why do we treat her badly by slowly adding toxic chemical to her? She asks for nothing in return. She just keeps providing nourishment, healing herbs, plants and fresh air for us. Even the ocean is healing because of the salt content. Its therapeutic and refreshing when we enter the ocean to feel the water and salt on our skin, meditate, look at the waves crashing onto the sandbar, sit in the sand running our fingers through it, or walk hand-in-hand on the sand.

Healing is abundantly given. Though it is not received as much as it could or should be. There are certain foods such as gluten preservatives, which cause inflammation in our bodies over a long period of time. This inflammation can be eradicated with the right plants and herbs. Many diseases, such as diabetes, high blood pressure and stress are caused through inflammation. Again, Mother Nature provides healing for us.

Inflammation affects our internal systems, intestines (leaky gut), sluggish digestion and low red blood cells. The Arma (toxins) build up. Many Ayurveda clinics are popping up in Australia and around the world to teach us about the Ancient Healing Modality of Plant and Herb Medicines.

I know my personal experience, if I eat a more natural diet my energy increases, my weight reduces, and my overall insight (intelligence) heightens. My wellbeing improves. I try to stick to a vegetarian diet as much as possible. I may eat chicken or fish once a week or monthly. It depends on what my body wants or needs. In saying that I have only eaten red meat once or twice in the last two years. It's not something that my body wants any more. Herbs and plant medicines hold a healing powers which strengthen and nourish us, so we can replenish our soul.

Fuel for the soul or food for the soul. This is one of my favourite sayings to write because if fits with meditation, mantra, and nourishment.

Brahma Kumaris, which I write about in my Chapter 14 (Meditation and Yoga), have a very special way of feeding the soul. They pray and sing mantras while preparing food. As you now know, everything has vibrational energy - food is no exception. If food is treated badly, then it will hold negative energy and when we consume we then hold that negative energy within us. If someone was preparing your food while angry and upset about something, then the food is made with anger and resentment. We then eat it the anger and resentment and hold it within us, festering.

There are plenty of restaurants around the world that have cottoned on to this. They now cook with love. When I visit Australia, I eat at Govindas, which means protector in Sanskrit. The food receives chanting from Hare Krishnas before it is prepared. It is always delicious.

Some Brahma Kumaris have followers of their beliefs with restaurants. They also chant over the food before it's made. I try to find these restaurants or look for staff who look happy before I choose a restaurant to dine at.

Each time we eat something we should be mindful of our environment. Look at eating time as a time when we nourish our bodies. Take time to connect with your food. Say a prayer over your food to clear any negative energy. Food that is processed has very little nourishment or prana. It has been handled many times, by the people who produce it, people who process it in factories, those who distribute it, and then finally it arrives at an eatery or restaurant. Send loving prayers to them also.

The prana from plants will be pushed out of it, which makes it acidic to our bodies. If our bodies are too acidic, we develop inflammation, hence disease. This is because cells in our blood thicken from the acidic, low-vibration food and block the flow of prana. Prana is not only our life force energy, but it is also in plant food which nourishes our bodies. Eating too much processed food, without prana is bad for our soul or us.

For more Ayurvedic principles on healthy eating go to chapter 12 or 13 on Doshas. This gives a full picture of your body type and what will be best for you. Remember, though, everything in moderation.

Exercises

- Do you have restaurants in your area who have staff who pray over their food? Research to find at least two and write them down.
- Visit one of these restaurants and note down how you felt after eating their meals?
- How different was the vibe of this restaurant compared to others you have dined at?

Golden Gem for your Spiritual Treasure Chest

I have created some prayers or mantra's you can use before eating your meal. Try this one: "Thank you, Mother Earth, for everything you provide for us to nourish and feed our bodies and thank you to all the people who cultivate and prepare our meals for me to eat. I give thanks to my mind for helping choose nourishing food and to my body for being able to prepare food."

CHAPTER 20

Angels and Channelling
They are always with us

"Since my illness, I've felt the presence of my angels."
—Fran Drescher

Angels appeared in my bedroom soon after my NDE, began my first angel connections. I woke and felt a feeling of everything being okay. It was like I was embraced in an incredibly warm, loving hug. I felt a deep sense of belonging. The room was filled with so much love. From that day on I never felt lonely again.

I felt a part of everything, earth, trees, ocean, moon, and sun; a deep connection to nature and every living being.

Angelic love was in the room. I started not only visually seeing angels, but also feeling them inside me. I was part of something else besides myself. During those early days, I would wake up at sunrise and see the sun, hear the silence. Thinking I should go and connect with the sun. I would then connect with the ocean. Then I would hear birds chirping and free, flying; fly high. I'd never contemplated such simple things so avidly before.

The feeling of love shined through everything I saw. Light between trees. Deep love and connection to universal energy. It was seven years ago that I truly discovered deep, deep love. It is part of who I am. The feelings are intuitive. I always had within me, but I have developed since then, finally gaining the understanding I needed. It's like the light switch for the *light* was suddenly switched on.

Buddha came to me a few months later. It was then that relived my NDE after it happened. Before that I had an internal calling, telling me to go to Bali. I checked emails and websites, wondering about this feeling that I had to go. Some guide said, "Go." I booked a flight on 11th March. I followed my intuition or inner-guidance system.

I stayed at a random place because I had no accommodation booked. Ubud Aura was the name of the place. It happened to be next door to The Yoga Barn. Ten lovely rooms, pool, manicured gardens, lush greenery with the smell of fresh rain, frangipani and burning incense. It was gorgeous in the morning. I strolled down a laneway and found Yoga Barn; a place I was always meant to find.

I did some yoga which had lovely energy. Then chose to try meditation. There were healers. One resonated with me; a little Indian in a turban. I had heard that Indian's use a traditional meditation which is the best kind. He was traditionally dressed in a robe and sikh. He began and said in a strong Indian accent, "We will do Ananda Mandala today," Ananda Mandala is a blissful circle in Sanskrit. The forty or so people attending held hands and sat up straight, forming a ring on the timber floor; The Blissful Circle.

We were guided, by him, to do deep breath work into each chakra. Odd things started to happen to me. He said, "Don't open your eyes."

I struggled to listen and follow through. I started to get pain. I thought about NDE. Then I began to feel it. All the pain. I had visions of it all happening again. I had to let go of hands and needed to stretch.

I had done the opposite to what the meditation required. I felt like fainting. I decided that I could push through the pain. My inner guidance said, 'sit up straight and take a breath'. It was like something channelling and guiding me. Immediately the pain disappeared, and I calmed. I took hold of the hands each side of me, sitting up straight and reconnecting the circle of meditators.

Buddha came. I know it was Buddha. I have no doubts in my mind about who appeared to me. I was dressed as an Indian. I wore a white sari with a scarf with gold trimming. Buddha gave me blessings, which is a hand over someone's head giving them the flow of energy. It flowed into every cell in my being. I felt a deep lightness and euphoric love flowing through me. As he was doing that, I could feel him and his energy. I was physically crying in the room at The Yoga Barn but, also in my vision. I know understand this as channelling.

Buddha said, "You have a beautiful, beautiful heart. You need to use your heart for healing." I did not know at the time what it meant, but I do know now. Buddha became my channel to heal. Visions with Buddha, Shiva (means energy) and Lakshmi, continue intermittently with me today.

During my many mediations Indian deities coming through

Why me?

What do they want? What do they want me to do? I was so confused.

I never even knew who Lakshmi was until it was explained after I saw her. She was Goddess Lakshmi, the goddess of health and wealth. In my vision, she was showering me with gold coins. It was strange to be seeing Lakshmi and other ascended masters. I was shown reiki and other pathways I should follow.

I know that this energy can come through us to help heal others. The energy is the frequency, and it is related to my NDE. I have a higher frequency since the NDE, allowing me to channel and see my angels.

Funnily enough, it makes more sense, as I write this. Imagine how strange it all felt to me at first. Now I know that I am supposed to tell people about it – to heal and to pull in divine energy. I am here to empower others and uplift them

At times I still struggle with it. Keeping my heart open is not always easy. Not everyone believes or understands. Some people have closed hearts. They want to project it back on the person trying to express and share love and light. They want to pull people down to their level, unwilling to bless their success.

I must keep going. I can't help those people or anyone if I jump into negativity with them. I can only help who is willingly wanting help. Those who are ready to open their hearts, see good and do good for others and the planet.

I desire to have everyone to be able to find the capacity and the power to be able to heal their own pain. I want them able to find a place of bliss and love and kindness whenever they can. Everyone can do that. They just need to be willing.

Some people are not as spiritual as they claim to be. Some cry about how broken they are. They will try to heal themselves, only to get sicker or live in more fear. They are the ones who do not truly believe in themselves. Please try to do it for yourself, without relying on others. Do not get caught up in the hype of the marketing of some, supposedly spiritual places. Make sure you let your inner-belief system guide you.

I've seen vulnerable people, trying to find their spirituality, taken for a ride on the wrong path and are worse off than before; in India, Bali Australia and worldwide.

You need to believe you can do the work yourself. I don't have to spend thousands of dollars on workshops and spiritual advisers for years. When you forget what you are doing, just flip to a chapter, or page and get back to the place of using your guidance again. Marissa Peer has many YouTube videos which explain a little about this.

To create awareness that my NDE came to teach everyone about the Light.

My NDE gave me an enlightened spiritual awakening, that now allows me to share the experience. The experience is love and peace. A place of love creates a wonderful happy life. This must include forgiveness to truly work. You must move on.

People are vulnerable and shouldn't be taken advantage of. To find spirituality and a way of meditating to find the *light* and a way to heal their body from within. The power is in you. Do not wait for someone to give you the right answers, for them only to be wrong. Read this book, take the gift of what I want to give. I want to empower you.

Becoming awakened is the inner knowing that you are in control of your GPS. Feel into you and allow your inner guidance system to show you the way. You will become empowered, find inner strength, resilience and know when someone is affecting your inner vibe or rises with your vibe. Don't hide from your vibe.

Find the inner-child, let it out and let go of what does not serve you. Remembering you were born with this is another key to finding it, your inner child is calling, 'come find me', and then we can live in harmony together. The inner-child is where the inner suffering started. Become connected with it to heal through love, inner peace and nurturing. This is *AWAKENING!* Wake up the child within.

Sacred Heart Meditation

I decided to develop this meditation as plenty of my clients were busy and didn't have time to do daily practice. Recording a nine-minute meditation, I began giving it to every client. Encouraging them to do it every morning when they wake up (sitting up) and every night (lying down) before they went off to sleep, it was a great success for them.

Soon after I made a handbook with healing affirmations to do daily as part of the transition, it too is a great success. I have been developing five yogic therapy practices to add to Sacred Heart Meditation, to help others shift the negative energy they take on from their environment and others. They go hand in hand. All up it will take 20 to 30 minutes a day. We all should have that.

The beauty of these practices is, they are very simple, easy to do and make you feel good inside. Once you feel good, you attract good, and you do good. Life is always moving and shifting, energy is moving and shifting within us. We must understand that if we don't clear the unfavourable from our mind, body and come into our spirit within, we still suffer in our thoughts and old beliefs (negative patterns).

When I teach meditation, I sometimes bring in the angelic realm. Each one of us has a guardian angel, and I love to teach this. Often people in group meditation come to me afterwards and share their angelic experiences. From angels speaking to them, to feeling of pure bliss, golden orbs, angels flying around the room; to feeling like someone is holding them, these experiences are real. Spirit guides and angels are all working together for the higher good of all of us and our planet.

Countless ancient scriptures come from India Veda's, Greek philosophy, Italian, from many religions and in the bible, just to name a few. Angels have been around since the world was created. Babies and small children are deeply connected. You may notice when a baby looks up and smiles at the ceiling or sky.

People share with me their children's experiences with spirit and things they can see. My own granddaughter shared with me the people she could see who were pink in colour. We sat down together and drew what she described. It was no surprise to me when we drew people. I too had my own experiences and although it was never encouraged to believe what I saw. I know now that it was true. We can connect with whoever we want at will, once we embrace it with love, trust and understanding it will flow.

We can receive high life forces energy and insight from those who have lived here before us. Whether they are angels or spirit, they exist.

To believe your heart has a higher intelligence you must first believe it to be true. Otherwise, you will block the pure essence of angelic spirit. When teaching Scared Heart Meditation, I first ask if everyone has meditated before. What is interesting is that people who haven't meditated before are the easiest to work with when it comes to receiving. I believe this is because there have been many other (beliefs) teachings taught on how to meditate and they are confused and unfocused. They try too hard. The mind gets involved and takes them away from feeling the love energy coming through.

Try this; gently close your eyes, feeling your breath enter both nostrils. Allow your breath to touch both sides of your throat as you gently feel the breath flowing into your magnificent lungs. Gently staying focused, continue feeling your breath. Command your mind using the power of your breath to feel your breath touching the lower part of your tummy.

As you feel into your inner being become present with the power of who you are as you connect with your breath, heart, and intuition (lower tummy). By using the power of your breath and commanding your mind, you will start to notice the difference between your inner being and your mind (thoughts). Allowing yourself the time for each to feel into you. After a few practices, your inner being will guide you. Don't allow your mind to control you. Control your mind by commanding it to your breath. It's your breath that holds power, the key to the *light*.

Meditation to lead you to help access the *light*- Your light within

Meditation activates the subconscious mind and takes it in relaxation (consciousness). Our mind and breath are deeply connected, and breath (prana) is the bridge between body and mind. Meditation improves consciousness, concentration, intuition, wisdom and higher intelligence. Breath also takes your mind into relaxation, calmness and when your mind is relaxed your muscles are relaxed. Then your body relaxes as we release stress and anxiety.

I have developed my own divine meditation which helps me connect with who I really am and my true inner being. This is how I found my life purpose and receive the right answers from my higher intelligence. In this meditation accessing the light means bringing yourself into superconsciousness, allowing the divine light to shine through you and give you what it is you need to know.

Sitting either in a chair or yoga mat whatever is comfortable. Gently close your eyes. Slowly, gently calmly relax. Bring your awareness to your breath. Visualise your heart, it can be any shape or form and keep breathing into your heart until you start to feel relaxed.

As you connect with your heart visualise the colour green in your heart. (You may wish to visualise Mother Earth flowing her healing energy into you). Keep this going until you feel the connection of lightness and calm. Some people feel tingles, start to have visions or just keep the vision of their heart. It doesn't matter, as this just means we are shifting through something to get us to where we need to be. Like walking through a jungle and pushing the jungle plants out of the way. Once you get to this place, then the mind is calm and relaxed; when the magic happens. You're creating space in your mind for the good stuff to come in. You may see colours or visions.

I had one client say they connected with their daughter and father who had crossed over. There was another who experienced different colours or white light streaming through their body. We all experience things in different ways.

Exercises

- Have you found the *light* yet, as you meditate?
- Continue to do the meditation, as suggested. Sometimes it takes time to master it.
- Are you feeling happier, lighter, warmer inside, this far into the book?

You can access *Sacred Heart Healing Meditation* on YouTube or email kerrythehealer@gmail if you would like a copy.

Louise Hay and Channelling

Louise Hay, Author, motivational speaker, Queen of affirmations and the Founder of Hay House Publishing. She has been inspirational in my learning to heal, connect and understand that our thoughts can change. Dr. Wayne Dyer is another, they both hold extraordinary knowledge about who we are and where we come from.

Working with clients at The Yoga Barn, Ubud, Bali opened many opportunities for me to connect, teach and offer guidance. What is amazing is that when I teach, I not only give out healing energy I receive it. Especially when a group is large. 20 to 40 people can move energy to the highest realms. I have tested this many times, especially when there is touch through hands or eyes. These are also ways to connect with heart and soul energies which are divine connection. It gave me opportunities to join with those who were suffering in their thoughts and feelings. It also made me look at the way I think and feel. I found that as I saw more clients, I realised that something from past hurts was healing in the process. Our thoughts are not who we are, we are unique, loving beings.

After a few weeks, I found that clients wanted a connection with self, but also a connection with others. Mostly they wanted reassurance.

I began using Louise Hay's affirmations and shared them with my clients. I printed them and have them on my healing room wall. Remarkably, the more I did this, the more I could feel Louise. It was like she was starting to channel through me.

Conversing with a friend, Heidi Henneman from New York, I was telling her that I had Louise Hay affirmations in my healing room and I used them every day with my clients. I told her I thought I could feel Louise since doing this. Heidi had been a friend since we met when she had sat beside me during meditation when I had first relived my near-death experience.

Heidi said, "You need to write a book about your whole experience, the NDE and channelling," pushing me to take the first step to write a book.

I was speechless. A feeling of 'yes' came over me. Then the thought of 'how?' came over me. Looking at Heidi, with her beautiful smile and bright eyes lit up in hope, I felt a deep inner feeling of joy. I connected with what she had said. I knew it was something I was here to do. Though, at the time I didn't know where to start.

I decided to leave it to my meditating time. In this way, I hoped to see what I needed to do next. Soon after chatting to Heidi I spoke to publishing companies. I found it overwhelming because I naively thought I would write it and things would fall in place. Surely someone would look at it and tell me if it was good or what needed to change. I thought I needed someone to critique what I had barely started writing. It was still a thought. That thought was manifested until I soon found the right path. Maybe Louise pushed me there. I wonder if she did.

Exercises

- Have you ever had a sensation of someone else in a room with you?
- Do you ever receive a flash idea (insight)?
- Do you believe in your own angel's guides? Who are they?
- Have you ever closed your eyes and felt the presence of someone's spiritual energy?
- Try meditating and breathing as deeply as you can. How do you feel afterwards?

Golden Gems for your Spiritual Treasure Chest

I love giving you a Golden Gem It is my gift to you. This gift is simple. I wish you inner peace and love. Spread this message to others that you would like to share it with.

Peace to you.

Send out love energy whenever and where ever you go.

Love and peace will be returned to you in many forms.

And the planet, planet be at peace, for the more people who are at peace, the more people will not act in a non-peaceful way.

This will then become a ripple effect, and the cause will be the planet is at peace (cause and effect) universal laws. A smile can also send a message of positively and shift energy. We could have "International Smiling Day" just imagine the shift in the planet.

Crystal therapy along with reiki, channeling and massage enhances the healing effect. I use crystals in my healing practice daily. Crystals have energy properties that work with our energy systems.

Below are some of my favourite crystals.

1. Clear quartz because its known as the master "the divine connection" healer for the crown chakra. It is the light of the soul.
2. Amethyst is known as the multipurpose stone and third eye chakra. I use this by placing it on the forehead as I reform reiki. Amethyst is for receiving insight, knowledge and balance.
3. Rose quartz . A beautiful pink crystal and very calming. It represents the heart chakra. The heart is the centre of love, forgiveness, kindness and compassion.

Holding crystals in your hands or placing them on your body will help balance physical, emotional and spiritual wellness. Crystals communicate with your body's energy field, or chakra. Some crystals alleviate stress, improved concentration and enhance our creative side. Crystals work with intent, so if your intent is to heal using crystals then so it is.

CHAPTER 21

Healing
We are all healers, some of us just don't know it yet

"True love is born from understanding."
—Buddha

Healing healers is something I strive to do. Without the health and wellbeing of all healers, they cannot guide their clients effectively. Many healers give continuously, not taken time out for themselves. Self-care is extremely important. That includes time out to nurture their inner being. If they deplete their own energy, there is nothing left to share with others.

By replenishing and giving to self is being selfless. If you are not energised then how can we, as healers, give our best. We must take care of the internal part of us and balance our mind, body and spiritual side of us. By not giving to self-first we are selfish. If you are not at your best and allowing yourself time to fill up your heart cup, then how can you be good and do good for others?

There is a side effect. It can lead to resentment, anger, jealousy, guilt shame, etc. Remember these are all low vibration and will block you. We are all healers, and we each have a Buddha, Jesus, Mother Mary, Mother Teresa, Shiva, Krishna, Yoda with us. We just need to allow ourselves to access these remarkable ascendant masters and spirit guides.

I have met people on my path who think self-care is a massage, getting your nails done or going to the hairdresser. There is nothing wrong with those things, I am merely explaining the obvious.

This can be part of self-care. However, this is external. Looking good is important. Self-care is balancing the three. Mind Body and Spirit. Self-Care and healing takes time, commitment and meditation. You cannot connect to yourself or inner being unless you calm your mind, close your eyes and feel what is going on inside you. Breath is a powerful healer that when we adapt to what it offers, we can heal and drop into who we are. It's the same for healers. They need to be in the right mind space, with inner peace and wellbeing to be able to pass that on to you. If someone is not balanced, then their energy is out of balance, and they can take you away from your vibrational space and into low vibration.

It's an inner journey with a never-ending path. What's the point on working on your physical if you're not working on the mind and spirit as well. Remember they are all linked mind, body and spirit. You cannot physically see your mind and spirit - you can only feel them. Balance the two with awareness and insight this is the key to the light.

Not long after my NDE, I was feeling confused about my transition. I felt the changes within myself but had no idea who I should seek for answers, or what I was supposed to do with my enlightenment. My mind spun like I was in a fantasy and I was a different being connected to Mother Nature. I was linked to angels and the spirit world. I felt the beauty of our planet and the universe. Everything was within me.

On the other side of those feelings of bliss, my life was sometimes lonely. I had not yet found a teacher or friend who understood what I was going through. How can someone be of comfort to you when they too are working on their life path? I found the answers within. Others who have had NDE know that relaying their story can often be met with scepticism. I was wary of anyone stealing my bliss.

This may sound harsh, there are plenty of people who are ready to rip others down just for the sake of it. These people are lost and confused. If they weren't and had knowledge of spirituality, they would lift others up and not tear them down.

Sending love and asking the divine to guide them to the good of their high self is something you can learn to do. This is for your higher good and good of others. Letting go of people who exhaust and take energy from you is a huge part of the transition.

People who want to take responsibility will and move with you. The ones who don't, won't want to move and that is their choice. The easiest way to move away from this toxic energy is to send a loving prayer to them through visualisation. They will feel something; however, it will be up to them to ask for help once they understand they are responsible for their happiness and not you.

One day, I was typing on the computer. I was responding to emails when suddenly my inner guidance said, "You need to go to Bali. You must go to Ubud." I looked up and asked the Universe, "By myself?"

My initial reaction was, oh dear I'm really into something I don't understand. Despite those first thoughts, I decided to follow my inner guidance. It was all I had in the world. My inner guidance was my one true friend, and I needed to trust that friend.

My inner child was also part of it. As she healed from her emotional pain, she became my inner teacher. She celebrated life with me by being my inner little champion. Whenever I feel lost or fearful, I meditate and allow her to come through. She now is my high energy retriever, the one who dances, sings and is playful. She plays with the universe.

The moments of joy and bliss are the moments you should listen and meditate on whatever you want to create; when the universe listens and returns it to you.

I wanted to book my flight to Bali and waited in front of my computer. I thought, when should I go? I looked up and said, "When?" I was yet to realise that I was speaking to the universe or God.

I received a distinct answer in my mind and body; go on the eleventh. Okay, I'm going to Ubud on the eleventh of March, not knowing why, how, where or any other relevant information. All I knew was that I needed to go. A week before departure I googled accommodation for Ubud, there I found Ubud Aura, which sounded perfect.

I arrive at Ubud Aura, and it's a lovely tranquil place with lush gardens, a pool, and beautiful kind staff. The first morning I was awake around 5 am because of the time difference to the sound of roosters crowing. I showered, sorted through my things, checked my emails and strolled to the restaurant for breakfast. The delicious fruit and omelette were just what I needed to nourish my body because I hadn't eaten for a whole day.

Getting to know the staff was exciting. They willingly shared their celebrations and ceremonies. I was aware of these rituals to the gods, as I had been visiting Bali for twenty-five years. It was only my third time I had been in the more traditional Ubud.

I took a stroll. On leaving the main gate of the resort, I looked to my left, thinking there was a street that way and a lane that looked interesting and mysterious to explore. I ventured down the lane and to my delightful surprise found a yoga studio, The Yoga Barn.

I felt drawn to The Yoga Barn, the perfume of flowers, damp vegetation from recent rain, sunshine filtering through high trees, gave it a lovely ambience. A good yoga class would energise me, so I decided to take a class. A good decision for my future me, I realised much later.

I discovered Hatha Yoga. It varied from the yoga I had been practising in Australia. However, it was a nice experience. I finished the class, making my way through to reception which was on my way out. I glanced up, and to my surprise, there was a poster of an Indian meditation teacher and healer who was guiding a meditation class. I had been meditating for many years, so this increased my interest.

On reading his card I thought, this man is a Guru. His name Punnu Sing Wasu rolled off my tongue. I was drawn to him and what he offered. I especially liked his turban, and he also looked cute. As I waited to go in, I yawned, hoping we would lie down during the meditation. I could have done with more sleep.

Seriously, was I wrong? The practice was something I had never been privileged to experience. We sat through forty-five minutes of eyes-closed meditation where we breathed deeply into our chakras or psychic centres. Two lovely girls sat either side of me. The one on the left later became a dear friend Heidi.

Trusting your inner guidance is like trusting your inner child

My inner being, inner guidance is what I call it when insight, heart and intuition blend. I was excited when I read about gut health being part of our digestive system (Fire Element) which is where part of our intuition lies. When the three communicate to each other, we are in flow. Yes!

This is when the magic happens, and divine energy flows loving through you; life force energy flows. Becoming into you (IN TUI ON) or into one. Your lower tummy (fire) is your GPS saying no not that way or don't do that with that person or be careful approach with care as you connect with a person.

Once in tune, your GPS will drive into your heart (soul) and then your mind's eye (third eye). Together they become your convoy or inner guidance. It's a good idea to test this out with family and friends. You will understand and have more clarity around how you feel in a certain situation. For example, notice how you feel when someone close to you is angry or hurt. One you feel in your stomach and one you will feel in your heart. You are on your way, letting your GPS guide you. Your inner child is deeply connected to our inner guidance. Its our joyful, our playful and our unconditional love for self and others. Its speaking our truth. Have you noticed children they are so honest and tell the truth about how they are feeling. If we don't nurture our inner child we become blocked and don't speak our truth of how we feel in fear of being judged. As a child we didn't care what others thought because we didn't understand or know about judgements or expectation of others. We are not taught to be self or love for self.

Breath meditation

The first couple of minutes were easy. Punnu's smooth voice was guiding fifty people into Ananda Mandala meditation. Ananda Mandala means blissful circle in Sanskrit. I felt pain, strangely where my pain had been during my NDE, anaphylactic episode. As my breath deepened, my pain increased. What was happening?

Punnu said, "Don't let go of your partner's hands. Don't let your eyes open. Stay with your breath and keep going."

I couldn't continue. The pain in my body was excruciating. I felt nauseous. Im going to faint I thought as I struggled with the pain. Rather than fainting, I let go of the hands each side of me. I had my legs out in front of me grimacing as the pain of my NDE was relived. I had no control over it. I curled into my body with my head in my lap with my eyes closed. Suddenly, I had an impulse(higher self) to take a deep breath. I sat up straight, crossed my legs and took a gulp of oxygen, letting it fill my body with the breath. As soon as that deep breath flowed through me, the pain immediately stopped.

Wow, I thought, what is going on? I was unable to control my thoughts or feelings. Something was inside me and had taken over me. I continued concentrating on my breath, trying to work out what had happened. I cried as I felt a deep inner love shine through my heart. It was as if I had died all over again. The feelings of bliss, love, and joy filled my heart once again in the same way they had after my NDE.

Tears of joy flooded my eyes. They were still shut when I saw Buddha. He came, dressed in a sari-type gown. He walked towards me with a loving smile that melted my heart. He gently placed his hands on my head in deeksha, a oneness blessing that filtered love into me.

He said, "You have a beautiful heart, and you need to use your loving heart to heal, heal others."

I don't want to leave the moment, it was such a beatific experience. I wanted to stay there forever, just as I had felt when I was happy to remain in nonphysical statem my spiritual self was ignited once again. Higher self came to me while I was living and breathing. As I was healing I was living, I thought as I transitioned into the lightness, the light inside me was again enlightened. I was not only feeling lovely I was beautiful, altering my clothes, hair, and feelings. I was wearing a scarf over my head, much like an Indian godess. Exquisite gold jewellery adorned my hair. An Indian sari draped my body. I was deeply connected to Buddha. I was deeply connected to the spiritual essence of the nonphysical world, yet I was in the physical. Though India had never been on my bucket list, I felt India and connected to that place in my heart. This experience was a huge part of my spiritual awakening. How can I teach physical and nonphysical spiritual guidance if I have never had the experience.

It took months before I followed the messages I had received through meditation. I resisted India for a long time, then by chance, or is it destiny, I travelled there.

After the meditation was complete, I wondered who this Punnu man was. What were his teachings? How did they give such a hypnotic meditative breathwork technique that allowed so many thoughts of Buddha to enter my mind and soul? Why was Buddha, of all people, channelling me? What did he really want me to do?

I realised that the love was coming from Buddha and channelling through my heart. I was awakening and felt the forces of love driving energy flowing through every bone, vein, internal organs; everything inside was waking up. I loved Buddha and many other deities but didn't understand what that realisation meant. I had travelled to Bali, to the mountains of Ubud and found Buddha. After the meditation, Punnu asked everyone how they felt and whether they would like to share their experience.

Thinking no one would ever believe what had happened to me I decided I would not share it. My mind was spinning like a washing machine. What was I supposed to do with the new me? I was no longer the person I used to be and had transitioned into a better me that felt good. But oh my God, what should I do now?

Punnu ended the session and mentioned he had a two-day program the next day. He asked if anyone would be interested in joining. "Just sign the program list to register if you are keen," he said.

I was more than enthusiastic. I thought it would be awesome, if I feel this wonderful from his meditation, imagine what I would receive from his program. I attended the next day. Within hours of Punnu and I had connected. I felt he had something very special that he should share with the world.

I asked him if he would be interested in coming to Australia. He glanced at his partner Catherine, asking her, "Do you want to go to Australia?"

Without hesitation, Catherine said, "Why not!"

Five weeks later they stayed with me on the Gold Coast, my Australian home. The wonderful experience led to fun, laughter, and connection. We offered meditation to Gold Coast Community, during which more and more things started to happen to me.

I had visions and feelings from the deities of India. I didn't understand or know at the time, but I was channelling Lakshmi, Buddha, Shiva, Ganesh, bright lights angels and many others. I didn't know or understand who they were. The only one I was familiar with was Buddha. He was my soul connection; part of me. He was the one who came to me and gave me my true love of self and the gift of the meaning to life.

He taught me to live a life of joy, happiness, and peace. I lost the suffering in mind because I had no expectations or attachments. I became aware that I was here to live a life of joy. Attachment to thoughts are beliefs, values and our personality which is formed, not by us, but by other's opinions.

Wow! That realisation hit home. I never felt like I fitted with my family or others. I used to think, why do some people hurt others and they seem to get joy from it? Why do people let someone do that to them? It all started to make sense as I became more aware of why I was here; what I was here to do.

Nothing in our life is done without a thought. If we bring in awareness to that thought and decide based on it, then this is what we become, what we create and where we will be. If an action is a doing thing and a thought is a thinking thing, then why aren't we all thinking good things and doing good things?

It wasn't long before I realised we just don't know, how can we practice something that we do not know. Once I had this realisation, I knew I was here to 'teach'. I needed to teach spirituality and guidance of who we really are what we are here to do.

This new knowledge was tinged with pain. I left my family and friends to share my knowledge. It was my purpose, my life and my divine connection to the universe. It was like a marriage between the two of us; me and the universe. Everyone else was part of the ceremony, sharing in the excitement.

Getting to know Punnu and Catherine was part of my transition of growth. They are both Healers and lived in Ubud for many years working at The Yoga Barn. Three weeks with them in Australia went quickly. I was sad when they left, especially Punnu. I felt a deep connection with him and knew he was going to be part of my journey.

Punnu and I began skyping, this gave me a sense of reassurance after they left. Everything was going to be okay. This was reaffirmed each time I spoke to him. One day while skyping I said to him, "I feel really stuck, I am doing the meditation and people are coming, but I still feel like I should be somewhere else. I didn't know where."

Punnu said, "Go to India."

"I don't want to go to India."

"Then come to Bali."

"That's not possible, with my work. Family and friends are here and what would I do?"

Lastly, he said, "You know what to do. Prayer and meditate to your divine for answers."

The next morning, I woke up and literally bounced out of bed. Jumping in the air, I yelled, "I know what to do. I will rent my house, sell my belongings and move to Bali." Seven weeks later I was in Bali, planning my next steps. I took a complete leap of faith from one side of me to my inner guidance. It was as if I were wearing angel wings. I was guided through every step.

Ubud is classified in the *Lonely Planet* website as a spiritual awakening. It certainly was for me. I was initially excited about meeting new people and living in a way that is far more relaxed than what I was used to on the Gold Coast. I slowly slid into this new form of being, and it wasn't long before I was doing other courses with Punnu; Reiki 1 to Grand Master Reiki.

Reiki

Reiki was the stepping stone to my healing work and spiritual being. I learnt to give healing energy through my presence. Previously my healing wasn't as loving when I was channelling, using crystals and massaging healing of energy points in the body; Reiki and channelling opened my eyes. Reiki is an energy exchange and we all carry this gift. We can channel healing energy which not only is healing for self, but healing for others. As we channel, divine loving healing energy can penetrate through the palms of our hands and onto the person/self. We receive this energy through our heart centre and transmit it through our hands and onto others. Its works on the same concept as a massage therapist or any therapy use with the hands.

After one of the Reiki courses on a late Saturday afternoon, one of the students, an Ayurvedic doctor, mentioned he could do a deep chakra massage. It would alleviate any pain I had in my body. Not knowing what to expect I booked an appointment.

I went for my first ever Chakra massage. I have never experienced anything like this in my life. It was so powerful I thought I was going to have an orgasm on the table. Wow, wow, wow!

All my energy centres opened. I was a light, floating being who could barely speak let alone stand to get dressed afterwards. When I finally got myself grounded, I walked downstairs. The Ayurvedic doctor was sitting there with ginger tea and asked me would I like to join him.

What a nice gesture. I had to ride my scooter home and could use something to heighten my energy. I felt my spirit had yet to return fully to my body. While sipping the much-needed ginger tea, the doctor said to me, "I would like you to come and work with me."

I almost spat out my tea in surprise. What could I do for a doctor like him? I asked, "What is it you see me doing for you?"

My life turned around when he said, "You are a healer, and your energy is amazing. I could feel it vibrating when I was massaging you."

"Mmmm?" I gasped, clearing my throat, embarrassed, I wasn't ready to share my orgasmic experience with him. To this day I have only shared the experience with a couple of friends.

Soon after I began energy and chakra healing and training in Ayurvedic massage. I learnt how our energy centres work and how energy (prana or life force energy) flows through our bodies and what causes the blocks.

Once we understand how energy works internally, as well as externally, we are on our way to finding our purpose of being; true spiritual being.

When I finally did go to India, I found Greens Ayurveda, Kerala India. Dr. Asghar said, "We would be happy to have you. See how you like it. If it feels right, stay and train for as long as you like." With those words, I was drawn to it and went.

For fourteen months on and off I was in India training. I wanted to experience everything that I was studying. Without the experience, I could not be authentic to my clients. I experienced deep emotional pain as the Panchakarma did its job and releasing past toxic, emotional and physical pain from my body. I was being transformed through the ancient Indian Healing process. Experiencing Panchakarma was because I wanted to deliver my experiences with integrity. It would be like a telling someone, "Yes this is amazing ice-cream," without tasting it.

As for the term Ayurveda; many people were confused about the definition of what it is. I wanted to simplify it in my teachings. I wanted to heal people in the best ways I could.

Some people want an assessment of their doshas, thinking it's about food and diet. Ayurveda and its principles heal from the inside out. It's about finding the disease, emotion or psychological, then targeting that particular area, to find the toxins and renew the cells. It is also about thoughts and feelings. They need to be addressed as well. Fears need to be released for healing to begin.

The example that diet in Ayurveda is like the size of a pea and Ayurveda is like the size of a football field, is apt. There is so much more learn. The one thing I would like to mention is that you, yourself know the answers. Step away from other's beliefs, and you will find you. Ayurveda is a process that helps us understand and remove what doesn't serve us, including toxins.

You may have a pain in your body like back pain. You have it for ages, and you think about it being there forever. But you have the power within to heal your body. We need the knowledge of the herb, plants, meditation, self-healing, and yoga combined. Ayurveda uses plants-based and herbed-based medicines combined with certain oils, coconut oils, sesame oil, and almond oil. They go externally to remove the toxins.

There are also some to consume or use as enemas with the other herbs. The toxins build in the colon. If the digestive systems can't release the toxins, they will be released somewhere else in the body and then create disease. Often these diseases come through from emotions like fear. Let go of all fear. Combine yoga and meditation with Ayurveda knowledge, and you have the recipe for a healthy life. Science is now supporting this. Essential oils are also good and combined with a good therapeutic and holistic approach, toxins can easily be removed from mind and body.

Disease and toxins are called AMA in Sanskrit, this can be in the form of swelling (inflammation), pain or emotions. AMA can give you depression, anxiety and leave a feeling of out of balance. Another reason to find a way to turn your fear words into positive ones. Ama can also cause weight gain and imbalance many systems in the body, including the immune system. Below is a brief outline of treatments I would recommend if you're starting your healing path.

Panchakarma

Panchakarma is an authentic Ayurvedic procedure which aims in the purification of the body. It is a cleansing and rejuvenating program for the body, mind, and consciousness. It is known for its beneficial effects on overall health, wellness, and self-healing.

Shirodhara

Getting a good night's sleep, relaxing, and just letting your mind be at peace, is something we all strive for.

Imagine, taking time out, lying on a massage table with the gentle, soft music playing. Strong healing hands stroke pressure points, massaging your head, squeezing out all the stress. Nice.

And then a stream of pleasantly warm oil, rich with herbal aromas falls on your forehead (third eye chakra), taking you into, at times, in a hypnotic peaceful state, bringing you immense calm and pleasure. Goosebumps already, eh? Fantasy, no. Ayurvedic science, yes! This is Shirodhara. It is great for headaches and stress release. Shirodhara has many healing components.

Inner Child

You were born with non-judgement, no fear or status, being happy and content with who you were. Then you were connected to the divine energy frequency.

Watching playful little children is one of the things that gives me joy. Nothing bothers them. They have a cry or disagreement and it's forgotten and forgiven in moments. From a few months old we are doing yogic asana's, child pose, baby pose, side twist, cobra, stretching and mudras.

Yes! We all had the yogic knowledge, and we all were little yogis. Yoga is part of our wellbeing and wellness. Ask yourself, how well is my being (wellbeing) or how well am I being? Little children are honest, saying things like, "I don't want to," "I don't like you," or "I don't like that," because they have no fear and are honest with who they are.

Over time it dissipates because we are punished for being honest and authentic. We are told to be something outside of us. We are not taught to trust what we feel. The exact opposite. We are taught to be, do, act like someone else. Not our true authentic selves. Once we move into teenager or adulthood, we fear being judged. Like a feeling of not belonging. We stop being honest and authentic and don't speak our truth. We are in *FEAR* of being rejected by our parents, peers and socially. We don't understand it, making us anxious and depressed. Not able to express our true feelings will will block our throat chakra. Unable to speak our truth because of fear will cause pain in the throat area or dryness, like choking. This is a sign, you are not being honest with self. Always speak your truth. If in the moment you cannot, take yourself away from the situation until you feel like you can. This is empowering and healing.

Dig deep and connect with your inner child. Feel the emotions of the inner-child. You will experience the reconnection once you do. The child and adult come together.

Your inner child says, "You can do anything, trust me!." Your inner child is not afraid of failure. Small children without fear of failure, do it anyway! Once we reunite with the inner child with the adult, they combine, finding joy, happiness, and inner peace. It feels like a resinence with home or family a feeling of safety.

GO FOR IT, LET IT GLOW! Light up your inner child and your inner spirit. They will love you for it. Let the little light shine!

Healers and healers

Writing some of this stirred my emotions. Not all people in Bali, India or any other country are kind and caring. In the early days of my transition, some people took advantage of my money, my life, and my ideas. I wondered why I was attracting those sorts of people. Once I worked that out how I could turn everything around I could be happy; happy with myself, happy with my life and happy with my life choices.

It was like bursting the seams of sadness and self-worth, once those seams opened the *light* began to shine through. The *light* is such a huge metaphor for me, as its part of my experience in my NDE. I am *light*. You are *light*. We all are *light*. The *light* is our gateway to our heart and soul. It is the access we need to have non-ego, non-resistance and non-attachment to outcomes.

This universe; part of us, always know what you think. It thinks that's what you want because the universe does not understand what you don't want. The universe provides you with what you want and sometimes instantly. Therefore, we need to have a new way of thinking. If we think in a way that's not good for us, then the universe will give us that. If we think in a good way that gives us goodness, the universe says here is some of that.

I have tried my different ways to communicate to the universe in a way that I can manifest whatever my heart desires. I can. You can too! Through self-love, self-awareness, and self-knowledge. These are the best ways to heal.

Remember the happier you are, the more you are in flow. When you align with the flow of life force energy (divine or happy feelings), you will feel something inside you that comes alive and WAHOO! "You're here for me, inner soul."

You are physical when being a materialist, but spiritual when in harmony with self. Find your inner peace or place of peace. Asking your inner self, are you at peace everyday, will get you there.

Daily clearing your energy is an exceedingly important part of the mind, body and spiritual connection. If you hold someone or something inside you, you become that. Everything is energy.

By daily visualising the colour purple around me or a white crystal flame burning away any negative energy charge, I clear my energy. Another way is to sit facing the sun and imagining the sun charging and lighting up your inner being, filling it with *light*. Feel the glow beaming into your whole body. I do this because the sun is positive energy, recharging our cells like a battery.

Think of yourself as a cell phone you need to charge daily. Your soul is you phone needing positive energy to charge it. Full charge will keep you from attracting negative charge or vibration. It's like knowing your body responds to your thoughts and cells.

I like knowing that my body had a higher intelligence that is connected to the sun, moon and whole universe. Feeding my body with constant communication to my trillions of cells enables them to be the driver of my GPS. I am the creator of my wellbeing, knowing this changes my energy and perspective.

Exercises

- How have you healed yourself?
- Write down five golden gems for your spiritual treasure chest that gives you self-love. Write the things that give you joy.
- Maybe a walk on the beach feeling the sand between your toes, staring at the twinkling diamonds on the water radiating from the sunlight. This may bring a feeling of joy to your heart.

Golden Gems for your Spiritual Treasure Chest

- I Am Vitality.
- I Am Healthy.
- I Am Divine Light.
- I love who I Am, and I feel free.

You can make your own by writing:

I love……………………………………..………………..

I adore…………………………………………..…..…..

For example, "I am a really good at my own healing, and I can focus on my inner light." "I love my body and know that it responds to universal energies."

Saying things like, "I am not good at this," or "I am not good at that," are negative and low vibration. Use uplifting healing affirmations. Pay attention to how you feel when you close your eyes, saying them to yourself; you feel you. Forgiveness will free anyone from suffering thoughts. Remember the law of polarity, everything has an opposite. The opposite to anger is forgiveness.

"It will set you free." You will feel light... "Feel the light within you," as you let go and flow. Make up your own healing affirmations. These affirm who you are and what you let go of.

Once you let go of any negative emotion you will understand how good you feel by not allowing your thoughts to rule who you are and what you want to feel. Be your unique self and not what others want you to be. We each have a gift to share to the world. Dream big, become fearless (not fearful). Fill your spiritual treasure chest up with golden gems that light up your heart. Love how you feel.

CHAPTER 22

Healing Affirmations
Affirmations are a foundation for healing

"Go Within and Let the Healing Begin"
—Kerry Clancey

Affirmations are ways of confirming something to your subconscious to change beliefs not serving you. Knowing and understanding that you have been programmed from a very early age, to do, want and be something you don't want to be, is a step toward affirming who you truly are.

You may have experienced the emotional pain of not being good enough, undeserving (self-worth), unable to be you without judgement of others. Let go of what others think and stay true to your heart. Speak your truth about how I feel, especially when other's expectations of who you should be, are pushed on you. They may expect you to do things their way or make you feel you are a bad person. This carries guilt, shame, and pain.

I understand it. After experiencing the joy of living, I can do anything I wish or desire. If you need more clarity, observe little children playing. They don't say, "You're too fat. You're too thin. Your skin is different from mine." They 'be in the moment' and have fun. Have pleasure with your life. Get your inner-child out and play, sing, dance. This is you.

Healing our painful beliefs (others beliefs or perception) which cause loss of self and purpose is paramount. I found my life purpose once I found my inner soul. My soul is the freedom to be who I want. I want to be *LOVE* and *Be Loved*. We all live for love.

You can choose to let go and say *YES*, or you can stay in *FEAR*, saying *NO*. I have followed these rituals. They are what gave me what I have today. The closer you are to your heart the closer you are to your soul; to divine, divine love.

What you put out you will receive. What you believe you will receive. Find whatever serves you and teaches you to be gentle with yourself. If you a have a feeling of *FEAR* or negativity, that's not who you are.

In that moment, acknowledge the *FEAR*, celebrate, do a happy dance and say to yourself, "I get it. I am in control, and I have the power to change my thought." YIPEE! Remember FEAR will cause you to feel dark, depleted and consumed by negative thinking. Bless FEAR for its reminder of who you truly are. Remember to bring out your inner-child. Have fun, sing, skip, do whatever you need to do to set your heart on fire with love.

Consciousness and subconscious are like brothers and sisters. They may fight with each other then be calm and loving. Consciousness is what gives us happy in the moment. My NDE proved as much, in that once I let go of all my beliefs (subconscious)I could easily master my consciousness.

As mentioned, *I AM* is exceptionally powerful, bringing us to a state of consciousness. *I Have* overrides the subconscious to bring in the good (belief) of self. It's not easy sometimes, but I have found making a daily ritual as part of healing is empowering and powerful. It also nourishes your soul and brings you to our true soul of being.

My daily ritual usually starts with meditation, as this is my way to my heart and soul, where I make a connection with the spiritual world. Yoga is important to me, however, depending on where I am at the time and how I am feeling, I always make sure I meditate. It brings me back to connect with myself; the way I find my answers. Sometimes, staying in my heart and positive is not easy. What is easy is sitting is a quiet place, feeling breath as it enters my body and connecting to my heart. By doing this, I find joy floods my heart and my life. It makes me feel happy.

Countless people feel disconnected. Some spend thousands of hours talking and working with life coaches, healers, counsellors, psychologist etc., though remain disconnected. Again, our heart feels. We are emotional beings.

I will remind you many times through this book to make it sink in. Look for places, things and connections with your thoughts and feeling that give you joy or happiness. Listen to music, play an instrument, go bushwalking, pat a pet, walk on the beach, sit in the sand; just feel. Connecting with Mother Nature is calming; a part of who we are.

By saying something to yourself while you are in a state of *love or peace* affirms the feeling. You can plant a new seed in your subconscious. Once you do this, your subconscious will respond next time to this if there is a trigger or past beliefs. You need to do this often for a more peaceful calm life. If your thoughts are telling you one thing and your heart tells us another, imagine the confusion in the Universe. What we put out, we get back. Feel the freedom within.

Watch what you think about (particularly if it is not good) or you may create it. A bit like we need the darkness to bring us back to the *light*. The darker side of us will always be there, however, what we choose to think is what will *HEAL* us or destroy us.

Many of my clients *HEAL* through their past loved ones, coming through while we are in session. It's a beautiful feeling for me. I love being the connector bringing it together. Sharing with others and helping them *HEAL* emotional pain, is a gift I am very grateful for.

You don't need to suffer to live. Saying daily affirmations override negative beliefs so do as many as you can. I am constantly looking for ways to keep my spirits heightened. By sharing the last paragraph, I hope you can implement this in your life and *HEAL*.

Doing daily affirmations helped me leave my old self behind. When I experienced nonphysical, I became who I am today; Kerry the Healer. Dying gave me a taste of pure consciousness and joy. Whichever way you look at it I was total BLISS. Love ran through me and to those around me. The energy of love and peace frequency was sensational.

Knowing that when we heal ourselves, we heal the planet, gives me the inspiration to keep my thoughts and beliefs in check. I make it a practice and teach this to others, loving my work and what I do. Contributing not only to self but to the planet and others, makes me feel good and fulfilled. As does seeing people shift their mindsets and connecting with their inner beings.

I love that I can breathe to connect to myself and Mother Nature. Understanding who I really am and not what others think and feel about me is important. As I mentioned earlier, this is their thoughts and feeling or beliefs, not mine. Today, I make life a spiritual adventure; a positive place.

You are a spiritual being, light being; full of goodness and love. You are here to have a human experience and *HEAL* whatever you need to *HEAL*. You can think like this; my religion is *LOVE*, my thoughts are *LOVE*, my heart is filled with *LOVE*.

Many people put their focus on the wrong in the world, not on what is right. Human wellbeing should not be from Facebook, Instagram or the media and the wrongs of the world. Sure, sometimes we all need to know what's going on. However, is it helpful to our inner being or wellbeing to listen to this daily? Wouldn't it be better to turn off the TV?

Instead, learn how to keep your thoughts, body, and spirit uplifted and balanced. Contented people and happy places are for us. Why not put that out there, instead of FEAR of something bad may happen? There are loads of studies proving we can alter our brain activity and rearrange our brain (neural pathways) by thoughts. Surf the web for some sites that explain it further (I have some at the end of this book) to find more information. People share such this information with some research and scientific study supporting it.

We can catch our emotions by listening to our thoughts then changing them. How remarkable and powerful is that? Knowing this excites me. Your mind can shift energy, from person to person, inside our body and inside our heart. Why not share this on social media instead of the diatribe that some share instead of kindness.

Golden Gems for your Spiritual Treasure Chest

Here are seven Golden Gems for your Spiritual Treasure Chest. These help with stress and anxiety:

1. Meditate to your heart (on video) Sacred Heart Healing Meditation.
2. Write five 'I AM' affirmations. Say these, every morning straight after your meditation. Hold your hand on your heart centre while saying these.
3. Write five 'I HAVE' affirmation so that you are ready for your subconscious when it decides to show up in your mind.
4. Say the affirmations each morning before you do anything else. This allows the mind to absorb what you are telling it before other things have a chance to get into your mind.

5. Be present with yourself. Ask yourself how you feel?. Tell yourself you are worthy of everything your heart desires.
6. Remind yourself daily that you are more than your body. You are a beautiful soul that is full of *light*.
7. Meditate into your heart. Make this the last thing you do each night before you close your eyes. Tell yourself you are a shining *light* being, full of love and goodness. You are filled with love. You are surrounded by love. Love flows to you and through you.

Within three to four days you will notice the difference how you feel. As your align with who you are, your reprogramming is turned on and tuned into the real you.

You are perfect just the way you are! It's easier to smile than to frown and we use less muscles when we smile. Our muscles, cells, and tissue hold memory, so when we are stressed, we hold that inside. Release and be at peace. Strive forward and protect your vibe.

CHAPTER 23

Learning to Live with the Light Consciously
It's not just bliss, peacefulness and joy

"Seeing the Light is a choice. Not seeing the light is no choice."
—Douglas Horton

I believe we are all universal *light* filled with love. My NDE taught me that. When I was in my spiritual being, I saw the light and became the light. I am full of light. It's within all of us. We can heal ourselves within by reconnecting. Each of us can channel spirit, just by quietening our mind and going into our hearts, feeling with our hearts and thinking with our minds. Using our breath to slow down our mind (thinking) and relaxing our physical (muscles) we can journey into the spirit within. We are spiritual beings who can access our inner being and come into wellbeing. Nonphysical feels like bliss and joy, so when we leave our physical and become that we understand the meaning of we are both, spiritual and material.

You cannot think love, you feel love. Just like peace or inner peace, it's a feeling. I realised that when we are not in alignment with the feelings of joyful love or lightness, we are not in a frequency that connects to our higher intellect; our connection to Universal Source Energy (the Creator or God). The name is irrelevant. It's our feeling of connection that is what will take us to where we need to be or feel.

There is an insightful video of where Jill Bolte Taylor speaks about her stroke. She is a renowned neuroanatomist, author, inspirational public speaker and undertakes brain research. She has enormous knowledge about brain function. In her video, she shares her experiences. One main connection she felt to another human was her mother. After her stroke, she'd lost the ability to communicate. Her mother climbed into bed with her and held her. She felt the connection and the healing love coming from this embrace.

Taylor discovered that when we send a feeling of love vibration to heal and love, we connect to something inside us. It can heal others just by sending healing love and connection through love energy. Connection is who we are.

As I mentioned in a previous chapter, I felt a deep connection with my grandfather when he was sick when I was around 8 or 9 years old. He was in bed sleeping, and I was holding his hand knowing that I could heal him and make him feel better. I didn't understand this at the time. However, my inner guidance new there was something inside me that would help him.

I have had many experiences with spirit, ascendant master and deities. I know when I meditate, I can connect with them. If I need guidance, they are there. I have had experiences with angels. I know that they are real. If I need their help, I can call on them.

I know that my thoughts are linking to my guidance system and to my inner being. These thoughts can be changed in a moment which also alters our vibrational frequency. Every cell in our body has consciousness; like water, like plants, like the universe, like all the elements, we are connected. When we disconnect from this, we don't feel good. When we connect to it, we feel good by connecting to the consciousness either within us or outside us.

Water & Crystal Therapy

Dr. Masaru Emoto, a missionary of water, a researcher from Japan discovered water has consciousness. He has written many books and conducted seminars on his theories of water crystals. He passed away in 2014. However, his research assistant Michiko Hayashi continues his work. I met Michiko at a Global Peace and Happiness Event in India. She is a remarkable woman spreading the message of water. We are water. Michiko and I share a vision, that all human beings be at peace and feel love and happiness. Our cells contain mostly water and that water holds memory. Fascinating isn't if. Our physical bodies are really amazing.

That's why water therapy works so well when we are stressed or tired. A shower after a hard day's work can make us feel better inside. A swim in the ocean is also stimulating as we are connected. It's because we have washed away the stress with water (consciousness). If we meditate either with eyes closed to go into our inner self or with our eyes open. Eyes open meditation is when you're thinking and focusing on the moment, living in the moment and having a joyful experience that connects you to the universal energy. It may happen when you cook a loving meal for your family, paint a picture, colour in, or garden on a sunny day. It's a place of feeling good, deliciousness, calmness, and happiness.

It doesn't matter if you need something symbolic, like a picture of an Indian deity, Jesus, Mary, Buddha, a butterfly or unicorn; it doesn't matter. What matters is your vibrational frequency of inner peace, love and joy. The things that give you the experience of peace, love and joy inside you. Once we find that material totem or symbolic thing that resonates with us, then go for it. Feel it, smell it, taste it, touch it. Use your five senses (channels) to create your inner peace.

We get so caught up in things like, 'I must do sound healing therapy', or 'I need to go to this country to sit in a temple for seven days to feel joy', or 'I need to see Jesus in a church'. We don't have to do that. I am not suggesting that you don't do these things. What I mean is if it makes you feel good and brings you joy then do it. Don't rely on others to fill your spiritual cup. Learn how to do it yourself without looking for something outside of you. All the answers lie withing you. We just need to understand that we can teach ourselves how to align with the universal source energy anywhere. Believe that we all have this inside us. That we can access it by just sitting under a tree in quietness and breath. We each have the capacity to heal, release and live.

Anywhere can start to feel inner-being energy through breath flowing through us. The feeling of lightness gradually drifts within us. Go into the flow and allow it. If you don't allow it, you are in the opposite. You are blocked. Say, "Let it go and let divine energy flow through me."

People who apply focus to a symbol or listen to music will cause their energy to flourish and uplift. The symbol takes the focus away from what they don't want to focus on. Then they move into a flow of energy. It's like the placebo effect (science and spirituality again). If you were given a tablet and told that it will make you feel better, then that's what happens.

This is because we shift our focus to getting better. We believe the tablet can heal whatever we need to heal. For many years people have been going to churches, temples, prayer groups and meditation sessions, just to name a few. It's fine if it makes them feel good and align them with their inner being and if they are filled with wellbeing.

It's not about what you do. If you feel close to Jesus without going to church, don't go unless you want to. If you freely meditate in your own back garden, you don't have to join a meditation session unless you want to. If you were told that a symbol of something will make you feel better, if you looked at it and you have the inner power to inhale that energy then you will do that. It's simple don't you think. A bit like saying, "I have the inner power to turn dirty water into crystal and purify it." Yes! You do. Holy water doesn't fall from the sky. It's blessed by someone who believes in their ability and the receiver believes in their capability also.

It is about how you feel and whatever makes you feel good. You allow whatever it is so you can connect to your inner being. Whether it be; in your lounge room in a favourite chair, under a tree in a garden, wading in sea water, or sitting in your car, if it feels right for you it is. If it takes you to a place of love, peace, and joy you have connected to your true vibrational universal energy.

This is our wellbeing, our true nature of self; our inner self. Some people find going to church soothing and connection where they connect to self. Others it may happen when looking out a window watching a waterfall or bright, perfumed flowers in the garden.

It doesn't matter what you use to get your loving energy to flow. Our conscience, due to other people's wishes and our upbringing, may make you feel like you should attend this or go to that. It is your choice, not theirs if you do.

You do not even need to visualise a symbol. You could meditate on your big toe and if that's what makes you feel the vibrational flow. Meditate in your special place to releases stress and worry. It will make you feel better and calm your mind. Remember, anything (and I mean anything) you use can raise your vibration if you stop resistant thoughts that are not good for you.

Chakras are Golden Gems inside us

Chakras are energy life force meaning 'wheel' in Sanskrit. Energy filters through like a vortex or whirlpool of energy that spirals into our systems. It pushes prana into our spine, channels, muscles, tissues, and cells, creating freedom of lightness and cleansing. If chakras are blocked, energy cannot move through our bodies. Its stays stagnant creating stress and blockages in the body.

There are 107 marma points in our bodies. In some cases, trauma to certain marmas can mean instant death or slow death. This explains a lot when someone is hit on the head or receive trauma to the head, and they die suddenly.

Deformity can be caused if a marma point is damaged or hurt. Severe pain caused through fall or hit are examples of trauma.

Marmas are Ayurvedic energy points which are a vulnerable and sensitive centre where pressure may be applied to release the toxic energy. They are like pressure points of acupuncture and aromatherapy.

These points are the power points of prana or life force which reflex on the surface body. These marmas are proof that we are not just physical but a field of energy. Some of the points control both the physiological and psychological process.

Marmas in the body are the same as the earth. Earth has sacred sites and energy points.

Through the power of gentle touch, medicinal oil there is a natural and traditional healing system. Many different marma points are explained in Ayurvedic text. Through manipulating the marma, prana can be directed releasing and removing blockages, improving energy flow and making a connection with the greater power of life and Mother Nature. Much ancient Vedic knowledge was lost and destroyed when foreign invaders tried to rule India, hence, destroyed ancient Vedic transcripts and people.

The knowledge of marma was part of the path of the warrior who learned to master his prana for both defensive and offensive purposes. It is part of the ancient Vedic code.

According to some information, marmas are places where muscle fibres, ligaments, bones, joints or vessels meet.

We have five elements Air, Fire, Earth, Water, and Universe. These are the elements connecting our five senses; taste, smell, touch, hearing, and sight. The Ayurvedic doshas are Air (Vata), Fire (Pitta) and Earth (Kapha) all are connected to the Universe and water.

We have 72, 000 nadis in our body. According to various ancient and tantric texts, the human body contains this nadis, channelling prana to every cell. Some are wide and rush. Others trickle prana through them. When they flow freely through our bodies, we feel a sense of freedom; we are vital and healthy. When they are week or congested, they struggle. In turn, we have weak mental and physical health.

Our spine is the largest nadi throughout the body, the spine is connected universally. In some meditations they ask you to keep your spine straight, this is to receive and clear the nadi. When we release this from the physical, we can come into the nonphysical; where our true essence lies.

The crown chakra is Earth (Element), known as the Sahasrara (Sanskrit) the crystals are clear quartz, rainbow moonstone, selenite, and amethyst. The crown chakra is our cosmic connection, spiritual communication, universal consciousness, expansion, connection to the divine, source energy, and higher self-awareness. Placing a crystal in a downward position for two minutes will help support and clear blocked energy.

This energy centre (chakra) connects to other dimensions. It's not linked to glands, it controls them. It knows we are connected to everything, no matter what. The crown is where we let go, connecting with everything in the higher consciousness realm. It's where I was connected to when I died, the place we journey to when we leave our physical. It's our waking up and awakening. We are both feminine and masculine energy, knowing and understanding that we have an inner power. Wear your crown to step into bigger power. You must go through all these chakras and clear them while you are living. Heal them, and you can shine your *light*.

When blocked we can feel neck stiffness, foggy brain, low energy, and nervousness. A Shirodhara massage is good for balancing, with meditation, forward bends and cobra pose.

Mantra for this chakra is:

I AM light,

I AM one with (something),

I AM oneness,

I AM divinely guided.

The third eye or (Ajan) is located in the centre of the forehead between the eyebrows. It is the pineal gland which is surrounded by tiny crystals floating in a crystal-clear fluid. It is the size of a small grain of rice and looks a little like the shape of a pineapple.

This is your intuition, if opened you will receive your messages and answers from within. Insight from the higher dimension is received through the third eye. You may be clairvoyant, clairsentience, see visions, past life, or even austral travel when this is open. Combined with the crown chakra, we have an inner knowing of who and what we really are. When opened you release negative energy, increase energy and gain clarity. Whether you are clairvoyant, clairsentient, or claircognizant.

The crystal for this chakra is amethyst or any blue crystal. St Germaine and Arch Angel Michael are the angels for this chakra. It can be unbalanced and give you digestive problems, overeating and appetite problems.

Healing affirmations or mantras for the third eye chakra are:

I AM in Harmony with life,

I AM connected to the universe,

I AM divinely guided at all times.

Make up your own mantra or song, sing it everyday and see what happens. You will feel better and connect with your inner guidance; divine self. Jive your vibe. Dance with your mantra, it will shift your blocked energy and make you feel good.

Golden Gem for your Spiritual Treasure Chest

Write down your own mantra or song to suit your true self. Store it in your Spiritual Treasure Chest for everyday use. For example, I enjoy listening to Ed Sheeran's song *Perfect*. I can feel my heart chakra opening inside when I hear it.

CHAPTER 24

Sound Healing Meditation
Tibetan Singing Bowls

"There is no organ system in the body that's not affected by sound, music, and vibration."

—Mitchell Gaynor.

Discovering sound healing was 'fall into my lap' kind of moment. I loved attending sound healing classes, finding it stimulating and relaxing. This kind of meditation was healing for me. I felt I would receive guidance. Sometimes I would fall into a deep sleep state.

The ancient brain entrainment methodology of Tibetan singing bowls is like Catholics using a church bell. Sound healing has become popular in the spiritual world, for those who are open to it. If you cannot connect openly with your heart, your heart will not receive the true benefit of sound.

Sound is everywhere. However, it is certain sounds that resonate with our hearts. Research and scientific studies have found that if a guitar, for example, can be played at 528 hertz it can connect with our heart. Isn't that amazing? Try sound healing meditation with Tibetan singing bowls. It's a wonderful enlightening experience. I should point out that there needs to be training done before using these bowls as they are of no use if the teacher has no understanding of why or what they are doing with the bowls. It like handing someone a guitar and say now play it. If we are not taught and understand the music and keys we will not play a happy tune. Sound healing and bowls work the same way.

On one of my trips to India, I decided to do a Masters in Gong & Tibetan Bowl Sound Healing Course. Not knowing what to expect, it was the most transformative thing I have ever done. I trained with Shiva Girish from Satyam Shivam Sundaram Goa, India, who is also a Tantra Yoga and Meditation Teacher. His teacher training was what I needed to give me firsthand information about how these wonderful ancient bowls heal our bodies. He taught me unique ways to meditate. Understanding the core principles and experiencing practising of sound was a huge education for me.

The many things I learned were; how Tibetan Bowls work, chakra healing and sound mantra. Using these bowls in my meditation sessions really hits a chord in the heart. Some clients say they have never experienced anything like it. My understanding and knowledge increased as I incorporated Tibetan sound bowl healing with crystal healing, reiki, intuition and channelling. Throw in some high vibe mantras or meditations, angelic music, and you have the recipe to heal within on a very high scale.

I found the key is to speak (counsel) clients first to see where they are at. If a client is open, they will receive a much higher sound healing. It resonates with their heart reaching a hertz of 528.

These hertz have a frequency which resonates with the planet our cells and the universe. Nasa recorded the sun and proved the sun makes sounds like OM. The moon even has its own frequency. How did they know that over thousands of years ago? As I mentioned the sun is masculine energy and the moon is feminine energy.

Instruments played in the right tone, hertz and frequency will strike a chord in our heart that heals. It also resonates on a cellular level; our cells rejuvenate and heal. Cells relax and calm and when this happens. They become happier and start to vibrate at a higher level; cells being part of consciousness. When they hear the sound, they send a frequency to the universe and vice versa. How cool is that?

We hold every thought, emotion, and feeling in our chakras. There are 114 chakras or energy centres throughout our body. Most people have heard we have seven. The human body is complex with its energy form. In addition to the 114 chakras, it works with 72,000 nadis or energy channels, along which vital life force energy flows. As mentioned, this is prana which comes from Mother Earth.

By now you would have more understanding of what we are made of and where we come from. We are connected to everything and everyone, including *EARTH, AIR, FIRE, WATER, and UNIVERSE.* Everything has energy, the words we speak, things we see, the food we taste, sounds we hear, the breath we breathe. Breathe 'prana' shifts just like everything else, inside and outside of us at every moment, every day and every second. If we are awake or become awakened, we can manipulate what doesn't serve our happiness or inner peace.

Your thoughts are made up of energy. If you allow them, they will lower your energy frequency by low vibrational thoughts or actions. As a result, you will become low in energy, tired and stressed. Each chakra spins like a wheel of energy that receives and transmits energy. Chakras are located on major endocrine glands and nerve plexus within our bodies. A chakra is the centre of activity and receives and expresses life force energy 'prana'. Each vital organ is connected to a chakra, meridian, channel etc. You may now understand that when I went into my spirit (nonphysical) that I was becoming the vibrational high frequency that we are all made of. What I mean is our internal organs are connected to energies or life force/ universe. When my major organs were shutting down, I was letting go of the physical to come into the spirit within (nonphysical). As I mentioned earlier, we are both. We are eternal, which is internal.

Each musical note, the seven musical notes and seven colours (rainbow) of the chakra correspond to the chakra's emotional and physical issues attached to them. Sound healing has the power to tap into our chakras and create healing.

Find your tribe and raise your vibe.

The planets play a symphony of sound, vibrating to a frequency. There are seven ascending notes CDEFGA or Do RE MI Fa So La Te. English notes. The highest healing frequency is 528 hertz. Solfeggio frequency or musical notes have boundless healing power. They liberate us from fear and awaken our intuition, even repairing our DNA. We can manipulate and change our DNA through sound healing and meditation.

The natural sound of the universe is 432 Hertz and has cosmic healing powers. In ancient times sound frequency (music) along with dance was used in many cultures as a form of healing or stimulus. Music and dancing make us feel good. Certain songs played will make a person feel like moving or dancing, hence, exercise with music. This opens the channels. Prana will flow easily and freely through the body. Music makes us feel good inside.

As Dr. Emoto's research proved, it's not the sounds or vibrations in the songs it's the words that change the energy vibration, hence, low vibe if low vibe words are sung.

Think about when you last felt like dancing. Where were you and who were you with? Take a favourite song and play it, noticing how you feel. When we reach a feeling of goodness, it's the best time to create and manifest. Notice little children when they hear music, they just want to move their bodies. You were that once.

Make a playlist on your phone of high-vibe songs and music. Start with five or ten songs. Grow your list from there. Listen to them to create and manifesting your dreams. Fill your spiritual treasure chest with your gold gems of music. Do what makes your heart sing, it will come alive. You will feel a sense of freedom and lightness. This feeling belongs to you. Feel it and heal it.

Align yourself with the frequency of peace and love energy. Your GPS or inner guidance will guide you to where the sound frequency needs to go. You will become love energy. For those who think they don't have time, remember it is your mind telling you so. Let it go. Get into the groove of becoming playful and free. Be playful like a child, let your little inner child feel free.

The sixth chakra 426-hertz keynote is A, resonates with the sound of the planets and the universe. It is connected to the universe and receptors in the brain. When stimulated, it can receive divine messages and insight, hence, intuitively. Intuition is to know what your next step is or to have an inner knowing of what to do. The sounds of bells or music will stimulate this chakra; insight and wisdom will be received. The element is kapha's Sanskrit name is Ajna and is located between the eyebrows in the middle of the forehead.

The fifth chakra 384-hertz keynote is G, resonates with communication to self and others. Saying positive things to the inner self and to other people is the best way to pacify this chakra. Also speaking the truth about how you are feeling will also keep this chakra balanced. Being in fear of speaking up will block this chakra. Known in Sanskrit as Vishuddhi or throat chakra.

The fourth chakra, the heart chakra is 528 hertz, resonates with the heart's feelings of love, kindness, forgiveness. This is a powerful healing sound that rejuvenates and replenishes on a cellular level. It's like laughing from the inside. The cells light up and no longer hold stress. Located around the heart area in the middle of the chest, in Sanskrit is known as Anahata.

The keynote is F, and the element air dosha is Vata. It is connected to our nervous system.

The third chakra 320 hertz resonate with the digestive system or fire element. The energy is roaring fire, meaning to have a great digestive system. This sound will help to give your digestion a boost, helping to eliminate waste from the body, reducing toxins. A sluggish digestive system cannot eliminate waste effectively. It is a sound vibration connecting with the digestive system allowing it to rejuvenate the cells and is situated around the navel area. The keynote is F, and the element is Fire (digestion) digestive system

The second chakra 288 hertz and resonates with hip, pelvis or genital area. This is our creative side, where we find ideas, sensual drive and reproduction, knowing who we are and how to use our creative insights. The second chakra helps us to use and develop our creative skills to serve our life purpose. Known in Sanskrit as svadhisthana or sacral.

The first chakra256 hertz resonate with the tip of the spine or coccyx. This chakra is our inner knowledge; knowing. This chakra is for grounding. When we feel disconnected, we sit on Mother Earth to feel a sense of reconnection. The dosha is kapha and is the earth element or Mother Earth connection. It is also connected to the lymphatic system.

Researchers such a Solfeggio and Dr. Leonard Horowitz developed a scale for music for the frequency of sound. The love frequency resonates with the heart. Love frequency can be fundamental to broadcasting all matter and energy into reality, according to the laws of physics. Much like the law of attraction; and law of polarity like attracts like.

If you use Pythagorean mathematics the heart chakra with a hertz of 528 reduces to 6; physical manifestation. Add 5+2+8 equals 15. 1+5 equals 6. 6 is a symbol spiralling from heaven or the universe into the earth, creating the love frequency that resonates all energy and matter. It resonates with the heart. Some people who are said to have died of a broken heart after a loved one has died before them, have their heartstrings stretched too long with the love frequency.

We resonate with sound. We are consciousness. We respond to either high or low, negative or positive, conscious or unconscious; all the same thing. If we change the way we communicate to either ourselves or others, add in some positive prayers and mantras (high vibe), we can vibrate to a frequency that matches the universe. Our fingers, hands and open channels all are interconnected and communicate with the universe. Our frequency within is communicating with a frequency outside. This is amazing. We are amazing. Words have power. Sound has power. Everything around us has power. We just need to learn how to access our power within.

Bliss, love, and light with the angels and spirits

Living with the light is like living in love all the time. Knowing when you're not in your loving state you do not love yourself within. I have inner knowing (clairecognisance and claireaudio) that I have been given knowledge and inner power to help me overcome life (human) challenges, overcoming an obstacle. Each time I do this I survive even the darkest of days. It has made me stronger, and I am more resilient having this knowledge. Once we understand this, we are living a life of happiness. The happiness within us. I know when its my energy or when its someone elses.

It's a step-by-step, day-by-day process keeping aligned. Everyone goes through tough times, however, it is how you perceive and believe that will determine the outcome or action. Remembering to take action when you are in spirit or 'inspired', meaning you are connected to universal laws that will send that back to you. Everything you ask for will come because everything is energy.

I read recently, there are over 650 Million light workers or people who have and enhance psychic ability or can channel spirits and tap into the afterlife. Many don't even know or aren't aware of their abilities. We are energy bodies capable of reaching powerful energy frequencies when we are in a place of peace and love. When we forgive we can access this very easily.

Our energy is our body containing light and lightness. Our light enables us to connect to the highest frequencies and connect with Mother Earth, the Universe, all five elements. It's like the mother and father of Earth and the Universe. We are the children.

Divine Feminine Wisdom is coming through because we have been out of balance for thousands of years (Age of Pisces) which is dominant. The divine feminine is emitting through the moon (especially super moons). It's coming through men and women who say, "We have had enough," (i.e. #MeToo movement.) Wisdom is emerging through our Wisdom Energy which is more powerful than the Masculine Energy. We are both divine feminine and masculine. The masculine is approaching into the feminine divine.

Keep yourself balanced with grace and forgiveness. Come into oneness (empathy, no separation of any living thing) to move into our power, mercy.

Angel energy and cosmic energy is being transported down from higher dimensions. Therefore, people are feeling the change. Information is being transported from angels and spirits through orbs or colours, visions, dreams, audio and inner feelings (clarecogniscence). There are portals of light some people are being drawn to. It's a fantastic and wonderful time to tune into your guides and channels. Orbs of light, light surrounding people or animals in photos; all of it is part of the movement to the higher dimensions. We each have a purpose and a spiritual contract, to serve and bring change; love and peace to the whole planet.

Energies like angels come when we trust. Thinking thoughts, sending them messages and deep knowing, is the key. Faith and trust. Believe and receive. You will be given what is right for you, receiving from angels, spirits, and guides. Have faith, trust, believe, stay in a place of love and peace. Believe we are all connected. These will get you to where you need to be. Feed your soul courage and encouragement, love, and lightness, and you will become that.

Grief is a natural feeling that needs healing

Grief must be mentioned because most people believe grief is what happens with the loss of a loved one; nothing else. To be honest, grief is one the most painful emotions we can experience. We suffer from grief because we do not understand it.

Grief can be debilitating, lower your lifestyle, wellbeing, and wellness. The emotion can be from the sudden loss of a person, relationship or loss of something personal. Whatever it comes from, it is to do with the loss.

Many ancients' scriptures (including Buddhism) write about non-attachment to possessions and people. We need to understand our emotions are what drives our GPS to travel the path ahead, reverse or do a U-turn. The choice is ours.

If we understand nothing is forever in the physical realm, including loved ones, we are eternal beings, then we can appreciate having them in our lives for the time we have. We return to source energy or life force energy (without the physical) when we cross over and unite. Understand, when we came into this world, we were playful, non-judgemental with no expectations or attachment; one day we shall return to that. The key is to accept the way things are; perfect for that moment. Daily change is inevitable.

Let's say you leave your home in the morning, and it is gone when you return (fire, cyclone, flood). If your partner, children, pet; anything that you love and care for was inside, they might be gone too. You'd be devastated. If our loved ones survived such tragedy then our focus would shift to, thank god your are alive. I could have lost you to the fire. Those who cope with such hardships understand their loved ones remain in spirit. When the human or living thing leaves our world as we know it, it's not forever. When some people experience this kind of grief, they will sometimes use it for the higher good and help others by using the loss to empower them and others. When we are in a state of love or loving the memories of a past loved one we are able to connect with their spirit, this is because we come into our spirit of being. An example is Denise and Bruce Morcombe used the death of their son Daniel to help others heal and this has also helped with their healing. People need to learn and believe this to be true. Once this happens, we can connect and communicate with those who have gone before us anytime. Sometimes we see them, though not in the way they had been in the physical sense. We feel and just know that they are there.

On a personal note, the loss of a child that I never met (16 weeks utero) is a particularly difficult form of grief. At the time I was so overwhelmed with sorrow that I fainted a few days later when I was out to dinner. I was taken to the hospital. The next day I saw a specialist in Gynaecology. As soon as he walked into the room, he said, "You need one of these," and he hugged me.

My tears flowed down my pale cheeks, feeling the stinging on my face from the tears still trailing them from the night before. As I lay on the examination table I looked up at the ceiling, and I thought, *how odd*.

There were pictures of racehorses on the ceiling. The walls were green, the ceiling white with the odd mural of racehorses. I didn't understand the logic of the hospital at first. Once I thought about it, I realised it was better than looking at a blank ceiling. I wondered if animals grieved, the thoughts taking me into a place that was preferable to the pain of my grief.

Soon after I had the knowledge, my lost child was a boy. He comes to me in my dreams. I kept the understanding to myself, but they were real experiences whether I shared them or not. He would have been born in August 2000 and be turning 18 as I am writing this book.

A few years after my miscarriage I went to a clairevoyant. There was no mention of this or other things that had happened in my life. She had no idea. Seeing her had been a random idea on the spare of the moment. We had no prior knowledge of each other.

Sitting in her bulky leather chair, I stared at her hands as she shuffled the angel cards. I could see butterflies, angels, horses and beautiful colours. A radiating light illuminated the crystal on the wooden mahogany table between us.

At that moment, my heart filled with love, knowing he was okay. The best of all was gaining clarity that he was a boy. In that instant, I could feel he was there with me. Strangely at the time, I could always feel him with me and around me, just like my grandparents, deities, and angels. I believe they come and go with you until you are okay. Finding the energy changing makes them move on, not forever, they do come back. Depending on our inner energy and whether its aligned with the spiritual realm will depend on whether they are there or not. Therefore, inner meditation and prayer are important in keeping you aligned with the spirit world. It's like when you need them, they are there for us, guiding and looking out for us.

By understanding grief and knowing that we don't lose someone or something, builds awareness of who we really are. We can gain intuitive knowledge and understanding by allowing our heart to open and receive. The heart of the matter is love, from every emotional trauma to every emotive joy. The negative, the positive, each emotion; is here teach us something and help us shift to where we need to be.

Setting up a small shrine or little reminder in a sacred space in your home or somewhere private is a good way to stay connected with loved ones have crossed over. For some a plant, flower or even a tree maybe reminders. I think of my grandparents when I see two butterflies together. I know they are present because I feel them in my heart. A sacred place allows you to feel the person in your heart and that's when they feel a connection in the spiritual realm. The only thing that will prevent a loved one coming into your heart is if your heart is blocked with the low vibration of grief.

It's impossible for low vibration feelings to live inside a heart full of love. I don't mean don't grieve, what I mean is don't let grief take over your life. Crossing over into the spiritual realm is a normal part of the birthing, living, and crossing over. It's part of it, it doesn't mean it's the end. It's the beginning of the understanding of who we are. If life is meant to be about love and not fear then why do we give so much attention to fear, anger, resentment, judgment of self and others? Reminding yourself daily; we are love and peace full of *light*. It is the key to knowing that we have the power within us to connect with the spiritual realm.

Where do you feel your emotions?

We feel our emotions in many ways. They often become pain and illness (disease), however, once we are aware that our emotions are our guidance to our feelings both good and not good. Emotions are energy and if low vibration effect our wellbeing then we feel low if our vibrational energy is low. This is what causes dis-ease. What this means is if your energy is low then you will attract disease, if your energy is high you will be in a state of ease. Love, peace and harmony are the key. They are high vibrational energy feelings. If it feels good do it! If it doesn't feel good then don't do it. SIMPLE ! Your GPS is your intuition guidance, trust, have faith and you will not make a wrong turn. Even if you do, knowing this will always bring you back to a state of high energy vibration. Remember, love, light or hate, anger. Which one do you choose. Knowing we have the inner power to change will prevent, wrong turns, dis-ease and feeling lack of something. Life is about balancing, know when your out of balance and when you are balanced. This is living life of fullness.

A good example is, you may have a headache, an upset stomach or a backache. You may ever experience loss of energy and tiredness. Ask yourself, "What feels good for me?" Your inner guidance kicks in, and you connect with self. It's natural for vibrational energy to flow through us. Be mindful of it. Our emotions are your inner guidance system (IGS) like our GPS, it guides us to where we need to be. Being mindful of when your (IGS) GPS has taken a wrong turn is also a way of getting back on the right path. Knowing when the path is wrong is a good thing. It should not be frowned upon. It is a way to learn who we are and should be celebrated.

The things we think will stop the flow if it doesn't feel good. Change a bad thought like 'anger' to 'calm' and bring yourself back to the feeling of joy and love. Suddenly that headache is gone. And you have returned to loving life force energy.

Finding something to focus on takes our focus away from what we were giving attention to (like a headache) (or a feeling we have been wronged) that was causing the energy not to flow.

When we reach true alignment, we manifest. The universe aligns, and we create. Sometimes we do this with awareness and most times we do it without realising; we create. We are privileged to be able to access much information to help us understand this. Science has now caught up with spirituality and provides the evidence to confirm it. If you listen or read about what psychic, mediums, channellors and many ancient scriptures, you will see that they all say very similar things. We and everything is connected, and we are all psychic, spiritual beings in a physical body. Once we learn this and understand we can bring ourselves back by returning to who we truly are momentarily.

Living in the moment of appreciation, focusing on the present and letting joy flourish through every cell of your being will make you feel good. Focus on things like trees, the sky, and chant, "You give me joy. You give me joy," whenever you feel low or have low vibration. Give it a go. You will be surprised at what changes and energy shifts by saying these words. Remember you subconscious will follow whatever you give it. You will change neurol pathways in your brain and reset your subconscious. The stored data will then change, and you will become that 'Joy'. I AM LOVE is consciousness.

Try not to watch anything negative on TV including the news. Don't read negative low vibe books, magazines or newspaper. It is not our job to judge others. Why would we want to if it lowers our vibration? Why would we want to give our energy away to someone else? Yes! This is true, while we are putting our energy judging or speaking in a low vibration, we are giving a piece of our heart and soul to another.

Another way to lift your vibration is to give gratitude to the universe. Knowing and understanding you are connected to this power will increase your inner power and wisdom. Say something like, "I know you are always guiding me, there for me and supporting me. I appreciate you continually looking down on me. I also acknowledge my connection with plants by saying you give me joy."

Look to the stars or moon and say the same statements. Affirm with yourself (inner-being) that you know and acknowledge you are connected. "I understand the *light* does not come down to the shadow. I understand that the *light* rises upwards." This shows you are affirming to the universe that you trust and have faith. You are being heard.

Our emotions are either low vibrational frequency or high vibrational frequency; all energy. We are made of energy and 80% water. Water has consciousness which is energy. Every word, we speak, think or write is putting something out as high or low frequency. Words or emotions (listed below) are low vibrations and low energy. If you are experiencing any of these feelings, you need to rethink those thoughts from negative to positive:

Annoyed	Fear Guilty	Bored	Concerned
Harassed	Irritated	Hesitant	Embarrassed
Intimidated	Anger	Impatient	Cautious
Exhausted	Destructive	Confused	Hostile
Envy	Greed	Miserable	Grief
Sad	Stress	Used	Shame
Ignored	Suspicious	Pressured	Jealous
Panic	Isolated	Wasteful	Weary
Tired	Disappointed	Anxious	Revenge
Lonely	Shocked	Frustrated	Guilt

Using low vibrational frequencies day to day to communicate lowers consciousness to almost unconsciousness. All the above words carry a frequency of low vibration.

To help you understand the frequencies better if we all reached a higher level of consciousness, we could effectively counterbalance those vibrating negatively. Dr. David R Hawkins devised a system of levels of consciousness. The more we learn about the scale, the better our understanding to bring peace to the world. This also benefits the planet; even global warming would ease. Shift consciousness moves the planet into peace and harmony. For example, by saying plastic is not good for the planet, it becomes just that. Find ways that uplift.

Scale frequencies Enlightenment down to Shame

Enlightenment (the very top) - frequency 700-1000

Self-realisation and divinity where only the deities and sages the likes of Buddha, Jesus, Mohammed, Shiva, Krishna have scaled. The highest consciousness humans can attain. They probably have an aura that affects others. People can feel their inner-peace and serenity.

Peace - frequency 600

Reaching beyond the limit of human experience and knowledge. Very few people attain it possible one in ten million. Some people who have experienced near death may reach this level during the experience, possibly enabling them to draw on it later. In this state, some people leave society to ensure their eternal bliss.

Joy - frequency 540

A state of persistent happiness, like spiritual teachers and saints. They operate on a higher level and make those around them feel their joy.

Love - frequency 500

Have an unshakeable belief in their connection to everything. They share compassion, love, kindness through their hearts. Most will give lifelong service to humanity, such as Mother Teresa, Dalai Lama and Gandhi. This is totally pure with lack of ego (low vibration).

Reason - frequency 400

Lucid, rational thinkers like scientists and doctors. They have surpassed the lower frequencies and contribute to the world with their theories and research. Einstein was one of these.

Acceptance - frequency 350

These are people exploring possibilities after having a shifting in their thinking. Setting new goals, changing jobs, moving towns, following long-held dreams. They have a willingness to use their abilities for good use and often to help others.

Willingness - frequency 310

People who are finding the knowledge of their thoughts and energy. They are disciplined and organised to achieve and manage all aspects of their lives in a peaceful way.

Neutrality - frequency 250

As the frequency suggests, they don't take sides. It doesn't bother them putting them sometimes in a place of imprudence or lethargy. They have little need to verify or prove anything, taking care of their wants but aren't that motivated.

Courage - frequency 200

At this stage, people look forward to their future rather than looking back at their past. They have the strength to pursue life-changing choice and are not overawed by their steps. They enjoy change.

Pride – frequency 175

Like ego, you feel good, but it is not a true feeling. You may have material things, power, fame, accolades that make you believe you are right about the way you live your life, the religion you choose, the things you believe in and force them on others.

Desire – frequency 125

Not the desire to do with goals, this is more about addictions. Desires for unnecessary things, like alcohol, cigarettes, food, lust, and fame; materialism. Desire can be good if it uplifts you. It can assist with rising above other low vibrations.

Fear – frequency 100

Fear holds us back from the good things in life. As I have said fear paralysis us, blocking our chakras. We don't want the fear, abuse or whatever it is but are unable yet to rise above it.

Grief – frequency 75

The consuming loss of loved one or self. You cry easily, feel sick in the stomach and can't think or function properly. You can be depressed and yearn for what you have lost.

Apathy – frequency 50

Helplessness often caused by victimisation or circumstances. You may be stuck in a situation you see no way out of like poverty.

Guilt – frequency 30

You feel you have sinned. You cannot see past your wrongdoings to fix them. Along with shame, you may have suicidal tendencies or suffer with depression.

Shame – frequency 20

Realising you have contemplated suicide and seriously considering it. You hold deep self-hatred. You feel you are not worthy of anything good in your life.

Anger – frequency 20

You may still be afraid or hold resentment that you haven't dealt with, some hatred. You tend to be angry because whatever you are wanting is not being met.

It is said through Dr. David Hawking's research that humanity's consciousness frequency shifted considerably during the tragic events of September 11, 2001, and before that with the Harmonic Convergence of 1987.

Each time something bad happens, we react differently. Some put their thoughts and energy into good things with reasoning and acceptance. The people at the bottom of the frequency of love scale deal with such things with fear, anger, apathy and can become self-destructive or harm others. Most of us may be marginally below 200, but we can always work towards gaining higher spiritual frequencies by practising all the things I have explained in this book. Mindfulness, kindness, containment of thoughts, acceptance, forgiveness, meditation, Ayurvedic therapies, sound healing, yoga, dancing, exercise, appreciating Mother Earth and enjoying joy and peace. So, I have shown you the scale from anger to grief, what about the other side of the scale?

Ancient text and scriptures can also cause us to become certain frequencies because they are calibrated within certain ranges. For instance; the Bible calibrates at 475 on average, though parts of it calibrate much higher, depending on whether it be psalms, proverbs or revelations. All teachings have some level of calibration. This is why miracles can occur when people truly believe in the text and the thoughts they evoke.

The Koran, before the fall of Mohammad, resonates at 700 and so do other texts, scripts or declarations of peace.

Anyone who reaches 600 or above transcends self-realisation. A Tibetan abbot once said that Peace is of the greatest importance in our world today. In the absence of peace, we lose what we have gained. In the presence of peace, all things are possible: love, compassion, and forgiveness. Peace is the source of all things. This is also the level of kinesiology.

Source: Dr. David Hawkins numerous books and seminars including Power Vs. Force and Dr. Hawkins June 28, 2003, Sedona Seminar.

Golden Gems for your Spiritual Treasure Chest

I love giving you Golden Gems.. Have you found the inner light? It's a sense of lightness. It feels like letting go in the moment. Let go of ego, "Let it go". I love this saying and sharing it with my clients. In saying this, ego can be used for good, such as confidence. This is ego. And we need confidence sometimes to push us through fear.

My four-year-old granddaughter sings, "Let it go." I don't think she understands the meaning; however, it brings joy. I sing it in workshops and retreats. There is a song from *Frozen* the children's movie 'Let it Go,' sung by Demi Lovato that has resonated with many. I encourage my clients to research the words of the song on Google. It's a great song. The word 'let it go' is a way to release negative emotion from your body. It's very effective and works well for many people.

There are so many animated children's movies and songs written in a way to teach. Many have soulful songs to touch our hearts. These are songs that recharge the spiritual soul, like delicately gently applying a massage to the soul. It is a great concept to teach these songs to children. The more they are sung, the more consciousness will shift. *Frozen* and *Inside* Out *are two com*ing to mind. I enjoy them both, and so do my grandchildren.

CHAPTER 25

How to find your spiritual place
Finding your spirituality, trusting your intuition and having faith

"A single conversation across the table with a wise man is better than ten years mere study of books."

—Henry Wadsworth Longfellow

Intuition to me means 'into you' INTU-I-TION. Allow your intuition to guide you. Let the sharp ideas flow, increasing your intuition with meditation; helping to your Spiritual Path.

The heart said, *"Love me."*

The soul said, *"Light me up."* Sing, "This little heart of mine, I'm gonna let it shine"

"It's time to *create*," said the soul.

The heart said, "I am with *you*. I hear you. I feel you. I see, touch and taste you."

When I teach Intuitive Classes, I remind people who they truly are. I discuss how you can manifest whatever you want once you are in tune (intuitive). People will come to you, showing up for you when you need them. Trusting and having faith is the key.

All your answers lie within you. Trust your gut feeling, inner guidance (IGS). If you are not feeling love then this is your intuition telling you its not right for you. The sensation of fear feels like a pull in the lower stomach, a heavy heart or a feeling of nausea. Our digestion is affected if it is not aligned. There are neurotransmitters in our lower tummy. They are there for a reason. Trust this feeling. If it doesn't feel good inside, then it's not going to be good. If your heart lights up with the feelings of love when you need answers then this is who you are and what you are meant to do. If it is not you have the answer. Trust your inner being. It knows the answers. Have faith and you can have and do anything your heart desires. Your third eye is deeply connected to this, and if out of balance we cannot receive loving divine messages from above.

The pineal gland (Third Eye) receives sharp ideas or intense answers and insight. They may come when you wake up in the morning when are walking or during meditation.

As I have said, "Wake up and awaken." Morning is the best time to receive because a rested mind is refreshed, the sun is out and your third eye will open easily. Do sun salutations (yoga). Once we know what we desire, we can inspire with inspirational action. Such as; I now feel what I want in my heart. I can see, touch, smell, feel it etc. 'In spirit' is being spiritual, trusting your inner spirit and receiving. Just like the universe; what you put out you will obtain.

Try this;

- Get comfortable by sitting or lying down.
- Start with breathing into 'you', feeling your inner being.
- Calmly and gently respond.
- Let go as you breathe.

It may take a couple of times before you really feel the inner you (separate from your mind). Allow your breath to take hold of your inner being by letting it connect. Use the power of your breath. Exhale toxins as you breathe out. Breathe in peace and love as you inhale. Plants and Mother Earth will purify your toxins and allow you to inhale purity (purification). As life-giving air enters your body allow it to feel freedom and lightness. You will begin to relax further, feeling calm and letting go of your thoughts.

Your body will feel gentleness and *light*. Scan your body piece by piece as you let go. Come into your heart by commanding your breath into your heart, visualising Mother Earth green being transmitted into your heart. At this point ask your intuition for insight on your next step. Ask, what is it you need to do? If you wish to continue, draw energy into your spine, the largest nadi in the body. Nadis are channels carrying prana or *life force* into our bodies, including cells. As you feel energy flowing through your body, don't second guess what is happening. Just keep going. Feel the shift. A connection with self will occur, as the mind lets go. Sometimes when I do so, I almost fall asleep. A similar feeling you are aiming for. Like the sensation moments before you sleep; you are neither asleep or awake. This is you.

I found that not all Ayurvedic Training Centres deliver what they say they do. The centres I resonate with are Greens Ayurveda and School of Panchakarma and Ayurveda, Kannur. Before you enrol in any Ayurvedic Courses, kindly make sure of the following features (I include these on my website):

- Do they have a true Ayurvedic hospital with all panchakarma procedures? Are their participant's genuine patients – Outpatient & inpatient?
- Do they conduct theory & practical classes by trained and experienced Ayurvedic doctors?
- Do you have practical classes at the hospital where you will be studying, where patients are not only being treated daily but also residing there too?
- Do they manufacture their own Ayurvedic classical medicine by traditional (vaidyas) Ayurvedic pharmacists?
- As a student do you have a chance to observe and examine the genuine patients in the presence of a qualified doctor (who will aid in your learning)? Is the centre approved by the Government? How many foreigners have studied here? Read their reviews, if any.
- Is the place like Greens Ayurveda, Ayurvedic School, Panchakarma and Ayurveda, where students come from all continents? Does it come highly recommended by former students?

Program Highlights (you should be looking for):

The opportunity to experience & train in most procedures after each theory class. Unique hands-on training enables you to master your skills. You should learn creative techniques and be able to have a full comprehension of the materials. Self-experiencing as a specimen patient as well as healer allows you to dedicate yourself and enable you to have a subjective feeling as a patient. All the classes should be conducted by Ayurvedic medical doctors. Treatments performed by certified Panchakarma therapists will be overseen by resident doctors. Practical and theory courses should be conducted directly by doctors.

As a successful student, you should then be capable of conducting, applying and managing all varieties of treatments. Certificates are awarded after the successful completion of training Ayurvedic lifestyle consultant

- Fundamentals and basics of Ayurveda
- Panchakarma
- Rejuvenation therapies
- Massage Shirodhara, different treatments
- Marma massage
- Medicine manufacturing
- Ayurvedic pharmacy
- Ayurvedic Nutrition and cookery program
- Lifestyle management and yoga.

Yoga meditation courses should provide a practical understanding of the relationship between spirit and energy matter. They should also teach ancient yogic philosophies, an important component of yogic studies. The vedas should also be taught. Remembering Ayurveda comes from deities, the vedics who were here before us. There are many ascendant masters from countless cultures, Australian Aboriginal, Chinese Philosophy, there are many. Polynesian (Hawaiian) is another. Maori songs are soul songs. Look at the Haka, it's made global impact putting New Zealand's culture and music out there, showing the world their ancient tribal philosophies.

You should perhaps think about study where scriptures and philosophies are treasured and passed down, just like many other cultures. Many overlap by using similar ancient plant medicines to heal the body, rejuvenate and replenish. Ayurveda is one of them. There are countless. Whether it be bush medicine in Australia, Plant Medicine in Bali or Ayurvedic Medicine in India. Its all here for us to share and heal. Live a healthy life of fullness.

I hope in time I will have the opportunity to research several other cultures and comprehend similarities. Living in Bali has given me insight, broadening my perspective on ancient traditional healings.

Where you decide to study should also deliver an understanding of the interplay between souls, divine and the material world. The series of classes in my course facilitate your inward journey efficiently and effectively. You should learn about:

- Consciousness and self-realisation
- Connection and relationship with Goodness (God) or the Universe. Just look up!
- The law of attraction- Use inspired action. Feel the inspiration in your heart; the universal law.
- The tree of life
- A spiritual lifestyle – Understanding we are all physical (material) and spiritual (loving).

Other things your study should explore:

- Make time & space for meditation to establish a daily practice. This is part of giving to yourself and loving yourself-care. Take time to be with you. You are the master.
- Harness your thoughts, emotions, and responses. Be the rider of your thoughts. Take hold of your reins and give directions. Remember your thoughts don't know fantasy from reality.
- Use your meditation skills in everyday life, five minutes morning and night. Just do it! Find your place of peace, breath into your body and discover the true feelings of you. Eventually, your mind will follow. Fear will no longer be in the driver's seat. Our change is on the inside, not what's outside.

Learning how to overcome anger

Anger is an expression of inner pain; an indication that all is not well in your world. It is one of the most powerful and destructive emotions. How can you change the anger within and use your energy in more positive ways? Learn how to:

- Understand the stress process and how to redirect your stress in a positive way
- Realise the power of your thoughts in dealing with stress
- Let go of inner pain by allowing yourself to feel it, then release it with ease.
- Use spiritual knowledge and awareness to transform stress

- Develop a range of practical tools (golden gems)to live a more peaceful life

Learning positive thinking is beneficial

There are various courses for those who are not sure that they are ready for meditation but would like to understand the workings of the mind better. If you want to gain greater clarity and learn how to manage your thoughts, such a course may be for you.

Look for workshops or classes that teach mind body and spiritual side of things. In my experience, if you focus on the physical, the benefits are with your physical. If you focus on the mind, they benefit the mind, and so on.

Find classes and teachers that focus on the three components; mind, body & spirit. You will gain an understanding of what's going on inside as opposed to what's going on in the outside. Like the planet, how can the planet heal if we just focus on what's outside? We need to shift focus on the way we think about our planet, Mother Earth. To do that, we change our way of thinking about the planet or Mother Earth. Your mind is just matter and our world matters!

Benefits include:

- Becoming a master of your thoughts and feelings. Mastermind means just that, become the master of your mind.
- Applying the gentle art of self-reflection and encourage personal growth
- Tapping into the natural positivity of the mind
- Finishing negative, energy-draining language and self-talk
- Developing a constantly positive attitude and feelings
- Know and discover your positive self and your power within.
- Accept yourself, identifying personal strengths, abilities, and uniqueness. You are perfect as you are.
- Develop effective strategies for building healthy relationships, letting go of fears and aggression
- Empower yourself, making the right choices to maintain inner balance

Stress-free living

Stress has been identified as a leading cause of many health problems. Largely psychological, rather than physical in origin and therefore much more difficult to prevent and remedy. Modern stress affects nearly all of us at some point in our lives. Regardless of its origins, stress drains your physical, emotional and mental energy. Learning to free your mind is the key. I remember listening to an Ayurvedic doctor in one of her lectures and she said, "Now that many people are becoming vegan the price of vegetables has increased. For the rich they can afford to pay for any food increases, so they tend to overindulge, then stress about their health problems because of weight increase. Where poor people stress about the price increase because they cannot afford it." Interesting don't you think? Both are at risk of health problems due to stress.

Learn how to:

- Identify different forms of stress and the effects it has on our wellbeing
- Identify the triggers of stress and how and why we react
- Use practical (golden gems) to enable inner change
- Move from fearing change to embracing it

I hope that these guidelines will help you choose the best course for your spiritual path. Trust your inner-being and inner guidance on the most suitable place for you to study. You are then sure to find your happy study place like I found mine.

Looking after yourself from within is an important portion of the spiritual transitioning process. For those who are awakened and understand frequency, may have been experiencing this change from birth. People like that can have unexplainable fatigue due to dealing with low vibrational or third dimensional, causing conflict within. It can be unsettling, causing friction in the body. Some may go through of feelings of knowing they don't belong here. For them, once they have the knowledge, it is a relief. Recognising that consciousness or spiritual awakening is moving quickly, rising high with the frequency of freedom, love, peace, and compassion, just to name a few, is paramount. Applying universal laws will provide an understanding of this shift or awakening.

Exercises

- Have you researched places and courses before beginning your studies?
- Do you dream of somewhere you believe you should study? Where is it? Describe what it looks like.
- From the lists above write down the five things you want to learn most, then when you are sourcing your happy study place, you'll know what core things you need to tick off.

CHAPTER 26

Books and People who influenced my life
Don't let your exploration stop with this book

"A teacher affects eternity; he can never tell where his influence stops."

—Henry Adams

Many people have influenced me in my studies and spiritual path. I recommend you study some of these inspirational people who are healers, teachers, yogis, inspirational speakers, and incredible human beings.

Years ago, someone who I had known through a mutual friend gave me the self-help book *The Monk Who Sold His Ferrari* by Robin Sharma. What a book! When I read it, I thought, that's me I wrote this book. There are others just like me who feel the same or have had life-changing experiences that have brought them into themselves with awareness and knowing. Louise Hay, *You Can Heal Your Life* is like the bible. I share it with my clients.

Others are; Wayne Dyer, *Change Your Thoughts Change Your Life* and *Ayurvedic Book on health and wellbeing*. *The Alchemist* was given to me by one of my clients a young German gentleman who was studying Ayurveda. He also gave me testimonial in the next chapter, coincidentally he bequeathed my name 'Kerry the Healer". Such a sweet soul and a pleasure to do a spiritual guidance and healing session with.

People always present themselves when they are meant to. I call them either angels of light; angels of learning. Whatever they are they are all here to take you to where you are meant to be.

Others who have influenced my spiritual journey

I'd like to share with you some people, videos and books I suggest you explore to find your own light:

People

- Jill Bolte Taylor – American neuroanatomist, author, stroke survivor, and inspirational public speaker. Studied severe mental illness to understand the brain.
- Dr. Masaru Emoto - Japanese author and water researcher. He believed water has consciousness. YouTube video.
- Louise Hay - Author, motivational speaker, healing with affirmations and Founder of Hay House Publishing. Use her affirmations in life.
- Oprah – Celebrity, and philanthropist. She has come from trauma too. I remember when she gave a talk about the little inner voice, which I interpreted as my inner child or the voice within all of us.
- Deepak Chopra – Talks and meditations
- Abraham Hicks - YouTube talks
- Anita Moorjami - Facebook and YouTube talks
- Hay House Radio
- https://www.meetup.com/Spiritual-Self-Transformation-Southampton-PA/pages/14224572/Dr_David_R_Hawkins _Levels_of_Consciousness/ccording to Dr. Hawkins' system the average human consciousness on the planet right now is just below 200, yet the collective human consciousness is above this line. This paradox is because the people vibrating at a much higher level of consciousness along this scale helps to counterbalance the majority of others vibrating below 200.
- The scale advances logarithmically. For instance, one person vibrating at love, which is 500 on the scale, counterbalances 750,000 individuals below the line, while one enlightened person at 700 counterbalances 70 million others below the line!

Videos

- *PLANTS can SPEAK! WATER has memory. The universe is conscious! Scientific PROOF!* - https://youtu.be/e_mjkb74Hqo
- *The Science of plant consciousness* - https://youtu.be/YND9UHjv7Jg
- Thoughts are energy. Use them wisely (law of attraction) -https://youtu.be/ySonf2ysDS8
- *The hidden power of plants-* https://youtu.be/BsWQck8vXJA
- *Scientists find Australian berry to cure cancer* -https://youtu.be/Yti2w1hBcZg
- *Australian Cancer Cure - In 48 Hours* by BlushwoodBerry- https://youtu.be/1iDYhNR5t2k
- *The Neuroscience of Consciousness* – with Anil Seth - https://youtu.be/xRel1JKOEbI
- *Mind Science Kept Hidden Documentary-* https://youtu.be/fSGONup-CYE
- *The FORMULA to MANIFEST ANYTHING* (edit)*Law of ATTRACTION Meditation* -https://youtu.be/6j57w-CGios
- *The Beginning of Everything, The Big Bang-* https://youtu.be/wNDGgL73ihY
- *Amazing Laws of the Universe* - https://youtu.be/8YgZMC0sALM
- *'Heaven is for Real' raises questions on faith* - https://youtu.be/Y4iV27yR5bU
- *Your Power is beyond Measure* by Abraham Hicks - https://youtu.be/hcakNbMkD-g
- *Discover your power - The art of being the full being that you are* by Abraham Hicks - https://youtu.be/AbcGLp1vPl4
- *Observe others, but don't get Involved* by Abraham Hicks - https://youtu.be/sM-opa97hj4
- *Heal Documentary-* available on Amazon
- Hay House Radio has a free app to download. It is really grounding as healers and psychics from all over the World share information and connecting with those in need. Feeling grounded keeps me connected to my inner spirit.

Books

- *Understanding the laws of the Universe brings certainty* by Abraham Hicks
- *Near Death Experience NDE - The Life After Death Explained* by Mark Janniro
- *Power Thoughts 365 Daily Affirmations* by Lousie Hay
- *The Book of Ayurveda: A Holistic Approach to Health and Longevity* by Judith H. Morrison
- *The Ayurvedic Cookbook* by Amanda Morningstar with Urmila Desai Personalised guide to good nutrition and health.
- *Change your thoughts, Change your life* by Wayne Dyer
- *You can heal your life* by Louise Hay
- *Angel Cards* by Doreen Virtue
- *The power of now* by Eckhart Tolle

CHAPTER 27

Testimonials
People who have been healed by Kerry Clancey

"The greatest healing therapy is friendship and love."
—Hubert H. Humphrey

These people have either been clients through my spiritual counselling, channelling, reiki, crystals or chakra healings. There testimonials give me great joy in the fact that I have helped these people in their lives.

Brandon, California, USA

"Kerry the Healer, or my 'spiritual mother' as I know her, is one of the most beautiful, kind, and loving souls I have ever had the honour of connecting with. She and I met during our 200-hour yoga teacher training in Bali where we were clearly drawn to, in order to meet and have the healing I had from her. I approached her one day after she had shared with the group that she was a reiki healer. I asked to have a healing done, not knowing what was in store for me. The next thing I knew, I was laying on her massage table in her healing room with crystals on my chakras preparing for the experience that would forever change my life. To recount the entire experience would be like writing a miniature book but to summarize; I was transported to another world within myself. A world where Kerry, in spiritual form, guided me through my own heart while slicing negative energetic chords anchoring me in negative, destructive emotional patterns. She helped me heal the relationship with my mother, with my adopted sister, and with myself. To say that it was the most profound experience of my life would be an understatement. My heart was blasted open and I realized that I was a being of infinite love, who is worthy of being loved and deserving of the self-love I never properly gave myself. Kerry has continued to be a guide in my life for many years now. She has helped me adjust back to the world after the healing. She is someone that I would trust my life with and could only recommend 1,000,000 times over to anyone who is genuinely in need of healing. She has helped heal my terminally ill aunt, who is now on the way to recovery, as well. I could go on and on about how incredible she is, but you will just have to experience it yourself. Thank you will never be enough to Kerry for the healing and understanding she gave me through her treatment. I love you Kerry and can't wait to see you again soon."

Sophiee, London UK. (December 2015)

"I met Kerry purely by chance, or by what I thought was chance, on a bus back from the Gili islands to Ubud (in Bali, Indonesia). When sitting next to her my whole body felt alive and active. I felt butterflies in my stomach, my arms and legs had pins and needles in them. I didn't know what the reason was. As we travelled to Ubud, I thought she was carrying some new high-tech aura cleaning device transmitting electronic signals or something. We then started talking and she told me all about her family, life and what she did.

She said casually in the conversation, 'I practice Reiki. I channel Angels.'

As soon as she said the word 'angels', I knew she was connected to something amazing. Her energy radiated to me making me feel warm and comforted, something I hadn't felt in a long time; it wasn't an electronic man-made signal I was feeling throughout my body but the sensations of pure goodness; Angels. I knew it was.

"When she left the bus the tingling sensation left my body and so did the butterflies; it was incredible. I knew I had to see her, I was in awe of her energy and beautiful spirit.

"A week or so later I saw Kerry for my first reiki sessions and the experience was unreal. I mean unreal because it's something I can't describe in words because I feel like what I felt and experienced can't be described and everyone will be so different when undergoing reiki because we are all so different.

"However, I can say this, the most powerful thing that happened during this reiki session was a connection to something higher than myself, Angels. I felt them and heard them. I closed my eyes during my reiki session, so I couldn't see, because my brain wanted to look to see that it was something touching me or breathing slowly beside me. But I refused to let it happen because I knew I had to put my belief into something else rather than myself and my brain for once. Thus far in my life, it hasn't helped me at all; always thinking through my mind.

"Seeing Kerry has given me this complete shift in my life. She has taught me so many things and I have had many experiences that I cannot describe how magical and out of this world they are. Most importantly, through reiki and Kerry's guidance, I have started to love myself, others, nature, and God. I now realise I am never alone, ever, and the Angels, and now, of course, Kerry, will always be there to help me and support me throughout my life no matter what happens.

"Thank you, Kerry, for everything, so much love for you and all you do ♡Lots of love, Sophieeeeee."

Poem written by Sophie for Kerry

When an Angel calls

"I didn't know she was an Angel, as she sat next to me on the bus, I didn't know she was an Angel until she opened her mouth,

I didn't know she was an Angel until she spoke her words,

Of God (Universe). Something from another time and place, I felt it in my stomach. I felt it in my heart, she was a god sent gift, an Angel at heart. Her words were kind, her soul was pure, she was a beautiful human being that for sure, I will never forget the day she grace me with her presence, she was a messenger from GOD. A soul worthy to be sacred and cherished, just like you and just like I, We all are, we all carry the message and power. We just have to find trust and believe it" Sophie UK.

Jorge, Spain (July 2016)

"Dear Kerry,

"Meeting you has been a great experience for me. I came to India looking for Ayurvedic knowledge and found an experience beyond my expectations. As I told you, I am a very mind focused person and meeting you has been a great gift for me. You have really helped me to open my heart, my chakra heart, and link it with the rest of my body, mind, and soul. Thank you so much for the healing session. It was a great chance to find the love inside me and spread it around the world and the universe. And I thank you for the kind and valuable task you are spreading around the world. The world needs more people like you, flowering and loving endlessly; helping other people to heal or find their own path in life. With all my love, Jorge x"

Chloe, London, UK (March 2016)

"I had never had any spiritual healing practiced on myself, so didn't know what to expect. However, after Kerry completed a crystal healing session with me it was evident, she was able to clear any chakra blockages and tap into negative emotions I was holding onto. I came away feeling lighter, happier and more mentally prepared for life's next adventures. I would recommend this for anyone stress/anxiety, or is curious to discover one's spiritual self xx"

Id, Bali, Indonesia (February 2016)

"I had a healing with Kerry. As soon as she placed the crystals on my heart my heart started beating fast. I felt so blissful and happy. My body was relaxed, and I felt I was with my divine. My third eye opened up. I felt my head being tilted and divine cosmic energy was being filtered through my whole body. My mind was free of thought as the energy flowed through my body. I saw a bright light which was flowing with me and beside me. This was a truly divine enlightened experience for me; pure happiness. Thank you so much, Kerry."

Maja, Germany (April 2016)

"I can highly recommend Kerry's energy healing massage! Kerry is an unbelievably nice and warm person! From the first moment on I felt so connected to her. I could confide all my problems to her. She opened all my chakras with energy and the help of angels and crystals. I felt the energy flowing in all parts of my body. That was an incredible feeling! Thank you, Kerry."

Laurens, Germany (June 2016)

"I had an amazing healing experience with Kerry this morning. Kerry, you opened up my heart and my soul. During your healing I felt something I cannot describe. For the last year, my brain was totally blocked until now, right now after the healing my brain is totally free. Kerry opened up the space and I am now flowing. My life starts to flow again, like a river which goes deep into the sea. Thank you so much, Laurens."

Matthew, Australia (2018)

Just by walking through the door I can feel the healing effect that Kerry has on me. No doubt have I felt better within myself after seeing Kerry or being involved in one of her sessions, Thank you Kerry

Ruth, Australia (2018)

Kerry's beautiful heart meditation class was the first time I met Kerry it has really opened me up to living in heart and choosing love in all moments. Attending Kerry's workshops has helped me follow and tap into my intuition and understand the power we have to heal ourselves sooo much gratitude and love for you!!

CONCLUSION

This book contains over fifty years of learning, knowledge and experiences I have lived through. My hope is that you read this and become empowered. I want you to believe that you have an inner power that can be accessed anytime, anyplace and anywhere.

Through understanding that you are life force energy and part of universal energy, you will come into alignment of who you truly are.

My near-death experience was not because I was to experience death, but to experience life; to experience what life has to offer. This allowed me to live a fruitful life filled with happiness, joy and inner peace. If this book changes just one person's life and inspires them to motivate others, I have made a difference.

It is not my aim to force others to believe. My purpose is to inspire others to become stirred by their own motivations. To use inspired action to move forward with a feeling of I know who *I AM*.

Remembering who we are and returning to that, is the key to feeling happier within. Whether it be meditation, breath work, sound healing, yoga, exercise, being around happy people, whatever it is; make sure you have a satisfying experience daily, with self or others.

Unwind inside. Put your attention to the inner world inside you. Release stress, stressing less sets you up for the day. Whatever meditational, mindfulness, transcendental, angelic, sound or guided, whatever resonates with you on a cellular, vibrational level will guide you to where you need to be.

Use mantra sounds to lift your inner vibration. Feel inside you as the sound transmits into your cells. These are all thousands of years old techniques. Experience your inner self. This is the key. Don't rely on others to fill your spiritual cup. Depend on your inner self-being. It knows the answers for you.

For me; I have become an eagle totem during meditation where I fly high across continents. Buddha has blessed me and sent me divine messages. Angels have sheltered and hugged me. My deceased grandparents have communicated with me countless times. Deities from India have showered me with gold coins. Shiva has placed his spirit body inside my physical body. I have been a Hawaiian dancer and angelic energy floating in the universe. You can access all this if you open your heart. I have seen unicorns.

I have felt severe emotional pain from other's hearts. Communicating with spirit world taught me how to go in and access my inner child.

Mother Earth has a message I want to include in this book. The creator/divine/God gave us a beautiful planet, with abundant food, love, and fresh air. It was man who slowly placed unwanted vessels into her. She feels it. Her pain is projected through, earthquakes, floods, volcanos, and other natural disasters.

Imagine if you are a mother. Someone puts cigarettes out on your outer core, throws plastic at you and pours harsh chemicals over your body. How would you feel? The good thing is Mother Nature has the capacity to heal through consciousness and positive messages. Put out positive messages to the universe that are uplifting, healing, loving and peaceful, to everything and everyone. Soon that what will be created.

Include plastic and chemical. If we keep putting negative messages about them it is harmful to Mother Nature. Create something positive by an optimistic message or a constructive idea. Create a sustainable program or invention that will improve Mother Earth. It will help to continue the expansion of consciousness.

We are all going to be awakened, enlightened and our psychic abilities with be heighten. By 2025 we will be using our psychic abilities more. Many of us will communicate more through thought than speech.

Thanks

I thank all the beautiful people in the previous chapter, who took the time out of their lives to send me a testimonial. Helen even sent me a lovely drawing. I also thank them for allowing me to help them heal or to teach them in some way. I too heal in the presence of others. All these interconnections with people are what creating love, peace and joy is all about. It is what I am all about; the way to find your *light*.

In the future co-creating, sharing knowledge with others is what I hope people will do. If it wasn't for the numerous wonderful people who came into my life, I would have been unable to write this book. When I cleared and cleaned up my stuff, I realised I could do anything. The past is past and the new is always coming. However, *live each day and allow the flow of ease and grace* is a message I share with you.

We are in a state of change. Everything has not been in alignment is the past. The new paradigm will come into a place of love, peace, and harmony. Let go and forgive. Don't hold darkness or low frequency inside. It's time to release and be at peace.

Mankind is moving into higher dimensions, carrying understanding of the new paradigm. It carries loving, kind, harmonious vibration. As we awaken, we will heal within. Only then will the planet reconcile. Through receiving this knowledge, we will gain wisdom.

If everything is not aligned with the new paradigm, businesses will collapse. Materialism and greed will cause those who are consumed by it, excessive emotional pain. The heavens have opened their portals and the planets have aligned with the frequency of peace and love. Darkness is being cleansed. Every dark energy (low frequency) is being cleansed.

We will all feel the change sometime in the next seven years. By 2032 the planet will be cleansed and in harmony. For all those who would like to live in peace and harmony, you will. For those who don't then they won't. Be inspirit. Be inspired and inspire others to do the same. I AM SELF – I AM LIGHT !!

I believe we all have something to contribute to our planet. When we find it, we can make a difference, not just ourselves but others as well.

Life can be a party. Life can be a blissful state or celebration.

Your choice, NAMASTE!

AUTHOR BIO

– Kerry (the healer) Clancey

Author, Writer, Ayurvedic Therapist and Lifestyle Consultant, Yoga Therapy, Crystal Intuitive Healing, Chakra Cleansing, Spiritual Guidance, Deep Energy Channelling, Reiki, Tibetan Singing Sound Bowl and Gong Master Healer, Meditation Teacher & Spiritual Guide. Grand Master of Reiki and Spiritual Channeller. Yoga Teacher. Degree in Counselling Social Work.

Kerry's healing journey began with a near death experience eight years ago, where she was left with the ability to channel, guide and receive messages from divine energies and angelic realm. This is when she knew her calling was to heal, empower, teach and guide others how to heal and tap into inner self; how to heal within. Her inspirational words, "Love yourself within and let the healing begin," were given to her in meditation to inspire others to heal within.

Kerry is an Australian who has studied and lived in Bali and India. India is where she was introduced to 'Indian Integrated Therapies'. She has studied at an Ayurvedic Study Centre in India to become an Ayurvedic Lifestyle Consultant. Her studies and teachings are Yoga Therapy, Marma Therapy and Chakra Therapy.

Kerry attained degrees in Human Services/Social Work/Counselling when she worked in Australia. As a Spiritual Guidance Counsellor she guides and connects you with your true spiritual self through cleansing and clearing chakras, marmas, nadis, creating our life force energy to flow freely through your body, creating inner peace and joy. She realised healing was her life purpose after her near-death experience where she was given clear messages to heal and guide others into their true heart of self realisation.

Kerry has been influenced by The Australian School of Yoga and Meditation, many Indian Gurus, Greens Ayurveda India, and studied Tibetan Bowl Sound Healing (Master)Reiki and Yoga Teacher Training at The Yoga Barn. She has travelled to many countries, worked with many healers from around the world and trained as a Hatha Yoga Teacher. Training in many healing modalities, including Reiki (Grand Master), Chakra Meditation, Chrystal Healing Therapy, Marma Points Massage and Tibetan Singing Bowl Healing Therapies and Healing. She is a channelor and through meditation can connect with spirits and guides.

Her near-death experience gave Kerry the awareness, knowing and spiritual guidance to connect with higher self and spirit guides and supreme energy as she works, making divine connections, channelling and providing a deep level of understanding at a soul and heart level to heal.

Today Kerry divides her time between Bali, India and Australia spreading her message of peace and love as she teaches people to find the *light*.